Cumann na mBan and the Irish Revolution

Cal McCarthy, from Cork, studied history and economics at University College Cork before going on to work as a civil servant. During a career break he completed his MPhil with a thesis on the 1918 election. *Cumann na mBan and the Irish Revolution* is his first book.

For my parents. Thank you for always encouraging me to form my own opinions.

Cumann na mBan and the Irish Revolution

Cal McCarthy

The Collins Press

Published in 2007 by
The Collins Press
West Link Park
Doughcloyne
Wilton
Cork

British Library Cataloguing in Publication Data

McCarthy, Cal
Cumann na mBan and the Irish Revolution, 1914-1923
1. Cumann na mBan 2. Women political activists - Ireland - History - 20th century 3. Ireland - History - 1910-1921
4. Ireland - History - Civil War, 1922-1923
I. Title
941.5′0821

ISBN-13: 9781905172146

Typesetting: The Collins Press

Font: Hoefler, 11 point

Printed in Finland

Front cover images; top: Demonstration organised by Cumann na mBan outside Mountjoy by Hogan, W.D. photographer, 23 July 1921. Ref No: hog165, courtesy of the National Library of Ireland;
bottom and back cover: members of Cumann na mBan marching.

Contents

ACKNOWLEDGEMENTS

Research for this text began in early 2005 as work on an MPhil thesis about the 1918 election was still progressing. As such, the book has been completed in less than two years, although like most of the more enjoyable chapters in one's life, the time has flown and it seems little more than weeks since the beginning. The people I met along the way undoubtedly contributed much to my enjoyment of the research and their input deserves to be acknowledged.

My thanks to John and Nuala Tutthill, who provided me with a home during my constant trips to Dublin. My thanks also to their new arrival, my godson J.J., who dragged me away from this text to make a very hurried trip to Holles Street one memorable February night. I also wish to thank globetrotters John and AnneMarie whose laughter at my spelling difficulties made me scared stiff of e-mailing them! My thanks to John Tuohy, who in their absence, corrected my spelling and grammar whilst proofreading some of the initial drafts. John also provided the index, thereby saving me a job for which I am far too lazy!

Gratitude cannot begin to describe what all researchers owe to the employees of the various libraries and archives we visit. Without the years that all of you have given to cataloguing, filing, microfilming, retrieving, etc, no meaningful historical research could even be attempted. The staff of the Boole Library, University College Cork (especially Peadar, Catherine and Mary in Special Collections), Seamus Helferty and his staff at the University College Dublin

Archives, Victor Lange and colleagues at the Irish Military Archives, the staff of the Pope John Paul II Library in National University of Ireland Maynooth, everyone at the National Library and the National Archives, Paul O'Brien and Niamh O'Sullivan at the Kilmainham Archives, Dan Breen at Cork Public Museum, along with everyone at Cork County and City Libraries deserve special mention with regard to this work.

I wish to express my gratitude to the Department of Transport who granted me a career break in order to study for an MPhil and extended it so that I could complete this book. My thanks also to those many colleagues who made my time at the department as educational as it was.

I am forever indebted to Mary and Derry Harrington and all at Leeside. Your support and steadfast friendship throughout my student life has made the continuation of study possible.

The History Department at UCC deserve my gratitude for my undergraduate and postgraduate education. I am indebted to my MPhil supervisor, Dr Gabriel Doherty, who has taught me that real facts are hard to come by. Gabriel was also willing to answer a number of annoying queries during my research for this book.

Finally I wish to thank those friends and neighbours who were always willing to help by lending me both their books and their intellects. Tom Curtis, Kate Gallagher, Billy Wiseman, Marie Curtin, Sarah MacSweeney, Michael O'Connor, Pat and Evelyn Mungovan, Cal and Geraldine McCarthy, Kitty O'Leary, Dan and Jerry O'Riordan, Maire MacCarthy Thompson (RIP), Timmy R. Murray, and the Sisters of Mercy Macroom, all deserve special mention.

Alas, no matter how much I may wish to pass the buck, I must make the traditional admission that all errors and omissions are entirely my own.

CAL MCCARTHY
January 2007

Acronyms

BMH: Bureau of Military History
CI: County Inspector
CO: Colonial Office
DC: District Council
DI: District Inspector
DOIF: Defence of Ireland Fund
GAA: Gaelic Athletic Association
GHQ: General Headquarters
GPO: General Post Office
HQ: Headquarters
IMA: Irish Military Archives
INAA: Irish National Aid Association
INAVDF: Irish National Aid and Volunteer Dependents Fund
IO: Intelligence Officer
IRA: Irish Republican Army
IRB: Irish Republican Brotherhood
IRPDF: Irish Republican Prisoners' Dependants Fund
IVDF: Irish Volunteers' Dependants Fund
IWFL: Irish Women's Franchise League
IWSLGA: Irish Women's Suffrage and Local Government Association
MP: Member of Parliament (London)
NAI: National Archives of Ireland
NDU: North Dublin Union
NLI: National Library of Ireland
NUI: National University of Ireland
NYPD: New York Police Department
O/C: Officer in Charge
PRO: Public Record Office (London)
RIC: Royal Irish Constabulary
SDU: South Dublin Union
TD: Teachta Dáil (Member of Irish Parliament)
UCC: University College Cork
UCD: University College Dublin
UCDA: University College Dublin Archives
UK: United Kingdom
US: United States of America
UVF: Ulster Volunteer Force

Introduction

The Irish organisation known as Cumann na mBan (Irishwomen's Council), was a unique and peculiar nationalist group in that its membership consisted entirely of women and girls. On the continent of Europe where nationalism was very much in vogue, no other women's nationalist group existed, or at least, was even remotely prominent.[1] Cumann na mBan were substantial players in the Irish revolution and many male revolutionaries subsequently acknowledged that they had contributed much to the Irish Republican Army (IRA)'s war effort. The British establishment, which Cumann na mBan sought to overthrow, also acknowledged the contribution of these female revolutionaries by outlawing the organisation, along with several other nationalist organisations in 1919.

Yet, for all of that, in terms of the historiography of the revolution, Cumann na mBan remains substantially under-researched. Like the Gaelic Athletic Association, the Fianna and the Gaelic League, Cumann na mBan contributed much to the revolution but they did not lead it, in either a political or a military sense. Thus, like those other organisations, they have not received a great deal of attention from the writers of Irish nationalist history. Unlike those organisations though, Cumann na mBan have received considerable attention from feminist and women's historians.

The seminal work dealing with Cumann na mBan is Margaret Ward's *Unmanageable Revolutionaries*. Although Lil Conlon wrote *Cumann na mBan and the Women of Ireland 1913-1925*, this was, by the author's own admission, not a history of the organisation but rather 'a pot pourri of bitter-sweet memories culled in the garden of yester-year'.[2] *Unmanageable Revolutionaries* was not a history of Cumann na mBan either, but a history of *Women and Irish Nationalism*. Cumann na mBan were, for the first time, examined in detail and Ward uncovered many valuable primary sources which remain key to our understanding of the organisation.

In the wake of Dr Ward's work, further studies focusing on women's participation in the Irish revolution began to emerge. Whilst these studies did not specifically deal with Cumann na mBan, they did, naturally, add to our understanding of the organisation's participation in the revolution. New biographies of such notable women as Hanna Sheehy Skeffington, Mary MacSwiney and Constance Markievicz appeared. Ruth Taillon contributed a meticulously researched account of the participation of women in the 1916 rebellion. Sinead McCoole wrote a short history, *Guns and Chiffon*, and then built upon that work with a very fine series of vignettes on the lesser-known women of the revolution entitled *No Ordinary Women*. These are just a few of the many recent texts that have built substantially on the historiography of Cumann na mBan.[3]

However, as most of this research has been undertaken by those who study women's history, it was intended to contribute primarily to our understanding of Irish women's history and not specifically our understanding of Cumann na mBan. In an MA thesis, 'Cumann na mBan 1913-1926: Redressing the Balance', Ann Matthews argued that in relation to Cumann na mBan:

> General history does not exactly do them justice. Feminist history has distorted their story. It is necessary to go back to the beginning using the primary sources and try to construct an alternative view of Cumann na mBan.[4]

This is a good point. When read in isolation, feminist histories tend to distort the story of Cumann na mBan because they were never intended as histories of Cumann na mBan. As such, they do not present a complete picture of the organisation but rather one that is necessarily confined within the parameters of the history of Irish feminism, or within the study of the historical gender dynamic. There was much more to Cumann na mBan than their partial intellectual attachment to feminism. There was much more to Cumann na mBan than their place in women's history.

This book uses the feminist and women's histories wherever they are relevant to the history of Cumann na mBan's participation in the Irish revolution. In addition, it draws on those primary sources, to which Matthews referred, in order to construct a broader history of Cumann na mBan's part in the revolution.

Since Ward's *Unmanageable Revolutionaries*, more primary source material has been made available to the public. Foremost among that material are the 'Witness Statements and Contemporary Documents' collected by the Bureau of Military History in the late 1940s and early 1950s and made available for consultation in 2003. Unfortunately only 30 sets of Contemporary Documents were contributed to the Bureau by members of Cumann na mBan. Not all those documents related to Cumann na mBan activities and similar documents (first-aid certificates, etc.) were already available in other archives. Cumann na mBan's Witness Statements are also limited, 82 of them being contained within the Bureau's collection. Alas, the overwhelming majority of these Statements come from Cumann na mBan leaders and not from the rank and file. As this leadership tended to operate in Dublin, Witness Statements from provincial members are hopelessly thin on the ground. In studying the Witness Statements, the historian should also be aware that they suffer from two principle weaknesses: misremembrance (deliberate or otherwise) and exaggeration. When it came to granting pensions to Cumann na mBan members, one civil servant commented that 'the inflated claims of the Verifying Officers can scarcely be reconciled with the moderate claims of the ladies'.[5] It should be stated, however, that the inconsistencies referred to may also have been caused by the deflated claims of the rank and file. Nonetheless, any historian working with accounts written retrospectively must be aware that misremembrance and exaggeration will be factors.

In an effort to counteract the weaknesses inherent in the retrospective accounts of the members of Cumann na mBan, this book also attempts to extract information from contemporary source material. In that regard, source material written by both men and women has been consulted. The archives of male contemporaries may be mostly irrelevant to Irish women's history but they are often relevant to the history of Cumann na mBan. Thus police and intelligence reports, contemporary newspapers and journals, and the papers of male and female political and military activists have also been consulted during the course of research.

From the beginning I sought to make this book as accessible to the casual reader as it is to more learned historians. Thus, throughout the text I have provided brief introductory accounts of the events which surrounded Cumann na mBan's evolution. These accounts necessarily oversimplify the history of some very complex events. However, every attempt has been made to stick to established fact where possible and refer to ongoing debate where necessary.

When naming individual members throughout, I have sought to use the names they used themselves at the time in question. There were occasions where it was necessary to refer to some women by their maiden names after they had married. In doing so, it was only intended to simplify the narrative. The names on all Witness Statements are reproduced as they appear in the Bureau of Military History catalogue.

Whilst historians have come a long way in terms of their understanding of Cumann na mBan's impact on the revolution, a considerable amount of work still lies ahead. Like many historians who have already written about Cumann na mBan, I hope that this work builds on existing texts and will, in time, provide part of the foundation for future study.

Historical Background, Origins and Foundation

The Cumann na mBan organisation was to become the most influential women's group in twentieth-century Ireland. For many it will appear odd that such a prominent women's organisation existed at the beginning of a century when society did not encourage the participation of women in politics. But Cumann na mBan emerged and came to the height of its power in an Ireland undergoing rapid political and social transition. The organisation had its origins in two powerful forces that were driving that transition: feminism and Irish nationalism.

The Emergence of Nationalism and Feminism in Ireland

Since the Norman invasion of 1169, various generations in Ireland had objected to, and rebelled against, government provided by England. The various rebellions against this government were often driven by economic factors, power struggles among Gaelic chieftains, or anger at a new English way of life replacing an older Gaelic one. The Irish people were never fully united in any rebellion against the British and indeed sections of the Irish population often sided with the Crown in order to advance their own political agenda.

However, at the end of the eighteenth century, in the wake of the American and French revolutions, a new kind of rebellion occurred. Throughout the summer of 1798 armed insurgents, mainly in Wexford, known as the United Irishmen, staged a failed rebellion against British authority. As their name suggests, the rebel leaders had an ingrained sense of Irish nationality. They did not consider themselves British and fought for an independent Irish Republic.

The British response to the 1798 rebellion was the Act of Union of 1800. The intention of the Act was to make Ireland an integral part of the United Kingdom (UK) of Great Britain and Ireland. However, Ireland was never integrated with the UK to the same extent that Scotland and Wales were. While Britain was almost entirely a Protestant island, the plantations of the sixteenth and seventeenth centuries, with the exception of the Ulster plantation, had never taken root in an Ireland that remained staunchly Roman Catholic.

A series of penal laws discriminated against Catholics, and thus against the Irish, more than any other nationality within the UK. The Irish were not fully included in the government of the UK until Catholic Emancipation in 1829 and by then calls to repeal the Act of Union were already prominent. In short, from the beginning, many Irish people felt excluded from the State to which they were supposed to belong and for some, a sense of separation from the UK was almost inevitable.

In 1848 and 1867 the Young Irelanders and Fenians (Irish Republican Brotherhood) staged failed rebellions against the Crown. Those rebellions were based on their concept of a separate Irish nationality.

From 1880, a group of mainly Catholic tenant farmers began to demand ownership of the land they rented. Although the landlord system prevailed throughout the UK, in Ireland it was aggravated by a religious divide. Many Catholic tenant farmers came to see Protestant landlords as having dispossessed them of their families' lands centuries earlier and a bitter feud followed where rents were withheld and violence often flared. The tenant farmers were organised into a group known as the Land League. When the Land League was declared illegal in 1881, the Ladies Land League took up the work of their male colleagues. This was the first mass women's organisation in Ireland and some of its veterans ended up in Cumann na mBan. Eventually, the land question was solved by a number of Acts of Parliament which provided tenant farmers with loans, by which they could buy the land they worked. The land war was not overtly nationalist. However, it did foster already existing divisions, between those who cherished the Act of Union (mostly Protestant landowners), and those who did not (mostly Catholic tenants).

In the midst of the land issue, Irish Members of Parliament at Westminster had formed themselves into a loose parliamentary party and began to demand a Home Rule parliament for Ireland. This parliament would sit in Dublin but would have only limited fiscal and financial powers, and no power to decide on Irish foreign policy. These powers would remain in the hands of the British parliament at Westminster. In 1886 Irish Parliamentary Party (hereafter 'Irish Party') MPs failed to pass a Home Rule Bill through the House of Commons. In 1893 another Home Rule Bill was defeated in the Lords. Finally, in 1911, the Lords' veto was removed and Home Rule was introduced again in 1912. This time the Lords could only delay its implementation and Home Rule was set to become reality in Ireland.

Ulster unionists, however, would not contemplate being governed by a Dublin parliament and pledged to resist the implementation of Home Rule by force. For that reason a number of unionist militia groups began to emerge all over Ulster. These groups were amalgamated into the Ulster Volunteer Force (UVF) in 1913. In 1912 some 400,000 Ulster unionist men had signed the famous, and biblically titled, 'Ulster's Solemn League and Covenant', pledging themselves to use 'all means necessary' to defeat Home Rule in Ireland. About 250,000 unionist women signed a similar pledge.

By 1913 the demand for an Irish parliament had become overwhelming. It had grown out of a sense of Irish nationalism and isolation from the UK. This isolation was caused mainly by a religious divide and further exaggerated by a rich/poor divide reflected in the system of land ownership that had prevailed in Ireland up until the dawn of the twentieth century.

Organisations like the Gaelic League and the Gaelic Athletic Association (GAA) had been rediscovered and, to some extent, invented cultural expression of this Irish nationalism. For many, the Irish identity had emerged as something necessarily separate from the British State to which they were politically bound. The stage was set for political conflict.

Against the background of the development of Irish nationalism, feminism was also on the rise throughout the UK. An increasing number of people were beginning to re-think the role of women in society. In 1876 Anna Haslam and her husband Thomas founded the Irish Women's Suffrage and Local Government Association (IWSLGA). The IWSLGA was a group of mainly middle-class Protestant women and as such they had no connection with Irish nationalism. Aside from their primary campaign for women's suffrage, they also campaigned for the right of women to retain ownership of property after marriage.

The role of women in formal education was also gradually redefined. In 1878 an intermediate education bill recognised the right of girls' secondary schools to receive State funding in the same way as boys' schools, provided their students could demonstrate equal academic proficiency through examination. In 1904 Trinity College admitted women to its degree programmes and in 1908 the National University followed suit.

Better education gave those Irish women who could afford it an increasing self confidence. Some became active in the Gaelic League, and Sinn Féin became the first Irish political party to admit women into their ranks on a similar basis to men. In 1898 women were granted the right to sit on, and vote for, the composition of District Councils.

In 1908 the Irish Women's Franchise League was founded as a more extreme and militant version of the IWSLGA. But the third Home Rule

Bill of 1912 still did not recognise the right of women to vote.

Whatever advancement women were making in the public sphere was soon disrupted, however, when Irishwomen identified what they considered more important political movements. In 1911 the Ulster Women's Unionist Council was formed and members pledged themselves to stand by their husbands, sweethearts, brothers and sons in defending unionists from the 'tyranny' of Home Rule. It was only a matter of time before their opposing image would emerge in Southern Ireland.

Origins of Cumann na mBan

In examining the origins of Cumann na mBan, it is necessary to begin by commenting briefly on the foundation of their male counterparts, the Irish Volunteers.

It is generally agreed that the Irish Volunteers were formed at a meeting in the Rotunda Rink in Dublin on 25 November 1913. The meeting had been organised largely by Irish Republican Brotherhood (IRB) men in response to an article written by Eoin MacNeill in the Gaelic League's newspaper, *An Claidheamh Solais.* MacNeill was a university professor and head of the culturally nationalist Gaelic League. In the aforementioned article entitled 'The North Began' he proposed that a Southern volunteer force be formed along the lines of the already existing UVF. Now, using MacNeill's respectable scholarly reputation, the IRB seized the opportunity to form an armed organisation in the South.

From the beginning, control of the Volunteers was a thorny issue. Moderates like John Redmond, who was the leader of the Irish Party at Westminster, saw it as an organisation which would only be used to defend Home Rule should the actions of the UVF make that defence necessary. IRB men saw it as another organisation they could manipulate and control in pursuit of an Irish Republic. What is perhaps of most interest to the historian is that as early as 1913 many Irishmen were willing to exert Ireland's right to a separate parliament by force of arms. The 1916 rising might well have been more popular than some have alleged when viewed in that context.

The meeting at the Rotunda Rink gave Irishmen an organisation through which they could express their support for Irish self determination. Some women were also in attendance at this meeting, seated in a separate gallery. Ward has argued that this segregation was symbolic of their relegation to a passive and observant role.[1] It might have been. However, it was also symbolic of the gender segregation which was commonplace (e.g., in churches) at many public gatherings of the era. It is also clear that those women who were seated inside the rink were afforded a courtesy which was not extended to the many men that stood outside the doors, at various overflow meetings.[2] There is certainly no evidence to suggest that the entire male leadership set about actively excluding women from the Volunteers. Indeed it would appear that Eoin MacNeill did envisage a role, albeit a very separate role, for women, within, or at least on the fringes of, the Volunteer movement. The Volunteer manifesto reflected the leadership's desire that as many nationalists as possible could identify with the new organisation and consequently stated that Volunteer ranks:

> ... are open to all able bodied Irishmen without distinction of creed, politics or social grade. Means will be found whereby Irishmen unable to serve as ordinary Volunteers will be enabled to aid the Volunteer forces in various capacities. There will also be work for the women to do, and there are signs that the women of Ireland, true to their record, are especially enthusiastic for the success of the Volunteers. We propose for the Volunteer organisation the widest possible base. Without any other association or classification the Volunteers be enrolled according to the district in which they live.[3]

The manifesto was nothing if not ambiguous. Whilst ranks were only open to men, there would be work for the women to do. There was no indication of what kind of membership, if any, the women would be granted. However, if the manifesto was ambiguous, the speakers at the rink tended to forget such ambiguity in continuously referring to Irishmen and the manhood of Ireland.[4] The organisation was sending out very mixed messages to women but one thing was clear. Whilst women would not be joining in the same capacity as men, the Volunteers were considering some kind of role for them. For the moment, however, they remained carefully ambiguous as to what that role was. Varying interpretations were still possible.

M.J. Rafferty later wrote that she 'joined Cumann na mBan in the "Rink" in 1913'. She also stated that Con Colbert had taken her name and the names of other women present.[5] Of course, Rafferty could not have joined Cumann na mBan in the Rink, as the organisation was not yet founded. However, the fact that Colbert took her name, and that she came to see this as her initiation into Cumann na mBan, does suggest that the women present in the Rotunda Rink were not entirely excluded from proceedings. On occasion, women like Kathleen Keyes McDonnell of Bandon and Margaret Skinnider of Glasgow actually joined, or at least worked with, the Volunteers until Cumann na mBan branches were founded in their local areas.[6] Indeed it could be argued that the bulk of the Irish Volunteer organisation, who later became the National Volunteers, had no difficulty in including women, albeit that their inclusion would be on an entirely different basis to men.[7]

Yet women did not publicly push to join the Volunteers. Had they done so, it is unlikely they would have been granted membership on a similar basis to men. And in the weeks and months preceding the inaugural public meeting of Cumann na mBan, those women who may have wished to find a role within the Volunteers cannot have been encouraged by the signals coming from the male organisation. Whilst the provisional constitution of the Volunteers did commit the organisation to securing the 'rights and liberties common to all the people of Ireland',[8] and to training, disciplining, arming and equipping a 'body of Irish Volunteers', it seemed to rule out the participation of women when it proposed uniting 'Irish*men* of every creed and of every party and class' for these purposes. The provisional rules of the Volunteers proposed inviting 'all organisations of a National tendency to take part', yet only on the 'broad basis laid down in the constitution'. That constitution seemed to suggest that the membership would be male. Furthermore, there did not seem to be a place for women on Volunteer committees which were to be ideally 'representative of all shades of Irish*men*'.[9]

Mary Colum later stated that 'a number of women had made representations to the male leaders who, uncertain how to respond, decided to couch any references as obliquely as possible, so as not to alienate any potential supporters'.[10] Whatever was going on behind the scenes, the public utterances of the Volunteers were confusing.

Thus it would appear that nationalist women entered into a debate around whether they should join the Volunteers, where their role would be stereotypical of their gender, or start a separate organisation, where they could define their own role as they saw fit. Some 50 years later Kathleen Clarke, whose husband Tom was a senior IRB member, claimed that it was the IRB who first suggested the formation of a separate women's organisation.[11] Further evidence suggests that the idea 'emanated from ... Thomas MacDonagh' who was also an IRB member.[12] Molly Reynolds later recalled that Bulmer Hobson, also of the IRB, had been aware that moves were afoot to form a women's auxiliary and had told her of the group's first private meeting.[13]

Whether or not the IRB had any involvement, it was clear that some women refused to work in a subsidiary capacity within the Volunteers, and so the idea of a separate women's organisation gathered momentum.[14] Writing in *Leabhar na mBan* (a Cumann na mBan publication from 1919) a contributor calling herself Siobhan Bean an Padraigh (Jennie Wyse Power) leaves the following description of the months after the foundation of the Volunteers:

> Many informal meetings took place to discuss the formation of a women's society whose aim would be to work independently, and at the same time to organise Nationalist women to be of service to the Irish Volunteers. The Ulster Women's Council was at this time working to assist the Ulster Volunteers, and it was found that their method in the main was practical and worth considering.[15]

These informal meetings were held in a room above the Queen's Theatre in Brunswick Street (now Pearse Street) Dublin, but did not, for some time, produce any new organisation.[16] The fact that the meetings occurred behind closed doors means that it is difficult for the historian to understand what precisely caused the delay in publicly announcing Cumann na mBan. Agnes O'Farrelly stated that these first informal meetings had begun four months prior to the inaugural public meeting but the women had decided that the formation of a society, 'did not seem to us then opportune. We feared to hamper whilst we were anxious to help'.[17] Eventually, it would appear that the executive was formed by Jennie Wyse Power. Elizabeth Bloxham later described that first executive's formative meeting as follows:

> The actual founding of Cumann na mBan was the result of a conversation between … Mrs Wyse Power and I think Molly McGuire (later Mrs P. Colum) and some others, whose names I don't remember, during one of my holiday visits to Dublin … It may have been during the Easter holidays of 1914. Mrs Wyse Power spoke of an executive and I asked how is an executive elected – She said 'We elect ourselves; that is the way an executive has to be elected' … She jotted down a number of names. Apart from the three already mentioned and Mrs Tuohy I cannot recall them.[18]

However, O'Farrelly's confession to a fear of hampering the Volunteer movement remains interesting. For the Volunteers, the acceptance of women was a difficult and possibly divisive issue. In order for the Volunteers to attract support from as broad a cross-section of society as possible, different shades of nationalism and political opinion would have to be accommodated within the support base of the organisation. Some of those opinions (male and female) would not tolerate the presence of women in a militia. Michael Judge may well have represented such opinion when he allegedly stated that:

> The movement was one in which there was no room for the ladies. There was yet no room for an ambulance corps, or any other corps, but in the course of a few months there would be uniforms and rifles would be wanted, and these for each member would cost at least £10. There were 200,000 Volunteers in Ireland, so that would mean that they would want at least £2,000,000 and the ladies could form a society, and then collect money for that, and put their hearts and souls into it.[19]

Whilst Judge's comments quite clearly dismissed any notion of women taking part in the Volunteer organisation, in the immediate future at least, it should be stated that he made those remarks just weeks before the inaugural public meeting of Cumann na mBan. Thus they can be interpreted in two ways: as either an announcement and endorsement of the agreed role of the forthcoming women's society, or the final rejection that forced the women into the open with their own organisation. Either way, for anybody who was not party to the backroom manoeuvrings between nationalist women and men, it was difficult to disagree with the *Irish Citizen*'s assertion that Judge's comments were audacious and inconsistent.[20] Either way, Cumann na mBan were coming out.

The Inaugural Public Meeting

The inaugural public meeting of Cumann na mBan occurred in Wynn's Hotel Dublin, on Thursday 2 April 1914. The attendance at this meeting was tiny compared to that of the inaugural meeting of the Volunteers. The *Irish Independent* and *Freeman's Journal* both concluded that the meeting was 'largely attended'. However, *The Irish Times* was more precise in its estimate that 'there were about 100 ladies present'.[21] By contrast, it was estimated that at least 5,000 men attended the inaugural public meeting of the Volunteers.[22] Ward has correctly pointed out that the timing of the meeting at 4pm was hardly convenient for working women. However, it is far more likely that the small attendance was better explained by two other key factors.

Firstly, there can be little doubt that in 1914 women were generally less politically active than they are today. They were not yet allowed to vote and whilst suffragettes were locked in an intensive struggle for this right, the suffragettes should not be considered a representative sample of Irish womanhood. Secondly, and more importantly, the meeting at Wynn's was hopelessly advertised. The two major nationalist newspapers (the *Freeman's Journal* and *Irish Independent*) did not advertise the forthcoming event in the week prior to its occurrence. Indeed Mary Colum later claimed that the founders of the movement had 'deliberately avoided' newspaper advertisement.[23] Unfortunately she failed to explain why these founders would avoid something which might have made their organisation numerically stronger. Perhaps she was merely attempting to gloss over Cumann na mBan's error in failing to promote itself. Or she may have been claiming that the lack of media attention for the new organisation was not a measure of societal indifference but was somehow the choice of its founders. Or perhaps her statement was a truthful one and Cumann na mBan did not wish to attract too much hostile attention from a public, or a media, who might have objected to their foundation.

Whether or not Cumann na mBan 'deliberately avoided'

newspaper advertisement, there is no doubt that the absence of such advertisement certainly meant that many nationalist women did not know that the inaugural meeting had occurred until after they read about it in the newspapers. The meeting was advertised in the *Irish Volunteer* but for some bizarre reason the announcement that the meeting was forthcoming did not appear until two days after its occurrence. In a very small and confusing paragraph, the *Irish Volunteer* of Saturday 4 April announced that a public meeting of the new organisation would 'be held in the large room, Wynn's Hotel tomorrow (Thursday) at 4pm'. As this was the first time any announcement of the meeting occurred in the Volunteer's official organ, the most logical conclusion for those who read it, was either that the meeting would occur on the following Thursday 9 April or on Sunday 5 April. It is interesting to speculate how many women may have arrived at Wynn's on these dates for a meeting that had already occurred.

The attendance at the meeting was small but it is likely that its attendees were generally more committed to Irish separatism than their male counterparts. This was a small but determined group of women with an intense desire for Irish self-determination. Unlike the men who flocked to the ranks of the Volunteers, this women's group would not provide much adventure, excitement or glamour for its members. Indeed, from the minute attendance it must have been evident that their activities would not meet with the same support as those of their male counterparts. Yet their resolve to assist in securing Irish self-rule would not allow them to be deterred. It is little wonder then, that Cumann na mBan were to become one of the more uncompromisingly nationalist (and later republican) groups.

Agnes O'Farrelly presided over the inaugural public meeting. For her time, O'Farrelly was a remarkably well educated woman. She already had a Masters degree to her name and was later to become a university professor. However, her views were a little conservative for many of the feminists who may have sought to further their own agenda through membership of the new organisation. O'Farrelly clearly identified a separate role for women when she insisted that the organisation's primary function would be to fund and equip the Volunteers. 'Each rifle we put in their hands,' she stated, 'will represent to us a bolt fastened behind the door of some Irish home to keep out the hostile stranger. Each cartridge will be a watchdog to fight for the sanctity of the hearth.' It was also decided that the new organisation would not take a direct part in the defence of Ireland, except as a 'last extremity'.[24]

Membership of the new organisation was to be confined to women of Irish birth or descent, and its name would be Cumann na mBan, which literally translates as council of women but the organisation itself tended to translate it as 'Irishwomen's Council. Cumann na mBan's first constitution, which had been drafted during the initial meetings at Pearse Street,[25] declared the organisation's aims as:

1. To advance the cause of Irish Liberty.
2. To organise Irishwomen in the furtherance of this object.
3. To assist in arming and equipping a body of Irishmen for the defence of Ireland.
4. To form a fund for these purposes to be called the 'Defence of Ireland Fund'.[26]

In addition to assisting in equipping and arming the Volunteers, branches were expected to 'keep in touch with their local Volunteer battalions, appear at the parades, and identify themselves with Volunteer work in every suitable way'.[27] For some, this separate women's organisation had been founded in order that women would not be cast in a subordinate role within the Volunteers. But now, although they were a separate and theoretically independent organisation, they had cast themselves in a subordinate role outside of the Volunteers. Some feminist opinion was voiced at Wynn's, and *The*

Irish Times provided the following account of same:

> A lady enquired if the principle duty of the new organisation would not be to collect subscriptions for the men. (Laughter.)
>
> Miss O'Farrelly – We will naturally keep in touch with the men's movement and do our best in helping to equip and arm them.
>
> Another lady suggested that the women should also learn to fight. There had been fighting women in Ireland before now, and there was no reason why there should not be again. In any event the women could do splendid work as spies.[28]

In the weeks that followed, suffragettes continued to object to what they saw as the subordination of the new women's movement to the Volunteers. Agnes O'Farrelly's inaugural address as published in the *Irish Volunteer* on 18 April, more than two weeks after the meeting, cannot have eased the fears of suffragettes with regard to the new movement. In the *Irish Volunteer* article O'Farrelly seemed to rule out any active participation in politics. She wrote that:

> In so far as politics are the history of the moment, and our actions must be guided by events arising out of them, we are political; otherwise we shall take no part in sectional politics, nor shall we take up the time of what is meant to be a purely practical organisation in discussing them. The surest way to prevent future discussion which might cause disunion among a body of women, all working in their various ways for the one great end of nationhood, is, it seems to me, to be perfectly frank at the outset as to the immediate circumstances which called us into existence.

Ward has argued that the O'Farrelly article:

> … dismissed any suggestion that the organisation would enable

> women to discuss current political events. It was acceptable for the male organisation to enter into debate, but not for their female counterpart, in case this led to 'disunion'. The political arena was to be reserved for men, while women's role was to 'put Ireland first' by helping to arm the men. Agnes O'Farrelly's emphasis did not challenge prejudices but reinforced them. In her eyes, nationalist women were simply extending their domestic concerns to the public sphere.[29]

Whilst this analysis certainly has a ring of truth with regard to O'Farrelly's acceptance of a status quo which did not encourage women to participate in politics, O'Farrelly had good reason for dismissing the idea of the new organisation even discussing politics. Indeed it would appear that she was quite willing to discuss politics herself and thus her acceptance that Cumann na mBan would not do so had more to do with practicality than the acceptance of prejudice. Her concerns with regard to disunion in the new organisation were well founded, as demonstrated by the *Freeman's Journal* report of the events at Wynn's:

> Mrs T.M. Kettle … thought that no sectional politics should be introduced into the Society. She found, she said in the chairman's speech a distinctly hostile (attitude) to the politics to which she belonged. The Irish Party had been referred to in a hostile and sneering manner.
>
> The Lady Chairman – No, no; quite the contrary.
>
> Mrs Kettle – Reference was made to the sensations of the day at Westminster and things like that.
>
> The lady Chairman said that in speaking of the sensations of the day in Westminster she referred to the two great political parties who were playing their own game. She realised and they all realised the difficulty of the situation for the Irish Party who had their complete sympathy. No sectional politics, she said,

> would be introduced into the organisation ... Countess Markievicz also deprecated any discussion of party politics.[30]

The fact that Markievicz agreed that Cumann na mBan should not discuss party politics is telling. The Countess was a committed feminist but she was also a radical nationalist. On this occasion it would appear she feared a split in the new organisation more than she wished to encourage its discussion of politics. In any case Markievicz and Kettle were not alone in voicing concerns regarding the discussion of politics and several other women also objected to the introduction of party politics into the new organisation.[31]

It is clear that Cumann na mBan (like the Volunteers and, later, Sinn Féin) had to work hard to hold many diverse shades of Irish separatism together within their ranks. A practical part of that effort was to avoid the discussion of politics. The Volunteer organisation had also expressed a desire that their movement would 'be of a non-party character'.[32] Thus, by the time O'Farrelly's inaugural address appeared in the *Irish Volunteer* on 18 April, she had added Kettle's views to the text that the latter had originally objected to.

Amidst all this political manoeuvring at Wynn's, some traces of the constructive nationalist organisation that Cumann na mBan would become were already evident. Conscious of the developing UVF threat to the homes of Northern Catholics, a motion that 'the women of the South should be ready to offer their homes to the women of the North in any great crisis' was passed unanimously.[33]

The provisional executive of Cumann na mBan, unveiled to the public at Wynn's, included some very noteworthy Irish women, some of them known women's suffrage campaigners. Nancy O'Rahilly was the wife of the famous Fenian Michael O'Rahilly. Jennie Wyse Power was a veteran of the Ladies' Land League, the Irish Women's Franchise League and Inghinidhe na hÉireann.[34] Agnes MacNeill was the wife of the Volunteer leader Eoin MacNeill. Mary Colum was a teacher in Padraig Pearse's St Enda's school and was married to the poet and Irish Volunteer Pádraic Colum. Louise Gavan Duffy was a noted Irish scholar who had been one of the first women to graduate from University College Dublin (UCD) in 1911, whilst Agnes O'Farrelly's academic pedigree has already been mentioned. These notable women were joined on the executive by Mrs Tuohy, whose husband Dr Tuohy, was well known in nationalist circles, and by a Mrs McDonagh O'Malley. Constance Markievicz was not on the provisional executive. At this point much of her energy was directed towards the Irish Citizen Army. The Irish Citizen Army had been set up by the labour leader, James Connolly, as a reaction to the violence that had occurred between police and workers during industrial strife in 1913. As Cumann na mBan developed, however, the Countess did come to hold 'an official position on the Committee of one of the branches of Cumann na mBan'.[35]

The gender stereotypes of the era meant that Cumann na mBan had identified for themselves a different role to that of the Volunteers. It was a role in which society had cast them and there is no doubt that feminists considered it an unequal one. In 1914, however, Cumann na mBan women accepted that role and went about performing those tasks which wider society deemed appropriate to their gender. Their desire to assist in securing Irish self-determination overcame the reservations of feminist members regarding the wider equality agenda and Cumann na mBan began to organise themselves across the island.

At Wynn's, the Central branch or *Árd Craobh* had already been formed. That branch would share its headquarters with the Volunteers on Great Brunswick Street and from there it would direct the activities of the various branches it hoped to set up. Whether Cumann na mBan could expand across the island or whether it would remain a group of diverse Dublin-based intellectuals remained to be seen. Like any stereotypical Irish organisation, and their brother Volunteers, one of the first items on Cumann na mBan's agenda, was the split.

Consolidation, Expansion and the Preservation of Unity 1914-16

As Cumann na mBan's inaugural meeting had been hindered by poor timing and advertising, it was only in the weeks that followed that many Irish suffragists began to make public their reservations regarding the new organisation. Among the first to voice her grievances was Mrs Hanna Sheehy Skeffington. Mrs Sheehy Skeffington and her husband Francis had been engaged in the campaign for women's rights for most of their married lives. Indeed their marriage was an unusual one (for the time), in that each added the surname of the other to their own and thus the couple were known as the Sheehy Skeffington's. In 1908 they became founder members of the Irish Women's Franchise League, an organisation set up to campaign for the enfranchisement of women. This campaign occasionally turned violent and, as such, Mrs Sheehy Skeffington was no stranger to controversy. In 1912 she was arrested for breaking windows and sentenced to two weeks in Mountjoy Jail, having refused to pay the fine. She was jailed again in 1913 after a fracas with a policeman but this time after a six day hunger strike, she was released.[1]

It was little wonder, therefore, that Sheehy Skeffington did not approve of any women's organisation that did not place the equality issue above all else on its agenda. She had already clashed with Inghinidhe na hÉireann regarding their emphasis of nationalism above women's rights in 1909.[2] Once again she made her feelings known when attending a Cumann na mBan meeting at the Mansion House in Dublin on 2 May 1914. The meeting was again advertised late in the *Irish Volunteer* of the same day but this time it occurred at 8pm and thus the attendance may have been larger than at Wynn's. During the course of the meeting Sheehy Skeffington was subjected to a number of speeches which were certainly too conservative for her liking. Eoin MacNeill seemed to drift between awareness and forgetfulness that he was addressing a female group when he told them that, 'the plain duty of everyone was to do his best in whatever way he was able to come out and take his or her place with their fellow countrymen or countrywomen and prepare for the defence of their country'. Alice Stopford Green paid homage to the Volunteers saying that their movement demonstrated 'that Irishmen believed in themselves, in their manhood, and, if rightly directed they could win the freedom of Ireland by their natural ability'. Whilst she also hoped 'that the women of Ireland would band themselves into a real body of Volunteers', she thought that this body's primary purpose should be to collect money for the arming of their male counterparts.[3] Stopford Green's views might well have reflected those of wider society with regard to the feminine role but they could not be expected to sit well with a suffragette activist like Sheehy Skeffington. When Sheehy Skeffington's turn to speak came, in the midst of what she inevitably considered an endorsement of the inequality between Cumann na mBan and the Volunteers, she expressed her objections passionately. The *Irish Citizen* (which the Sheehy Skeffingtons had founded) of 9 May reported her outburst as follows:

> Suddenly a 'Volunteer' speaker began to ask questions – awkward ones. Was the Irishwomen's Council to have a place in the (Volunteer) executive? What were the liberties that Irishwomen possessed? ... Uproar ensued as Mrs Sheehy Skeffington put these points; the men for whom rifles were to be procured at the

> sacrifice of 'fur coats' howled to have the insolent one put out; the chair explained that the liberties of Irishwomen did not form a part of the constitution of the new society, and were entirely 'out of order'; that the only question of interest at present was the buying of rifles for men, and that nothing else was of the slightest importance to the truly womanly – and the unwomanly in the audience smiled to themselves and thought deep thoughts on the nature of men who cannot buy a rifle unless a woman collects the money.

The 'unwomanly' may have smiled to themselves, but it was one of the few occasions that Cumann na mBan made them smile. Cumann na mBan was a nationalist organisation and had identified its own primary purpose as the arming of its male counterpart. In 1914 there was no room for the discussion of women's rights within the organisation, or in nationalist circles generally. The *Irish Volunteer* of 9 May alleged that Sheehy Skeffington's words had not met 'with the approval of the majority of the meeting'. Suffragists may have complained loudly of Cumann na mBan's subordinate role from outside of the organisation, but Cumann na mBan's refusal to discuss such things, and the radical suffragists refusal to join an organisation that would not permit such discussion, meant that they could not complain from the inside. The *Irish Citizen* did maintain a habit of referring to Cumann na mBan as 'slave women' and Mary MacSwiney, herself a committed suffragist, did attempt to justify Cumann na mBan's position with regard to nationalism and feminism.[4] However, the absence of Sheehy Skeffington and women who shared her views from the membership of Cumann na mBan meant that the organisation was never forced to re-think its priorities. Instead they dealt with divergent views on women's role in wider society in the same way they had dealt with divergent views on Irish nationalism; they refused to enter into any potentially divisive internal debate.

The Early Expansion

Cumann na mBan's expansion began with the incorporation of Inghinidhe na hÉireann (Daughters of Érin) as a branch on 23 May 1914. Some Inghinidhe members had already been in attendance at the initial private meetings of Cumann na mBan on Pearse Street and had therefore been interested in the new movement from the beginning.[5]

Inghinidhe na hÉireann had been founded in 1900 by a group of Dublin-based nationalist women. Most famous among them were Maud Gonne who had previously been involved in campaigning on behalf of Fenian prisoners and Jennie Wyse Power whose home had been a safe house for Fenians.[6] The organisation had a strong culturally nationalist agenda and it had a considerable impact in the promotion of Gaelic culture through the teaching of Irish to children and the organisation of Irish entertainments. The Inghinidhe were so committed to the promotion of Gaelic culture that every member had to select a Gaelic name by which she would be known within the organisation.[7]

In 1910 the Inghinidhe spearheaded a campaign to provide school meals to some of the poorer children in Dublin in an effort to force the authorities to take up their responsibilities under already existing legislation. On occasion their nationalism had gone beyond cultural and charitable expression and they had become involved in various fracas caused by anything from the distribution of anti British army recruitment literature, to protesting against the visits of English monarchs. They were the first Irish organisation to produce a women's newspaper, *Bean na hÉireann*, which first appeared in November 1908. The newspaper reveals that the organisation certainly had a strong leaning toward militant republicanism and thus they were never supportive of the Home Rule agenda at Westminster. When the Inghinidhe were partially merged with Cumann na mBan it is hardly surprising that the new organisation became a little more culturally directed. And there is no doubt that its intellectual heart (in Dublin) also came under the influence of some advanced militant republicans.

Inghinidhe na hÉireann were the first of many nationalist organisations that would sacrifice their own independence in order to present a united face of Irish separatism to the British government. Of course there was resistance from some Inghinidhe members and many years later Sighle Humphreys did admit that they could rightfully have claimed 'that there was already a woman's organisation doing all that the new Society intended doing'.[8] There were even those who did not agree with the incorporation of the Inghinidhe and consequently did not join Cumann na mBan.[9] Thus, whilst the Inghinidhe did lose much of its membership to Cumann na mBan, for a brief time it remained a very small and independent body of Irish women.[10] But, in the end, Constance Markievicz seems to have been able to broker an arrangement between the two organisations. She chaired the first meeting of the Inghinidhe branch of Cumann na mBan. That night 30 members were enrolled.[11] Likewise in Cork, the existing Inghinidhe branch was used to launch Cumann na mBan's first public meeting. That meeting was itself used by separatist men to re-launch the Volunteer movement in the southern city. A previous attempt to inaugurate the Volunteers in Cork had resulted in the violent break up of the meeting due to a misunderstanding regarding Eoin MacNeill's sarcastic assertion that the Volunteers should cheer Carson for his role in founding the UVF.[12]

Across the island, however, expansion was slow initially. Although its pledge to assist the Volunteers had cast it in a role which traditionalists would have deemed more appropriate and feminine, Irishwomen did not seem enamoured with the new organisation. In their attempt to appeal to as broad a cross-section of women as possible, Cumann na mBan had sought to find a middle ground between radical feminism and traditional concepts of the female role. Yet, even that middle ground seemed a bridge too far for many nationalist women, or perhaps for their families. One of Cumann na mBan's early organisers later recalled parents who 'did not mind their boys taking part in a military movement, but who had never heard of and were reluctant to accept the idea of a body of gun-women'.[13] Cumann na mBan did distribute leaflets urging women to 'join the Volunteer movement' but the leaflets did not have enormous effect.[14]

Throughout 1914 and 1915 Cumann na mBan boasted an impressive rate of expansion through the columns of the *Irish Volunteer*. But it is suspicious that Cumann na mBan sources are the only indicators of such an expansion. Like many other organisations of the time, Cumann na mBan may have wanted to project an exaggeration of national strength in order to encourage new members into what was falsely perceived as a strong and vibrant society. By July 1914 Cumann na mBan claimed to have 30 operational branches. By October they had increased that claim to 'upwards of 60'. It is interesting that a more precise figure could not be arrived at for October and thus it would appear that the figures quoted in the *Irish Volunteer* can be questioned, to some degree at least.

In all likelihood, Cumann na mBan did have upwards of sixty nominal branches. However, many of these were branches in name only. They may have had a few enthusiastic members but not enough to keep the branch active. Throughout 1914 and 1915 most RIC County Inspectors did not report the existence of Cumann na mBan branches in their areas. They frequently reported on the political activities of everyone from the United Irish League (the Irish Party's local organisation) to the Fianna (a nationalist Boy Scout organisation), but Cumann na mBan were not doing anything to bring them to the attention of the police. It is quite likely that some County Inspectors knew of the existence of Cumann na mBan branches in their various counties but did not report their knowledge to Dublin as they simply did no consider women as a threat to the State. Their failure to identify the threat of a women's nationalist group may well have been borne of their preconceived notions of feminine passiveness but it is clear that in 1914 and 1915 Cumann na mBan were not challenging those preconceptions.

In one of the few police reports of pre-1916 Cumann na mBan activity, the County Inspector for Kerry reported that in March 1915:

> Miss McCarthy of Dungarvan visited the county ... and delivered lectures of a pro-German anti-recruiting nature at Killarney, Tralee and Dingle. She formed branches of Cumann na mBan in Tralee and Dingle.

The *Irish Volunteer* of 1 May 1915 gave a more detailed account of the activities of Miss McCarthy, and one which correlated with the Kerry inspector's report:

> During the months of March and April the Southern Branches were visited by Miss McCarthy, organiser for Cumann na mBan. She held successful meetings in Cork, Killarney, and Limerick where the society has flourishing Branches and also established promising new centres at Tralee and Dingle. She is at present visiting Wexford, meeting with members of existing Branches at Enniscorthy and Wexford town, and arranging to organise Branches in other districts.
>
> Miss McCarthy's tour having proved so successful and so helpful to country Branches, it is hoped to arrange shortly for a similar tour in other parts of Ireland.

Thus throughout March, April and May, McCarthy moved through three southern counties on Cumann na mBan business, yet only one RIC inspector reported her presence. Because the inspector general reported Cumann na mBan activity in both Cork and Limerick in March, we know that the County Inspectors for Cork East and for Limerick must have been aware of the existence of

Cumann na mBan branches in their areas. Yet neither reported McCarthy's activities. Therefore it is safe to assume that Police reports, prior to the 1916 rising cannot be considered accurate assessments of Cumann na mBan's national strength. But whilst the small columns which appeared in the *Irish Volunteer* were accurate for individual areas and named branches, whose members were, after all, among the newspapers readership, they should not be relied upon when providing national assessments. For example, the Killarney branch which were described as 'flourishing' in May 1915, was restarted in April 1916 along with the Enniscorthy branch, both of which were inactive for a period.[15]

Perhaps some of the more interesting admissions of Cumann na mBan's failure to expand in line with the Volunteers came from the organisation itself. On 11 December 1915 their column in the *Irish Volunteer* clearly stated that whilst every district in Ireland could boast of a company of Volunteers, 'in many parts of the country the women are still inactive'. By February 1916 Cumann na mBan hoped their flag day might raise awareness of the organisation in those areas where it had failed to establish itself:

> We should also like to remind Branches that the flag day, which we hope every Branch will be able to organise, has been initiated not merely for providing funds for the organisation but also for propaganda purposes. The fact that the Cumann na mBan is not well known in some districts is all the more reason why their flag should be produced, so as to rouse curiosity and enquiry.[16]

One of Cumann na mBan's earlier organisers later recalled that it was local Volunteers who were often the instigators of Cumann na mBan's organisation in various districts. Volunteer officers who saw potential in the women's auxiliary and wanted a branch in their own area sometimes took the initiative ahead of local women:

> There would be some contact before I would visit these places – A Volunteer might be up in town (Dublin) and ask Mrs Wyse Power to form a Branch. I would always have some place to go and someone to meet when I arrived at the town.[17]

In an era when women simply were not used to political activity, local Volunteers were often centrally involved in the formation of Cumann na mBan branches all through the revolutionary period.[18] Indeed Bridget O'Mullane later testified that many of the first members of the branches that she formed were handpicked by local Volunteer officers.[19]

For all their expansionary difficulties at home Cumann na mBan did meet with limited, but surely unexpected, success among Irish communities abroad. Branches were set up in Liverpool, Glasgow, Manchester and London and enquiries regarding the initiation of branches were received from as far away as Australia and the USA.[20] But whilst these branches must have brought financial benefits to the organisation at home, their political fervour and overall usefulness is debatable. We know that the Glasgow branch was involved in the shipment of weapons and explosives to Ireland. Margaret Skinnider later testified to having carried them over.[21] Likewise, the chief purpose of London's first Cumann na mBan branch was gun running. That branch later lapsed when most of its members moved to Ireland as hostilities escalated. However, the London organisation did re-emerge in 1920.[22] But some other overseas branches were likely to have been little more than social circles for expatriated Irish women. Lilly Farrelly of the Liverpool branch left the following account of activities there:

> As far as I can remember it was about 1916 that the Cumann na mBan started in Lpool, it was in the Irish Foresters meeting rooms in Seaforth St, Lpool. Dancing, Irish language classes and First Aid Classes etc. Quiet pleasant evenings were held there

> until trouble broke out and fires started at the Lpool Docks. People got very frightened and Irish homes were raided and arrests were made. So nearly all clubs had to close. Two of the Cumann members were arrested … but were released no charge, so that was the end of Cumann na mBan club.[23]

Whilst Farrelly's account portrays an organisation that was centred on Irish cultural activities, but was unwilling to maintain those activities under threat of arrest, she was incorrect on at least one detail. We know that Liverpool Cumann na mBan existed in 1915. And we know that they were quite an active branch as they sent a delegate to the Cumann na mBan convention in October of that year. Indeed the list of branches which sent delegates to that convention is surely our best indicator of how many active branches existed by October 1915.

The convention was held at 2 Dawson Street, Dublin, on Sunday 31 October 1915. This was the same day as the Volunteer convention, something which was surely intended to facilitate country members who may have been able to travel to Dublin with Volunteer neighbours, family or friends. Cumann na mBan had expressed the wish that 'all branches should be represented at the Convention',[24] yet when the day came only the most enthusiastic attended. Represented at the Cumann na mBan convention of 1915 were the branches of Ardpatrick, Athenry, Belfast, Ballylanders, Cork, Castlebar, the Central and Inghinidhe branches, Drumcondra/Fairview, Limerick, Liverpool, Lusk and Tralee. The only branches who decided to demonstrate some kind of unity with their comrades by at least dispatching letters of regret for their non-attendance were Glasgow, Dingle, Drumcollogher, Castlegregory and Westport.[25] The Central branch had changed their address on no less than seven occasions since their foundation but the address of the convention had been announced in the *Irish Volunteer* of 23 October and that address had first been mentioned in the edition of

16 October, therefore it is unlikely that the correspondence of any active branch (active branches surely kept abreast of address changes) failed to reach the convention.[26] Thus an organisation which had boasted 'upwards of 60' branches twelve months previously was now faced with a situation where only thirteen branches were active enough to send one or more delegates to Dublin and only five more were capable sending a letter. Of those eighteen branches, three were Dublin based and eight – Athenry, Castlebar, Westport, Glasgow, Drumcondra/Fairview, Tralee, Dingle and Castlegregory – had only begun their operations in the five months prior to the convention.[27] Indeed the enthusiasm of the Castlegregory Branch may well have waned in the months after the convention, as they appear to have gone dormant for a period before being restarting in January 1916.[28]

The membership numbers for any of the branches are difficult to ascertain, although we do know that at least some had membership rolls in excess of 100.[29] However not every woman on a Cumann na mBan roll was automatically an active member. In February 1916 the Inghinidhe branch boasted 60-70 members on roll and yet had only organised 42 of those members into active squads.[30]

Where police do report membership figures, their estimates are usually lower in the rural districts although quite high in urban areas. However, a sample of sufficient size cannot be extracted from police reports until nearly six months after the convention. In March 1916 police reports indicate the presence of one branch of 130 members in Cork, two totalling 46 members in Galway, one of 30 in Offaly, one of 40 members in Mayo, one of twenty members in Westmeath and one of only eight members in Waterford. As police were more likely to be observing active members, we can say that the average active membership per branch was approximately 39 members. Adjusting this figure to take into account the sixteen Irish branches that attended or wrote to the convention, we can say that Cumann na mBan had no more than about 650 active members in

Ireland. Adjusting for the 43 branches Cumann na mBan later claimed to have had in the immediate aftermath of the rising, we arrive at a figure of 1677.[31] Thus, in late 1915/early 1916, the organisation had between 650 and 1,700 active members.

The 1915 convention also elected the organisation's first president and vice-president; Jennie Wyse Power was elected in the former capacity and Nancy O'Rahilly in the latter.[32] Once again there was no place on the executive for Markievicz. In the month prior to the convention the Countess had been publicly critical of the subordinate role of Cumann na mBan, saying that, 'these ladies auxiliaries demoralise women'.[33] By now Markievicz was still channelling most of her energy into the more militant and less gender stereotypical Citizen Army.

Prior to the rising Cumann na mBan was a fledgling organisation characterised by partly active branches which drifted to and from its membership, and a small number of continuously active and thriving branches. As one would expect, it often painted a much rosier picture of its health than was really the case. But even among the Cumann na mBan records the reader will find enough contradictions to ask some serious questions. If the organisation was thriving and teeming with active members then why was the proposed summer camp called off in September 1915?[34] If rural branches were active and flourishing, why did the Central branch make numerous appeals for affiliation fees to be paid up? Why did the organisation issue an urgent appeal for funds in August 1914?[35]

Pre-1916 Cumann na mBan were hardly a strong national organisation representative of Irish womanhood. Yet the relatively poor state of their health is largely explained by one factor, the same factor that meant their brother organisation, the Irish Volunteers, were also in declining health: the Volunteer split of 1914.

The Volunteer Split

A few days after the passing of the third Home Rule bill in

September 1914, John Redmond, a member of the Volunteer executive and leader of the Irish Parliamentary Party, urged Irish Volunteers to join the British army and fight in the First World War. Redmond's appeal caused a schism on the Volunteer executive. Eoin MacNeill, along with about 11,000 Volunteers refused to endorse Redmond's position. They retained the Irish Volunteer name, though the press and police began to inaccurately refer to them as Sinn Féin Volunteers. It is estimated that the great bulk of the old movement (approximately 170,000) supported Redmond calling themselves' the National Volunteers, and commonly referred to as Redmondites.

For a time Cumann na mBan tried to remain neutral in the Volunteer feud. No support for either position was publicly announced. Four years after the split and just as Cumann na mBan and the IRA were entering the most intensive phase of their guerrilla war against Crown forces, Jennie Wyse Power reflected upon the Volunteer split as follows:

> Our mandate from that first meeting was that we were strictly non-political. For many weeks after what is known as the Volunteer split, Cumann na mBan made no move to stand by the Irish Volunteers only. This was not due to want of sympathy with the stand taken by them but from practical reasons. However, the time came to test our organisation and we decided to call a convention. This was held in November 1914 … A resolution from Ardpatrick Branch (Co. Limerick) was tabled pledging the organisation to neutrality as between the two sections of Volunteers. It was seconded by Miss Agnes O'Farrelly M.A. The resolution had practically no supporters. I can only remember the speech and vote of Miss O'Farrelly in defence of it. Miss McSweeney BA, Cork, and Miss Madge Daly, Limerick, led the Convention by their strong denunciation to help the side that had gone over to recruiting for England. The decision cleared the road for the work of Cumann na mBan, and the

newly-elected Executive issued a manifesto to their Branches recording the fact that in future their sympathy and practical assistance would be given to the Irish Volunteers.[36]

But Wyse Power was being a little misleading. The manifesto to which she referred had appeared in the *Irish Volunteer* of 17 October and was originally made public on 5 October.[37] It had not been issued by a 'newly-elected Executive', but by the provisional executive that had been in place since before the inaugural public meeting at Wynn's. An extract of the *Irish Volunteer*'s report of the meeting which first discussed the manifesto reads as follows:

> At a specially convened meeting of the Central Branch of Cumann na mBan ... on 6th inst., the manifesto issued by the Provisional Executive of the Organisation was heartily endorsed by the overwhelming majority of the members. Mrs Dudley Edwards and a few others resigned on the declaration of the result of the voting. The following is the manifesto :...
>
> As the Women's section of the Irish Volunteers we wish at this time to remind our members that they should abide loyally by the constitution of our Organisation.
>
> We came into being to advance the cause of Irish liberty and to organise Irishwomen in the furtherance of that object. We feel bound to make the pronouncement that to urge or encourage Irish Volunteers to enlist in the British Army cannot under any circumstances be regarded as consistent with the work we have set ourselves to do … we call on Irishmen to remain in their own country and join the army of the Irish Volunteers.[38]

This above meeting was called in the absence of moderates like O'Farrelly, and thus was later described as 'caucus' by Bridget Dudley Edwards, who as reported, resigned in protest.[39] The *Irish*

Independent gave the following account:

> The Central Branch, Cumann na mBan at a general meeting of the members approved by an overwhelming majority of a manifesto issued by the Provisional Committee of the organisation. Mrs Dudley Edwards led a small minority who disapproved of the manifesto. Most of her followers subsequently resigned.[40]

Wyse Power tells us that she presided over the above meeting although she inaccurately states that it occurred after a general convention in November. She records that the split was not in-substantial. Referring to the first reading of the October manifesto she states that:

> This was first read at a general meeting of the Central Branch (Dublin), where I presided, and was adopted by 88 members present, as against 28. This vote was an index to the state of our organisation, or, rather, the working part of it.[41]

The above statement seems to allude to a portion of Cumann na mBan which was not working. We have already seen that by October of 1915, only a handful of branches were active. It would appear that many branches ceased activity when the Central branch declared in favour of the Irish Volunteers. Even in the active Central branch the declaration had not met with unanimous approval.[42]

The convention which Wyse Power was to claim 'cleared the road' for the manifesto in favour of the Irish Volunteers, did not actually take place until 13 December, two months after the Central executive had already issued its dictat.[43] In reality it was little more than an attempt at glossing over the decision with a veneer of democracy. O'Farrelly, and a few other delegates from Ardpatrick still argued a more moderate stance, but effectively they were attempting to shut the gate when the proverbial horse had bolted.

Cumann na mBan had stated its position two months previously and most moderates had already walked out. There could be no back-tracking. Subsequently, O'Farrelly resigned from Cumann na mBan, although she remained active in the Gaelic League.[44]

The split in the Central branch reflected, to some degree at least, what had happened in the Volunteer organisation. In the case of the Volunteers the Redmondite faction had walked away from the executive. Soon after they had done so, numerous companies of Volunteers across the island declared in support of Redmond and thus the National Volunteers were formed. It would appear logical that something similar may have occurred in Cumann na mBan. In *Leabhar na mBan* Wyse Power explains that whilst many branches became moribund, none associated themselves with the National Volunteers:

> In justice, however, I must state that many Branches after the convention's decision became defunct. But in no instance did any of these Branches become in any way associated with the National Volunteers. The failure of the moribund Branches to follow us in this period was, I consider, due to the decadent spirit of nationality at the time.

But again Wyse Power is presenting an image of a unity which simply did not exist. Even the strongest branches of Cumann na mBan were somewhat fragmented. In Limerick the Redmondite faction did not have control of the branch committee and so they 'resigned in a body' and set up an organisation known as the 'National Volunteers Ladies Association', which appears to have been unique to Limerick.[45] But in several other places Redmondites did have control of branch committees and thus those branches associated themselves with the National Volunteers. Lusk was one branch which declared for Redmond and their letter of withdrawal from Cumann na mBan was printed in the *National Volunteer*, the new newspaper of the Redmondite faction) of 17 October 1914:

> My Committee have directed me to inform you that we have withdrawn from your organisation, 12 D'Olier street, and that we will have nothing further to do with you. We condemn your policy of supporting the manifesto issued by minority of Provisional Committee I.V.
>
> We, with the other National women of Ireland, owe a deep debt of gratitude to Mr Redmond and the Irish Parliamentary Party for the glorious work they have done for Ireland and we pledge ourselves to support them in every way.

The following week similar declarations were made through the pages of the *National Volunteer*, by the Naas and Athy branches. The Naas secession made the columns of *The Irish Times* [46] but it was the Athy branch announcement which gives a clearer indication of the future activities of these Redmondite branches. Their statement of support for Redmond came from the 'Athy National Volunteer Nursing Corps (Cumann na mBan)'.[47]

Thus it would appear logical that many other Redmondite branches formed themselves into nursing corps within the National Volunteers. These nursing and ambulance corps were certainly formed in a few places, among them, Waterford, Tralee, and Tipperary, whilst first-aid classes likely to have been attended by former Cumann na mBan members, were run by several National Volunteer companies.[48] The membership of women was definitely one of the features of the National Volunteers that distinguished them from their Irish Volunteer counterparts. Meanwhile, the Red Cross were also forming branches in Ireland during 1914 and 1915 and it is likely that their membership included some ex-Cumann na mBan members. Indeed nationalists in Bandon had been particularly worried about the Red Cross drawing from Cumann na mBan's pool of potential members.[49]

There were also a number of other organisations which may have picked up some of Cumann na mBan's membership. The first was the Volunteer Aid Association which had been formed around July 1914.[50] In *Leabhar na mBan*, Wyse Power states that the membership of this organisation was composed 'exclusively of fashionable women followers of the Irish Party'.[51] Her assertion was only partially correct. Whilst the Volunteer Aid Association was associated with the parliamentary movement, it did have many male members.[52] Indeed its formation had initially provoked some hostility from within feminist circles as it appeared to be undermining Cumann na mBan by setting out to do the work which the latter had identified for itself.[53] Through the columns of the *Irish Volunteer* Cumann na mBan's reaction was to remind readers that they were the 'only organisation belonging to the Irish Volunteers' and that branches should check with headquarters before accepting any offers of assistance from other organisations.[54] They need not have worried as the Volunteer Aid Association never appeared to rival them in terms of its membership numbers or geographical penetration and it soon vanished from the public eye. The second organisation which doubtlessly picked up some former members, was exclusively female and began as a direct reaction to the split in Cumann na mBan.

When Bridget Dudley Edwards led her followers out of the Central branch meeting that approved the October manifesto, she did not walk out on her sense of national duty. By the end of the month she was appealing for the foundation of a 'Women's National Corps' and by April 1915 she was already a member of the women's section of the 4th battalion of the National Volunteers in Dublin. Using that position she organised the Women's National Council, whose primary purpose was to collect money in order to arm and equip the National Volunteers.[55] This organisation does not appear to have had an enormous impact either and outside some limited accounts in the *National Volunteer*, its activities were unreported.

It is certain that Cumann na mBan lost more than half its membership during the Volunteer split. As already mentioned, just two weeks after the appearance of the manifesto in October 1914, they had claimed 'upwards of 60' branches.[56] Yet in 1919 the organisation claimed that immediately after Easter 1916 they had 'about 43 affiliated branches'.[57] Thirty-one newly-formed branches were named by the *Irish Volunteer* after the split and before the Easter rising.[58] Thus, by the organisation's own figures, a maximum of twelve original branches survived the split. Of the reported 'upwards of 60' this accounts for approximately twenty per cent. If the organisation had lost 80 per cent of its branch network, the resignation of members from surviving branches meant that it had probably lost an even larger proportion of its membership. Subsequent recollections of anti-Redmondite members from Cork, Dublin and Wexford indicate that in those areas the organisation had lost at least half of their initial membership.[59] Indeed a former member from Enniscorthy later recalled the meeting where she and a friend had sought to rally other members against Redmond's declaration as follows:

> I gave my speech and asked any member that was against Redmond to stand on my side of the hall, but Mrs Green and I were standing alone. It was my first big disappointment. I was heartbroken. When we told them at de Lacey's they said 'Try again and form a new Branch'. I did, and a few members came back.[60]

By October 1915 it is clear that Cumann na mBan had not become a widespread national movement. Indeed one senior member later wrote that 'before 1916 there were only a few branches of the organisation here and there throughout the country'.[61] Any advancement they had made was greatly negated by the Volunteer split and a subsequent haemorrhaging from their ranks. Yet they did survive the split. They were still the women's auxiliary of the increasingly republican Irish Volunteers. But what did this auxiliary do?

Early Activities

The early activities of Cumann na mBan were, unsurprisingly, based around the four primary aims they had identified for themselves. Their own organisation was part civilian, part military. They were hardly an army but they were not a sewing circle either. They had a strong nationalist ethos and as such did their utmost to organise nationalist women all across the island. Thus, in the early months the civilian positions of 'branch secretary' and 'lady chairman' were to the forefront of the organisation. In those early days their activities revolved almost entirely around fundraising for the Volunteers, and first-aid classes.

On Friday 24 April 1914 Cumann na mBan launched the Defence of Ireland Fund at the Mansion House. It began with the following impassioned appeal issued by the Provisional Committee to the Irish people:

> Fellow Countrymen and Countrywomen,
>
> We make a strong appeal to your patriotism and to that sense of nationality which neither wars, nor famines, nor oppressions have been able to crush in our people, to help us arm our men and organise our women.
>
> It is not necessary to point out to you that the heart of the country is with the National Volunteers …
>
> We want to arm and equip this disciplined national force, not as a menace to any section of our countrymen, for the rights and well being of all are equally important to us, but as a means of gaining our clear political rights and of securing and defending the liberty of Ireland … We appeal to you to support the Defence Fund, not as you would wish to respond to any ordinary demand on your patriotism but in a spirit of sacrifice and in recognition of a supreme opportunity that has never

come before and may never come again in our lifetime …[62]

Although the fund was launched by Cumann na mBan, and the women's organisation made sizeable contributions to it, it was not organised and administered entirely by the women. Indeed in the early days, as Cumann na mBan were still a fledgling group, it was the Volunteers who organised collections throughout the island in aid of the new fund.[63] But, little by little, as new Cumann na mBan branches appeared, the women's organisation began to make an increasing contribution to the fund and Cumann na mBan branches throughout the country began their own collection work. House to house and church gate collections were organised and an increasing number of women rattled collection tins at various nationalist events. In October 1914, Cumann na mBan raised rural awareness of their organisation's activities when their collectors raised £6 2s 1d in a collection on Jones' Road, before the All-Ireland final between Clare and Laois.[64] Fundraising in some branches was on a particularly large scale. During a three-day Fete in July 1914 the Limerick branch raised £220 for the Defence of Ireland Fund.[65] Considering that the average wage of a domestic maid was £10-14 per annum; cooks, housekeepers and chauffeurs made around £25 per annum whilst doctors were paid up to £200 a year, this was not an insubstantial sum.[66]

With the Volunteer split, the control of the fund might have become an issue. But it appears that Cumann na mBan's HQ did continue to control the purse strings, most likely because the women in charge of them were generally part of the Irish Volunteer faction. In London, Min Ryan was one such woman and she hastily made her way across the Irish Sea with the funds of the London branch in case the Redmondite faction would take control of them.[67] Throughout the latter end of 1914, the *National Volunteer* complained on several occasions that Cumann na mBan continued to collect for the fund but were not providing the Redmondite faction with any money. Eventually the Redmondites began their own fundraising activities and we have already seen that some former Cumann na mBan activists were to the forefront of same.

When the Volunteer split occurred, however, Cumann na mBan's method of fundraising was slightly altered for very practical reasons. Máire Nic Shiúbhlaigh (Marie Walker), a well-known Irish actress who worked with the Central branch in those early days, later recalled the early fundraising activities and the effect the Volunteer split had had upon them:

> Essentially, Cumann na mBan was founded to help in establishing the Volunteers. At the beginning, before belief in the wisdom of insurrection rather than debate became widespread, it was not the military organisation it later became. Apart from frequent classes in first aid, stretcher bearing and, occasionally, field signalling, a great deal of time was given over to the gathering of funds in support of the rapid expansion of the Volunteer organisation. Since there was a certain degree of opposition to the movement in certain circles – after the Volunteer 'split' many looked on the refusal to join forces with the British in France as a treacherous 'stab in the back' – the most effective way of doing this was by organising entertainments. Door to door canvassing was almost certain to meet with failure.[68]

The organisation of, and participation in, dances and concerts by Cumann na mBan did more than raise money for the Volunteers. The importance of such events, usually held in conjunction with the Volunteers, should not be underestimated. Ireland had long had a separate identity to Britain in terms of its religion and its segregated system of land-ownership. However, with the penal laws almost entirely abolished, and the Land League having secured the ownership of the land for Catholic farmers, the sense of a separate Irish identity was in danger of decline. But with nationalism becoming a new driving force in European politics, it was bound to take root in Ireland. The organisation of cultural events by groups like Cumann na mBan, the Gaelic League and the GAA ensured that this rooting of Irish nationalism was deeper than it would otherwise have been. The sense of a separate Irish identity (whether real or imagined) was expressed vociferously at Cumann na mBan fundraising events. Nationalist flags and emblems festooned the walls of dancehalls. Lil Conlon mentioned a tricolour hanging in City Hall, Cork, at one such event in February 1915.[69] This was over a year before the flag flew over the GPO during Easter week 1916. Meanwhile 'Tableaux depicting historical epochs' were regularly presented on stage.[70] These fundraisers were patronised by the Irish youth and thus that youth was indoctrinated with Irish nationalism during the course of their normal social activity.

Nic Shiúbhlaigh's account also gives us an idea of the primary importance of first-aid training to Cumann na mBan in the early days. Classes began in Dublin and spread quite rapidly to provincial branches. In the organisation of such classes the Limerick branch demonstrated an amusing impudence in their desire to acquire the necessary training. They succeeded in obtaining government grants for attending first-aid classes put in place by the authorities at the outbreak of the First World War.[71] First-aid classes in Kildare, Cork and Dublin were also run under the direction of the Department of Agriculture and Technical Instruction and it is safe to assume that similar grants may well have been attained elsewhere.[72] In Dublin, M.J. Rafferty later recalled that the Central Branch collected £16 for guns via departmental grants.[73] Thus a peculiar situation soon developed where Cumann na mBan were being trained and funded by the very administration they later sought to destroy.

By September 1914 the nursing sections of the organisation were urged to wear a uniform consisting of a washing frock, nurse's cap, apron and cuffs. An armlet was also recommended, on which the words 'Cumann na mBan' were stencilled or embroidered above a green cross.[74] The colour of the cross underlined Cumann na mBan's nationalist ethos and it would appear that the famous red cross was avoided for very specific reasons. Cumann na mBan had applied to the headquarters of the Red Cross in Geneva for affiliation. However, they had been told that the Red Cross could not recognise a country without a standing army of its own and therefore they were told that their application should first be directed to the British Red Cross.[75] Their strong sense of a separate Irish identity would not permit such an association with a British organisation and thus it was 'decided to have nothing to do with official Red Cross work, with a reservation that whenever the Red Cross was needed' they 'would use it without permission from anyone'.[76] In October 1915 these green cross sections of Cumann na mBan were formally attached to the Dublin battalions of the Irish Volunteers.[77]

In Dublin foot drill became a part of Cumann na mBan's training in the early months. The aim of such drill in any military organisation was, and is, to instil discipline and promote teamwork. In this regard one aspect of this training is worth mentioning. The officers who gave orders to the women during those early drills were frequently male Volunteers. Indeed this situation would appear to have prevailed in many Cumann na mBan branches right up until 1919.[78] This process is bound to have acquainted the members with receiving, and obeying without question, orders from Volunteer officers. Thus, to some extent at least, a chain of command which reached outside of the women's organisation was established in the minds of many of its members.

One of the more important occasions on which the women were to display their foot drill was during the 'pilgrimage' to Bodenstown in July 1915. This annual event was, and is, essentially a gathering of various Irish nationalist bodies at the graveside of Theobald Wolfe Tone. Wolfe Tone was a founding member of the United Irishmen and is regarded by many as the father of Irish republicanism. In 1915 Cumann na mBan's comparative lack of numerical strength was displayed by the participation of only 100 women from the Dublin branches. However, the increasing respect of other nationalist bodies for the women was equally demonstrated by the salute afforded them by both the Irish and the National Volunteers.[79] The next great nationalist demonstration occurred with the funeral of O'Donovan Rossa, a former Fenian who died in America, in August of 1915. This event saw a stronger Cumann na mBan presence with branches from Cork, Limerick, Belfast and even Liverpool represented.

Cumann na mBan's public appearance was to become increasingly militaristic with the adoption of a uniform of Volunteer tweed at the 1915 convention. They had first worn this uniform in public at the *Aeridheacht Mhór* at St Enda's College, Rathfarnham, on 5 September 1915. Some of the wives of those Irishmen serving in the British army did not approve of Cumann na mBan and were able to vent their anger by hurling stones and mud at the now identifiable members. One such attack occurred at Limerick railway station as a contingent of Cork Cumann na mBan made their homeward journey from a Volunteer review in 1915.[80] In addition to the mud and stones, the nickname 'grasshoppers', was also hurled at Cumann na mBan members' parading in uniform.[81] Uniforms were to be provided at members own expense and thus the 1915 convention declared them 'optional'. Most members made the uniforms themselves and the variance in tailoring skills meant that some of the early garments were badly made; 'as if they were cut out with a knife and a fork'.[82] They were not worn by every member and indeed one member of the Central branch later wrote that prior to 1916, 'they were the exception rather than the rule'.[83] Likewise the Cumann na mBan badge, a rifle upon which the letters 'C na mB' rested, cost 8d each and is not likely to have been attained by every member. The appearance of the uniform and badge were testament to the organisation's increasing militant republicanism.

With the First World War well underway, the military activities of Cumann na mBan were largely centred around the tactics of the conventional warfare of that period. Thus, whilst the modern reader may question the wisdom of activities like semaphore signalling, at that time it made perfect sense. This signalling, involving the use of flags, was practiced in many branches with the desire that those women who demonstrated themselves capable of signalling twenty letters per minute, would then progress to training in Morse code.

It was only after the Redmondite split that the more extreme republican element of Cumann na mBan began to diversify into other areas like rifle practice and gun maintenance.[84] In that area, some Belfast and Dublin women became expert. Indeed during a handicapped shooting competition with the Volunteers in Belfast two Cumann na mBan members took first and second prizes. Even without the handicap, Miss Kelly's score was the second highest overall.[85] The Belfast branch was particularly active in relation to target practice with live ammunition. But this does not appear to have been the norm in other branches as such practice was deemed to be optional. Where it was to be practiced, it was recommended that miniature rifles be used or that service rifles be converted to a smaller .22 calibre.[86] This optional practice, with modified firearms, must have seemed pointless to many branches and there is no evidence to suggest that it was widespread. Knowledge of the workings of and care for firearms generally, however, was far from pointless and all Cumann na mBan branches were expected to provide the necessary training. Members of ambulance sections were expected to be capable of loading and unloading the rifles of fallen men to whom they may have had to attend in the heat of battle. There can be little doubt that the training of women in firearm maintenance was of enormous benefit to the republican movement in the years that followed.

It was also after the split that Cumann na mBan's organisational structure took on a much more militaristic bearing. In December 1915 the organisational objectives of Cumann na mBan were set out as follows:

Branches should be formed into squads of 6, including squad leader. Six of the best signallers should form a special signalling squad. The rest of the squads should be comprised of First Aid and Home Nursing only. The squad leader should be chosen for having the best knowledge of the work in which the squad is engaged in. Two squads form a section, which is supervised by a Section Commander, who is also selected on merit only. The Branch Commandant will direct and supervise generally.

MOBILISATION

The Squad Commander should have the names and addresses of her squad, and the Section Commander should also have the names and addresses of the whole section.

The Commandant issues orders to the Section Commanders, whose duty it is to call up the members of their squads. When mobilisation orders are expected members should leave word at home as to where they can be found, if they are going away from home. Quick mobilisation is most imperative, and should be practiced often and at all hours, until you can bring out your Branch on parade at the shortest possible notice … organise your Branches in the way prescribed.[87]

It should be borne in mind that these were only the organisational objectives of Cumann na mBan and did not necessarily reflect the reality on the ground. It is quite likely that the more active branches attempted to adhere to them, whilst smaller and more inefficient branches did not.

In 1915 Cumann na mBan began their relentless propaganda campaign by publishing three nationalist pamphlets entitled: The Spanish War' by Theobald Wolfe Tone, 'Why Ireland is Poor' and 'Dean Swift on the Situation'. These pamphlets reproduced arguments originally made by Wolfe Tone and Dean Swift questioning the wisdom of British government and army recruitment in Ireland, as well as economic reasoning which appeared to demonstrate that Irish poverty was a consequence of British rule.[88] A fourth title in the publication of which the organisation was involved was an account of the life of O'Donovan Rossa, written by Mary MacSwiney's brother, Terence.[89]

By the beginning of 1916 Cumann na mBan had become a small but reasonably well organised and partially trained, quasi-military organisation. They had survived the Redmondite split and were even announcing the formation of a few new branches. Whilst only sixteen Irish branches could be deemed active in October 1915, the organisation did maintain a gradual expansion into 1916.[90] Yet if Cumann na mBan's numerical weakness was portrayed by the poor attendance at the 1915 convention, so was one of its major organisational weaknesses. Cumann na mBan's very existence depended on the existence of the Volunteers. As testament to their subordination to the Volunteers, the Cumann na mBan convention of 1915 greeted the Volunteer convention in Irish, their words translated as follows:

> Cumann na mBan congratulates the Convention of Irish Volunteers on all they have done for Ireland's cause and they promise to help them generously and firmly in every effort they make to keep the people of Ireland working in the service of Ireland.[91]

The Volunteers response was cordial but revealed exactly which organisation would lead and which would co-operate:

> The Irish Volunteer Convention wish Cumann na mBan well and it is their prayer that Cumann na mBan will continue the work that they are engaged in, in co-operation with the Irish Volunteers.[92]

In short, Cumann na mBan would help the Volunteers and the Volunteers valued their co-operation. The male organisation did not pledge any such co-operation with Cumann na mBan, however. They would lead and the women pledged themselves to follow. The night of the convention, Cumann na mBan women catered for a Volunteer reception.[93] Whilst they worked, the Volunteers, and probably some of Cumann na mBan's leadership, enjoyed themselves. The future of Cumann na mBan depended on the future of the Volunteers, although the reverse was not necessarily the case.

Cumann na mBan and the Rising

The rebellion on the streets of Dublin during Easter week 1916 is often regarded as the birth of the modern Irish Republic. For many years the leaders of the rebel forces were portrayed as heroes who went to their certain death so that Ireland could be free. Then in the 1970s, as a new generation of militant republicans began killing and dying in Northern Ireland, the more popular portrayal became one of a group of destructive dreamers who tore a city asunder in a fight which could never have resulted in victory. Both arguments were based on the assumption that these leaders knew the rising could not succeed. Yet in more recent years we have begun to acknowledge that the rising did not go according to plan and thus its failure was not as certain before the event as the benefit of hindsight would have us believe.[1]

The rising was essentially planned by the IRB and executed by the military organisations which they had infiltrated, namely the Irish Volunteers and the Irish Citizen Army. It was intended that these organisations would rise, in pursuit of a fully independent Irish Republic, all over the island on Easter Sunday 23 April 1916. However, due to a series of confusing orders and counter-orders, the rising did not generally spread beyond Dublin and did not begin until Easter Monday. On Easter Monday 24 April, the Citizen Army and the Irish Volunteers began seizing a number of strategically positioned buildings around Dublin city. The 'Irish Republic' was declared and its provisional government was installed in the General

Post Office (GPO) on Sackville Street (now O'Connell Street). The British army were taken by surprise as many of its senior officers were attending a race meeting which occurred on the bank holiday Monday. They organised quickly, however, and soon their numerical supremacy and superior weaponry had the rebels in disarray. On Friday, Padraig Pearse, head of the Provisional government, ordered the surrender of all rebel garrisons and the rebellion ended.

Although the rising failed for many different reasons, many of those reasons occurred in the days immediately prior to its commencement, when confusion had prevailed across Ireland. The rising began on Easter Monday but the confusion had begun the previous Thursday.

A Nation Confused

On Thursday 20 April 1916, the IRB circulated a document around various nationalist quarters in Dublin. The document, now widely believed to have been a forgery, was a British order for disarmament of the Volunteers. The IRB hoped that Eoin MacNeill, the official leader of the Volunteers, who was not party to their plans for a rising, would not allow this disarmament to occur without a fight. At first their deception paid off and MacNeill issued an order for a general mobilisation on Easter Sunday. Later on Thursday, however, MacNeill learned that an insurrection was planned and cancelled the mobilisation order. By Friday he had learned of plans to land arms in Kerry on Easter Sunday and changed his mind, believing that it was now necessary to fight as plans were already well advanced. What MacNeill did not know was that the original plan had called for the landing of arms as early as Friday and the German ship bearing those arms had cut all communication and would stick to the original timetable.

In Kerry, Sir Roger Casement, who had procured the arms in Germany, was arrested on Friday. The German ship that carried those arms was intercepted and escorted to Cork Harbour by the

British navy. There its crew scuttled the vessel just outside the harbour, sending an estimated 20,000 rifles to the bottom. When MacNeill learned of these events he again countermanded the order to rise on Sunday. Late on Saturday he issued an order cancelling all previous orders for the Sunday mobilisation. The *Sunday Independent* repeated that order stating that, 'owing to the very critical position all orders given to Irish Volunteers for tomorrow Easter Sunday are hereby rescinded'. In adjoining columns news of the arms seizure in Kerry was also published.

Meanwhile the Military Council, those IRB, Volunteer and Citizen Army members who had planned the rising, met in Liberty Hall, Dublin. They confirmed the cancellation for Sunday and issued a new order to begin operations at noon on Easter Monday. Many women, and some Cumann na mBan members, carried these orders and counter-orders up and down the country.

In the midst of all this confusion Cumann na mBan were left out in the cold. Some branches had planned for mobilisation on Sunday but they had no idea that a rising was intended. Ruth Taillon's well-researched study of the women of 1916 gives the following account of Lily O'Brennan's confusion in the days before the rising. O'Brennan was a member of the Central branch of Cumann na mBan and was also the sister-in-law of Eamonn Ceannt, who was one of the leaders of the insurrection:

> Máire Nic Shiúbhlaigh's Cumann na mBan Branch had not made plans to participate in the Sunday 'manoeuvres'. Lily O'Brennan had therefore invited Máire to join with her and accompany Eamonn Ceannt's 4th Dublin Battalion ... On Easter Sunday Máire awoke to read the countermand order...Máire and Lily spent the day at the Ceannts' making up first-aid kits and assembling equipment for the Volunteers ... That evening, Lily O'Brennan and her sister Áine Ceannt attended eight o'clock Mass. Áine then had the opportunity to

explain that a messenger had come for her husband Eamonn during the night and that the days manoeuvres had been called off. Lily was annoyed, but she did not realise that anything other than major manoeuvres had been planned.[2]

O'Brennan was not alone in her ignorance of the planned rising. Indeed it would appear that most Cumann na mBan and Irish Volunteer members were completely unaware that a rising had been planned. As far as they were concerned they were going on major manoeuvres and only the high-level leadership knew differently. It seems that Sorcha McMahon and a few other Cumann na mBan officers were aware of the imminence of the rising, and Markievicz, although her involvement with Cumann na mBan was now peripheral, was aware of all the original plans and the altered plans for Monday. She had been appointed as one of James Connolly's 'ghosts'. All the leaders had been assigned these 'ghosts' in order that plans would still be carried through if they were killed or detained. Markievicz was to take a more militant role than Cumann na mBan would have afforded her during the rising. Instead, she attached herself to the Irish Citizen Army for the duration of hostilities. Within the ranks of the Citizen Army, no official differential was made between the roles of women and men. Thus a few of the Citizan Army women involved in the insurgency of 1916 were armed and did involve themselves in fire fights.

Whatever the leadership of Cumann na mBan did or did not know about the intended insurrection, it appears that the women's orders to mobilise were countermanded on Sunday and then reissued for Monday. Thus when the rising began at 12 noon on Easter Monday, at least one Cumann na mBan branch were effectively mobilised. They were the Inghinidhe branch. Prior to the rising, the branch had been split into two groups. One was attached to the 4th Volunteer battalion the other to the 3rd.[3]

These two Inghinidhe groups were mobilised on Dublin's south side at the Cleaver Hall on Cork Street in Dolphin's Barn and on Merrion Square. From the Cleaver Hall, 25 Cumann na mBan members marched to Emerald Square where they joined A company of the 4th battalion.[4] From there they marched at the rear of A company into the distillery at Marrowbone Lane, which was a part of Eamonn Ceannt's South Dublin Union command. Along the route they were joined by Lily O'Brennan of the Central branch who had been unable to join with her own group on the north side due to the continued confusion regarding their mobilisation. O'Brennan was still under the impression that she was engaged in manoeuvres. She later recalled entering the distillery in Marrowbone Lane:

> I heard a knock. It was the butt-end of a rifle on the high wooden gates. Then rang out the clear commanding order from the captain in charge of our unit: 'Open in the name of the Irish Republic.'
>
> A wicket door was opened. There was a parley and delay, but Captain Séumas Ó Murchada and his guard forced their way in. The big gates flew open and the Volunteers and Cumann na mBan filed into the courtyard, the horse and cart rumbled quickly over its cobblestones; then the gates were quickly closed, and army manoeuvres at once began …
>
> I knew, now, that we had thrown down the gauntlet to the British Empire and that, placing our trust in God, we looked for victory.[5]

The second Inghinidhe group was mobilised and paraded on Merrion Square on Easter Monday morning.[6] They were to join with Eamon de Valera's 3rd battalion and enter Boland's Mills. Instead, having waited for some time, a courier from Boland's arrived to tell them their assistance would not be required and they could return to their homes.[7] As the week progressed de Valera's garrison had the dubious distinction of being the only rebel garrison which did not admit any women. There has been some debate as to de Valera's attitude to female combatants. In 1966 Commandant Joseph O'Connor wrote that:

> It was arranged that as the units were marching to their positions Cumann na mBan, who had paraded at Merrion Square, should join with the Companies and enter the bakery with C company, from whence they would operate. Unfortunately the arrangement fell through. I think it was the fact of remaining so long at Earlsfort Terrace that made us anxious to reach our new positions before twelve o'clock. This is the explanation of how we were deprived of the assistance of Cumann na mBan.[8]

But this explanation seems a little flimsy. If de Valera was able to dispatch a courier to the Cumman na mBan assembled on Merrion Square it would have been as simple for that courier to ask them to join in as to go home. Subsequently, in a Dáil debate on the 1938 constitution, de Valera did admit that he had turned some Cumann na mBan members away from his garrison due to their lack of soldierly training.[9] This was not de Valera's only reason for refusing the women's services however. According to the recollection of another man under his command at Boland's, he also believed women should be spared from the horrors of war.[10] It should be remembered that this attitude to women and warfare was common and indeed may even have been considered chivalrous at the time.

Yet de Valera may not have been completely opposed to making use of Cumann na mBan when he needed their services to carry dispatches. One member, although not in the vicinity of Boland's herself, later recalled that although de Valera had sent the women home, some had remained in the area and 'in a very short time Commandant de Valera was calling for them to carry dispatches'.[11] Another testified that she had carried a dispatch to Boland's Mills although she had not been admitted to the interior of the garrison.[12]

With the Inghinidhe branch effectively mobilised and in position before noon on Monday, one would expect that the Central branch were similarly efficient. Their story, however, was a little more complicated. The Inghinidhe were assigned to the 3rd and 4th battalions south of the River Liffey (Boland's Mills and South Dublin Union) and the Central branch was to take up positions on the north side.[13] They were not mobilised at any specific point, but instead in a general area stretching along Palmerston Place (which joins Upper Dominick Street across Phibsborough Road from the Broadstone railway station) and Middle Mountjoy Street into Mountjoy Street across the road from the Black Church.[14] The intention was that members would not draw attention to themselves by congregating in a large group. For this reason they were also forbidden from wearing uniforms.[15] Somewhere near the Broadstone, Sorcha McMahon and other senior members had set up their HQ. From there, Cumann na mBan officers sent various girls to the homes of Volunteers, with news of their loved one's mobilisation. The Central branch had been attached to Ned Daly's 1st battalion prior to Easter week and it seems that they were to link up with that battalion on Easter Monday. It was only when a message arrived from Daly stating that the women were not needed that Sorcha McMahon ordered the demobilisation of the group.[16] The group demobilised between 5 and 6pm and were ordered to reassemble on Tuesday.[17]

In the midst of all the confusion surrounding the orders and counter-orders the timing of the Central branches mobilisation also went a little askew. Some were mobilised for 11am, others for 12pm, and some were not even given mobilisation orders but proceeded to the Mountjoy Street area, where a Sunday mobilisation had previously been ordered.[18] Thus, unlike the Inghinidhe members who had initially paraded at 10 and 11am, some Central branch members were only getting into position as Volunteers were already seizing buildings.

At the time of the rising the only other branches in Dublin city were the Fairview and Columcille branches.[19] Prior to Easter week the Fairview branch had been attached to the 2nd battalion. Most of that battalion mobilised on Stephen's Green and marched into position at Jacob's biscuit factory.[20] The Fairview branch was also to mobilise on the Green at noon. However, as orders were late in arriving at the homes of their senior officers, the mobilisation did not occur on time and any women who did turn up at the Green found that the Volunteers had already departed. They then either returned to their homes or found their way into other garrisons.[21]

Thirty members of the Columcille branch mobilised at the Fianna hall on Merchant's Quay, across the river from the Four Courts garrison and just east of the Mendicity Institute. This branch was only about three weeks old and had not been attached to any of the four Dublin Volunteer battalions. As such, they received no specific orders during Monday. At 6pm, two Columcille members made their way to the Four Courts garrison across the Liffey. There, they were instructed to make contact with the Central branch further to the north of the quays. By then the Central branch had already been demobilised and thus the Columcille members returned to their homes. They met again on Tuesday morning but were still without orders. This time it was decided that individual members should do 'what seemed most urgent at the time by bringing all the ammunition ... down to the barricades'.[22] Columcille members were not the only ones who made their own way into action. As soon as hostilities had commenced the real story of Cumann na mBan's participation began. All over Dublin, and even in points beyond, individual Cumann na mBan members began to mobilise themselves.

On Their Own Initiative

At the beginning of the rising the only Cumann na mBan members in position with the rebels were those with Ceannt in the South Dublin Union and Winifred Carney in the GPO. Carney was a member of Belfast Cumann na mBan and a veteran of the trade union movement. It was in the latter capacity that she became acquainted with James Connolly and before the rising he had asked her to come to Dublin and act as his secretary during hostilities. Some women of the Citizen Army were in position across the city and although some were also members of Cumann na mBan, they were not under the command of Cumann na mBan at that time.

Thus, at the commencement of hostilities, Cumann na mBan members all over Dublin were left out of a fight in which they wished to be involved. It was not long before these women began to seek out ways in which they could become involved. In and around Dublin city centre little groups of Cumann na mBan began to gather. As they were individual members they were outside the formal command structure and had to depend on their own initiative in order to make their contribution.

With the Fairview branch orders having arrived rather late, it was Monday afternoon by the time some of them turned up at Stephen's Green. There, Constance Markievicz spotted three of them wandering around looking to join in the fight. Their names were Nora O'Daly, Bridget Murtagh and May Moore and they were welcomed by the Countess, as it was feared that the Citizen Army garrison at the Green did not have enough first-aid workers. They joined about half a dozen other women who worked at the first-aid post in the summerhouse.[23]

On that first day Margaret Skinnider, a member of Glasgow Cumann na mBan but attached to the Citizen Army for Easter week, and Constance Markievicz later alleged that the women came under fire from British guns situated on the roof of a nearby building. Their white dresses and red crosses (it would appear that Cumann na mBan used the red cross symbol during Easter week) apparently made them easy targets for the British soldiers.[24] Skinnider's account of the Easter hostilities was written in 1917, however. Therefore it is as likely to be republican propaganda as it is a truthful reflection of what she saw. Markievicz's account of the incident was written nine years later and remarkable similarities suggest that it was either drawn directly from Skinnider's reminiscence or from Markievicz's corroborating memory.[25] It should also be remembered however that one woman, Margaretta Keogh, was killed by a bullet (perhaps deliberately)[26] and that Skinnider herself was seriously wounded later in the week. British soldiers do not appear to have been too chivalrous to shoot at women. However, the comparative lack of female casualties does suggest that they generally did not do so.

Elsewhere, other members also drifted into various garrisons. We have already seen that Máire Nic Shiúbhlaigh had been invited to join Lily O'Brennan's branch for the Sunday manoeuvres. She had spent Sunday at Ceannt's preparing first-aid dressings. On Monday morning she and five other women met at the Sinn Féin office and Inghinidhe branch HQ on Harcourt Street. Rumours abounded regarding various Volunteer groups and where they were positioned. Eventually the women decided to make their own way to Jacob's factory. There, Ceannt who had failed to link up with the Fairview branch at the Green, had not made provision for the arrival of the now unexpected women. Nonetheless, he was glad of Nic Shiúbhlaigh's offer of assistance and permitted her group entry to his garrison. Nic Shiúbhlaigh was the senior Cumann na mBan officer present and thus she took command, although the women whom she commanded were Inghinidhe members and not part of her suburban Glasthule branch.[27]

The Inghinidhe women who were to have joined de Valera in Boland's Mills also made their way back to HQ at Harcourt Street. There, they awaited further orders from de Valera. Eventually, when it became apparent that no such orders would arrive, they were ordered to make their own way in to any garrison where their help would be accepted.[28]

Likewise, the Central branch which had initially disbanded or been demobilised on the north side, issued orders later in the day that their members should get into whatever garrisons they could.[29] This order was most likely issued in response to a directive from the

GPO that women should be allowed to involve themselves in the fight, wherever they volunteered.[30]

Ned Daly had, unlike de Valera, responded to this directive, and had some women in his garrison at the Four Courts by Monday evening. Among them were Éilis Ní Rian and Emily Elliott. They were joined by up to eight other members of the Central branch[31] and a few from other branches as the week progressed. Daly's attitude to the presence of women in his garrison is still debatable. It is true that he initially refused their assistance. It also seems that he dispatched a courier to the Broadstone with instructions for the Central branch to demobilise. The group was ordered to remobilise on Tuesday but we cannot say whether or not this was Daly's idea. However, Josie Wall subsequently explained his refusal in terms of his own confusion regarding orders and counter orders.[32] Wall's account would require the reader to believe that Daly had occupied the Four Courts on Monday morning, but had then come to believe that the rising was once again called off. It should also be stated that another Cumann na mBan veteran later claimed that Daly had told her immediately before the rising that 'if there was going to be fighting, they would need all the women they could get'.[33] As a brother of Kathleen Clarke and Madge Daly, it is certainly true that Ned Daly was used to being in the company of militant female republicans.

In the GPO, Winifred Carney was joined by up to 33 other women (not all Cumann na mBan) by the end of the week.[34] Among them was Elizabeth O'Farrell who, we will see, went on to play a very important part in the rebel surrender. Also at the GPO was Louise Gavan Duffy, who was an executive member of Cumann na mBan in 1916 but remarkably (perhaps because she was preparing an MA thesis) had not received any formal mobilisation orders. She too made her own way into the city and although she first expressed to Pearse her disapproval of his actions on the grounds that he could not succeed, she subsequently joined up with Cumann na mBan personnel in the GPO.[35]

Leslie Price, who later married the famous west Cork IRA leader Tom Barry, was another member of the Central branch who found herself without orders when hostilities commenced. On Monday morning she had not received any mobilisation orders but proceeded to the Mountjoy Street area where she had had orders to mobilise on Sunday. Having made her way there, she then waited for about half an hour, until she and her group heard a rumour they had been ordered to disband.[36] She and a comrade then made their own way to the city centre where they remained on duty in various garrisons in and around the GPO for the duration of hostilities.[37]

By the end of the week some Cumann na mBan members were present in all the rebel garrisons in Dublin with the exception of de Valera's command at Boland's Mills. Even beyond the Pale, individual members were on the move and trying to mobilise themselves. In Enniscorthy, Cumann na mBan joined the local Volunteers when they seized the town's Athenaeum on Thursday morning. Under the command of Mary White, they 'fitted up the top story … as a hospital and preparations were made to receive the wounded'.[38] Approximately 20 Enniscorthy women were initially involved in the action, but 'membership' was to increase to approximately 50 during the week.[39] Cumann na mBan were also involved in the extension of Wexford operations into Ferns and it was during the evacuation of that town that one Cumann na mBan member was 'badly injured' in a car accident.[40] In Cork and Limerick Cumann na mBan carried many of the confusing orders and counter orders between the various Volunteer commanders. Later in the week Limerick's Daly sisters made their way to Dublin and were dispatched back to Limerick and Cork with an appeal for Volunteers in those cities to rise. Aside from a brief occupation of their own hall in Cork, those Volunteers did not rise and the women's appeals fell on deaf ears. Later in the week, Cork Cumann na mBan, along with the Liverpool branch, did send food parcels to Dublin.[41] Belfast

Cumann na mBan had been mobilised to join the fight in Dublin but on Sunday morning they were told of the cancellation at Coalisland railway station. Some members (most famous among them were James Connolly's daughters Nora and Ina) still decided to make the journey to Dublin hoping for action there.[42] In Galway Liam Mellows mobilised local Volunteers for a brief skirmish. Approximately fifteen to twenty Cumann na mBan members were involved in Mellows' activities during the week.[43] These women even appear to have voiced their own opinions when surrender was discussed.[44]

Back in Dublin the women of various branches joined up with women from the Citizen Army and together they began their work in support of the insurgents. Throughout the week Cumann na mBan were engaged in three major activities: nursing, communications and catering.

We have already seen that a first-aid station was set up in the summerhouse at the Green. On Tuesday that station, along with the rest of the rebel garrison at Stephen's Green was moved to the Royal College of Surgeons due to the intensity of British fire from overlooking buildings. Elsewhere temporary hospitals were springing up all over the city, like Father Matthew Hall near the Four Courts garrison. Cumann na mBan staffed another field hospital at the rear of the GPO and before the garrison fell, sixteen women were evacuated from it under the Red Cross flag. Not all temporary hospitals were staffed by Cumann na mBan and Red Cross nurses were greatly praised by the victorious British military after the rising. Whilst it is unlikely that all Red Cross nurses refused to treat Volunteer casualties, it was alleged that one temporary hospital was closed by the British military for providing treatment to the rebels.[45]

Catering work was not easy in a city that was gradually being reduced to ruins. Food was increasingly hard to come by and as the week progressed Cumann na mBan members had to use much initiative to find it. The women frequently navigated their way through the crossfire on the streets and in and out of ruined buildings in their search for food. In Marrowbone Lane they came into possession of stolen/commandeered cattle. One of the animals was killed and a remaining cow provided milk and butter for the week. In the GPO, the women were confined to an upstairs room where they did all the cooking. Although the GPO garrison had seized a considerable amount of food from surrounding hotels, Desmond Fitzgerald kept a strict watch on the women, ensuring that rations would last as long as possible. In Jacob's factory, biscuits were the order of the day and the women scoured the plant for as much variety as possible. They also found a cocoa that 'looked horrible but at least it was sustaining'.[46] While their catering continued, they were stationed in a ground floor room well away from British fire.[47]

Cumann na mBan were never armed and their combatant role was not directly in the firing line. There is a report of armed women relieving tired snipers in the GPO. However, it is most likely that this reference is to Winifred Carney who was a crack shot (and was described as being armed with a typewriter and a Webley revolver)[48] or to other women of the Citizen Army. It was also alleged that some of the women who surrendered at Marrowbone Lane did carry weapons.[49] This is consistent with reports of the women in that garrison being involved in the loading of Volunteer rifles.[50] Nonetheless, it would appear that most, if not all, reports of armed women involved in fire fights must have referred to Citizen Army members.

Throughout the week and even before hostilities began, Cumann na mBan carried dispatches all over Dublin and beyond. Again, the work was not easy and demanded courage from those who undertook it. Yet there are no reports of any Cumann na mBan member ever refusing an order to carry dispatches into dangerous areas. Indeed one Volunteer later recalled that by Thursday all dispatch work was performed exclusively by Cumann na mBan.[51] On Friday it fell to Elizabeth O'Farrell to carry the most famous message of the week. She carried Pearse's surrender to the British army on Moore Street. A short time later she returned to the GPO with what might well be the most momentous message that any Cumann na mBan member ever carried. Its contents were brief but definitively spelled the end for the provisional government of the so-called Republic:

> From the Commander of the Dublin forces to P.H. Pearse
> 29th April 1:40pm
>
> A woman has come in who says you wish to negotiate with me. I am prepared to receive you in Britain Street, at the north end of Moore Street, provided you surrender unconditionally. You will proceed up Moore Street accompanied only by the woman who bears you this note, under a white flag.

When O'Farrell had accompanied Pearse to Britain Street, she was dispatched to the other rebel garrisons with orders for them to surrender. When she reached Jacob's factory across the Liffey, Máire Nic Shiúbhlaigh was ordered to ask the women to leave as their being taken prisoner might upset the men. She later recalled:

> I gave the girls MacDonagh's order. They did not want to leave. I could understand their feelings. They were my own; I did not want to go myself. I told them what MacDonagh had said. He was anxious to have all the girls out of the building before he surrendered. He feared that we would be arrested. If this had been the only consideration, I would have ignored his plea, and stayed; but he thought that the sight of girls being arrested might upset the men – he wanted everything to go as quietly as possible. On the other hand, Sara Kealy said that it might be useful for a few girls to stay behind. They could write letters for the men and take messages to the relatives. She announced her

decision to remain. I did not press the matter.[52]

Essentially the seventeen-year-old Kealy was disobeying an order from a superior officer, an action which portrays the partly civilian character of her organisation. And all over the city other women were doing likewise. Many of them had made their own way into the fight and were determined to end it on their own terms. Some of them left the garrisons and melted back into civilian surroundings but others refused to be treated any differently to the male combatants and portrayed a single-minded determination to ignore gender specific values of the day. At the GPO the women were reluctant to leave and only did so after a direct appeal from Pearse. Some of those who left the GPO went to the Four Courts where they were later taken prisoner.[53] Three women remained in the GPO and were taken prisoner there. At Marrowbone Lane 22 women surrendered to British forces having refused to escape via a tunnel the Volunteers had constructed for them. Nell Gifford later explained that many female combatants felt that: 'the Republic promised us equality without sex distinction, so we were all adjudged soldiers, women and men, whether we worked as dispatch carriers or Red Cross units.'[54]

But how efficient were these soldiers? And what was their effect on the outcome of the rebellion?

A Beginning at the End

For Cumann na mBan the rising had been a significant organisational failure. The auxiliary that had hoped to assist the Volunteers had proven itself somewhat inefficient and almost totally lacking in military organisation. Whilst two of its Dublin branches had mobilised on time, only one of them had successfully placed personnel in a rebel garrison at the beginning of hostilities. The Central branch had received demobilisation orders from the Four Courts and thus their absence from that garrison was not the fault of

Cumann na mBan. What was their fault, however, was the hopeless disorganisation that prevailed across the city as women tried to join in the fight. Members of the four Dublin city branches wandered the streets without orders and without leadership. Cumann na mBan was far from an effective military machine.

Elsewhere, Galway and Wexford were the only other counties in which Cumann na mBan members played their part in military hostilities. Indeed in these provincial areas it could be argued that the branch organisation and mobilisation was much more effective than in Dublin. Yet Cumann na mBan's failure to mobilise nationally can hardly be blamed on the women's organisation. There was simply no point in mobilising unless the Volunteers were also mobilised, and the Volunteers were not mobilised across the island. There was little point in doing anything anywhere, independently of the Volunteers.

For all of that organisational failure, Cumann na mBan were significantly present in every garrison, except Boland's Mills, by mid-week. It is impossible to arrive at an accurate assessment of the numbers of Cumann na mBan who took part in the rising. Estimates of the numbers of women, and not necessarily Cumann na mBan women, involved vary from Margaret Ward's of 90, to Sinéad McCoole's and Ruth Taillon's more recent figures, of up to 200. As Taillon compiled a list of names, hers is likely to be the most accurate assessment and also takes in those women who were involved outside of Dublin. R.M. Fox, the Citizen Army historian, has named 26 Citizen Army women present in the Dublin garrisons. We also know that some women who were not members of either organisation assisted the rebels during the week and that many non-combatant women were taken prisoner after the rising. In her study of Central branch activity, Sighle Humphreys named 43 members of the branch who were involved. We know that 25 members of the Inghinidhe branch marched into position at Marrowbone Lane at the commencement of hostilities. A further six members of that branch found their own way into rebel garrisons as the week progressed.[55] Thus 31 members of the Inghinidhe branch served in rebel garrisons during the week. Add to this the comparatively small number of women from the Columcille and Fairview branches that made their own way into the fighting, and we can say that 80-90 Cumann na mBan members fought in Dublin. We have already seen that the Enniscorthy garrison consisted of up to 50 women. Lil Conlon's previously mentioned estimate of Cumann na mBan belligerents in Galway was fifteen to twenty. Thus, in all, approximately 150 Cumann na mBan members were deployed in rebel garrisons in Galway, Dublin and Wexford during Easter week. It is also worth noting that Sighle Humphreys' list of Central branch participants indicated that most of them were unmarried, and thus they were most likely younger women.[56]

In the end, however, the number of Cumann na mBan members involved in the rising is not as important as their impact on events. It is fair to say that the presence of Cumann na mBan in the various garrisons during Easter week cannot have had a very significant effect on the outcome of the rising. No doubt some Volunteers lived longer because of the first aid administered to them by Cumann na mBan members. Likewise, were it not for their cooking and carriage of dispatches, there would have been fewer men available for the firing line. Were it not for Cumann na mBan's fundraising activities, the Volunteers would not have been as well armed as they were but it should be remembered that significant money from abroad had also helped to arm the male organisation. For all these reasons there is little doubt that the presence of Cumann na mBan did prolong the duration of the rising.

Yet their prolonging of an enterprise that was already doomed to failure cannot be viewed as having had a significant effect on the inevitable outcome. With or without Cumann na mBan, the rising would have occurred, the rising would have been crushed within days and the leaders would have been executed.

But it is not fair to suggest that Cumann na mBan's activities during Easter week were insignificant in themselves. Their primary significance was not the advancement of republicanism but rather the unintended advancement of feminism. The determination of nationalist women to place themselves by the sides of the men, during what came to be regarded as the birth of a new nation, ensured that this new generation of republicans could not ignore changing opinions regarding the female role in Irish society. Cumann na mBan had proven that some women were ready, willing and able to play a part in revolution and that there was no rational reason why they should not continue to do so.

In the months that followed the rising, even those feminists who had been sceptical of Cumann na mBan's subordinate role began to treat the organisation with a little more respect. Whilst the *Irish Citizen* had previously described the organisations subordination to the Volunteers as 'slavish', after the rising it grudgingly conceded that, unlike various constitutional nationalist groups in which women were involved, at least Cumann na mBan was a women's organisation, and was led entirely by women.[57] In October 1916 feminists argued that the women who had fought during Easter week and did not confine themselves to Red Cross work had proven their capabilities and thus their right to vote.[58]

The presence of women among the insurgents did not escape the attention of the mainstream media either. The pro-unionist *Irish Times* declared that 'a large number' of female prisoners who surrendered at the South Dublin Union were subjected to 'very hostile demonstrations' from the public as they passed through the gates of Kilmainham Jail.[59] It is also worth noting however, that the mainstream nationalist newspapers, the *Freeman's Journal* and *Irish Independent*, did not appear during the rising and when they re-emerged in early May neither was overly concerned with the presence of women in the rebel garrisons.

Even the families and friends of Cumann na mBan members, who may have frowned upon these women's political and quasi-military activities, might have been prompted to reassess their own gender stereotyping. Nell Humphreys was one of those whom it would appear had begun to reassess her definition of what was 'unwomanly'. Her glowing tribute to the women of the rising is understandably biased, as she was arrested in the aftermath of the fighting, although she had not participated. But, nonetheless, the account reveals a woman who is not alone proud of her nationality, but also proud that her gender was so well represented among the rebels:

> I used to feel ashamed of Sighle as being unwomanly when Anna told me that at times it was difficult to keep her from taking a shot herself, that the way she gloried when the enemy fell was actually inhuman, and her nerve during the whole thing was wonderful. But it is only the spirit of the age, every girl in every centre, the GPO, Jacob's, the College of Surgeons was just as cool and brave. They gave the men *invaluable* help and kept things normal.[60]

Finally it should be stated that the Easter rising of 1916 was not in any way democratically mandated. As such, Cumann na mBan had proven their utter disregard for the democratic system. However, unlike the Volunteers, Cumann na mBan members did not even have the vote. Their disrespect for the embryonic democracy that then existed in Ireland is of little wonder. Crucially for them, the provisional government of the Irish Republic had proclaimed that Republic to 'Irishmen and Irishwomen', and had stated that future governments of the Republic would be elected by 'the suffrages of all her men and women'. This was a clearer commitment to the establishment of a woman's right to equality of suffrage than had ever been given by any British administration. Whatever Cumann na mBan might have thought they were fighting for on Easter Monday 1916, some of them later claimed that they were aware of the provisional Republic's stance on gender equality.[61] And in the years immediately after the rising they continually reminded their own members, and Irish women generally, that the Republic proclaimed at Easter 1916 had guaranteed women equality of suffrage.

Cumann na mBan had not seriously affected the outcome of the rising. They had proven themselves as inefficient as every other nationalist organisation that had participated. Yet they had gained the respect of many Irish republicans. Indeed Leslie Price and Brid Dixon had gained sufficient respect for Seán MacDermott to insist that they be promoted on the field and treated as officers.[62] The rising was over but Cumann na mBan were only at the beginning of their strongest and most influential phase.

From the Gun to the Ballot Box 1916-18

When the rising ended about 77 women were taken prisoner. Not all of them were Cumann na mBan. The vast majority of women were released on 8 May, little more than a week after their arrest. It would appear that their gender was the primary reason for British leniency. Nonetheless, a handful of women were detained for a few months. Most famous among them were; Helena Maloney, Brigit Foley, Nellie Gifford, Madeline ffrench-Mullen, Kathleen Lynn, Nell Humphreys, Annie Higgins, Mary Perolz, Countess Plunkett, Nell and Kit Ryan, Kathleen Browne, Winifred Carney and Mary MacSwiney. Some of these women had not been involved in the insurgency but all were known Irish nationalists. With the exception of the future president of Cumann na mBan, Constance Markievicz, all female prisoners were released by Christmas 1916.[1] Markievicz was sentenced to death for her leading role in the hostilities, although, as we have seen that role was performed in her capacity as a member of the Citizen Army. Her sentence was later commuted to life imprisonment on account of her gender. Sinéad McCoole has proposed an interesting theory for the Countess' reprieve:

> The verdict of Markievicz's court martial was unique; having been found guilty and sentenced to be shot, the court recommended mercy for the prisoner solely and only on account of her sex. In October 1915 the Germans had executed Edith

> Cavell, a nurse who had harboured British prisoners in occupied Belgium, and the British had protested against her execution. It may, therefore, have been politic to commute the Countess' sentence.[2]

It was alleged that Markievicz claimed she would have preferred to have shared in the fate of the male leaders, all of whom were executed.[3] However, it was also alleged that, at her court martial, she broke down and begged that her life be spared on account of her gender.[4] Whichever case is true, she was reprieved from execution by the gender specific values which impacted upon the politics of the era. Those same values spared Cumann na mBan the severity of punishment suffered by the Volunteers and thus the organisation survived Easter week virtually unscathed.

The liberty of female separatists in the aftermath of the rising was viewed by some as of enormous assistance to the republican movement. Indeed, Cathal Brugha was later to acknowledge that in the aftermath of 1916, when most male leaders were imprisoned, 'it was the women who kept the spirit alive ... and the flag flying'.[5] Whilst there is some truth in Brugha's statement it should also be acknowledged that the entire male separatist population was not imprisoned and that most of those who were were released by Christmas. Between Easter and Christmas, police still reported some concerns regarding the activities of both male and female separatists from various organisations.[6] Nonetheless, women generally did play a much more prominent part in republican activity after the rising. But to what extent were Cumann na mBan involved in this activity?

Propagating the Republic

After the rising, republicans had to spread their doctrine to a population that was substantially hostile. They had to convince Irish people that the loss of life and destruction of Ireland's largest city had been in the best interests of Ireland. By the time of the general election of

December 1918 it is clear that republicans had succeeded in removing anti-republican hostility from many Irish people and replacing it with sympathy, or even support, for the 1916 rebels. Later, one former Cumann na mBan member from Louth was to write:

> We consider that the change over of the public from open hostility in 1916 to the sympathy which carried the 1918 elections, was due in large measure, in Louth anyway, to the activities of Cumann na mBan.[7]

It is true that Cumann na mBan's activities had a huge propaganda value all over Ireland. They may not always have set out to propagate the Republic but oftentimes their actions had precisely that effect.

After the rising over 2,500 men were imprisoned. This left many of their families in dire poverty. As an organisation who had listed among its primary objectives the raising of funds for the Volunteers, one would expect that Cumann na mBan might have come to the aid of Volunteer families. And in the short term they certainly did. Immediately they emptied their own coffers of some £200, which 'was used to stem the need of the first weeks want and misery'.[8] But then the officers at the top of this fundraising organisation did a curious thing. They went outside Cumann na mBan and formed a separate group to raise funds for the families of the imprisoned Volunteers. This group was known as the Irish Volunteers Dependants' Fund (IVDF) and was founded by Sorcha McMahon, Áine Ceannt and Kathleen Clarke. All three were Cumann na mBan members, with Clarke on the group's executive. The foundation of the IVDF might well be interpreted as an admission of the inadequacies of Cumann na mBan. It seems most likely that senior members like McMahon and Clarke doubted the ability of the women's organisation to maximise fundraising potential. It is little wonder that they did because, with regard to this activity, Cumann na mBan had two major weaknesses.

Firstly, they were an exclusively female organisation which ensured that one half of the population could not involve themselves in this vital appeal for aid. This was not consistent with the 'all hands on deck' approach which was urgently required. It is logical that the women wanted as many people as possible involved in fundraising and not merely Cumann na mBan members. As such, the IVDF's first appeal for funds was signed by John R. Reynolds, a Volunteer who had been a part of the GPO garrison during Easter week but had escaped imprisonment after the surrender. However, when the IVDF's appeal appeared in the newspapers, the British military ordered Reynolds to leave Ireland.[9] As work on behalf of prisoners continued in Cork, women signed all the cheques by 1917 as it 'was considered too dangerous for men to sign'.[10] It was quite clear that the British authorities would not allow male republican suspects to involve themselves in fundraising activities. However, crucially for Cumann na mBan, they did allow the women to continue those same activities and thus fundraising work for the IVDF fell almost entirely upon the shoulders of Cumann na mBan members. Indeed Kathleen Clarke made it clear that in those early days, every woman, with the exception of Padraig Pearse's elderly mother, she selected for administering the fund was a Cumann na mBan member.[11] Thus in many ways the IVDF was 'used as a cover for reorganisation' of Cumann na mBan.[12]

But Cumann na mBan's second weakness in relation to fundraising was simply that they were not present, or were only nominally present, in many parts of Ireland. In the months following the rising, police reports indicate the emergence of IVDF branches in three counties where Cumann na mBan had not yet established a noticeable presence, namely Louth, Monaghan and Kilkenny.[13]

In the rising's aftermath another organisation pledged to assist Volunteer families also sprang up. This organisation was founded by influential women, men and clerics and was known as the Irish

National Aid Association (INAA). Cumann na mBan members were also key to the administration of this fund.[14] The INAA was much more widespread and successful than the IVDF. In his report for June of 1916 the Inspector General of the RIC described the INAA as, 'having a wider scope' than the IVDF. He also reported that it was supported by the Roman Catholic clergy and by nationalists who had not previously been connected with republicanism. That being so, by 30 June the INAA had collected almost four times the amount of money that the IVDF had.[15] By July the Inspector General's report indicates that the INAA had now surpassed the efforts of the IVDF by a multiple of nine. Clearly the IVDF had been sidelined by a wider and more extensive body, and as both bodies were engaged in similar work anyway, the most sensible solution was a merger of the two.

However, Kathleen Clarke did not initially consider this proposed merger a sensible one. She had come to see the IVDF as a sacred torch passed to her by her dead husband, Tom. She had suffered enormous personal loss in the aftermath of the rising. Not only had she lost her husband, but also her brother, Ned Daly, and the unborn child which she had been carrying. She was also very ill herself and her autobiography describes an out-of-body experience where she claimed to have floated upwards through the clouds until she heard her husband and brother send her back to Earth to continue the work that they had begun.[16] The Irish Republic and its dead martyrs were, understandably, important icons for a woman who had lost so much in their name. She saw the IVDF as republican property and would not allow it to merge with a fund which was partly administered by non-republican parliamentarians. As such, she insisted that a number of personnel whom she considered parliamentarian be removed from the INAA before she would merge her organisation with it. Although her sister Madge Daly, of Limerick Cumann na mBan, argued that these influential INAA men should be used in order to collect more money, Clarke resolutely refused to work with them.[17] Her refusal was borne more of emotion than of pragmatism but it was a determined one nonetheless. However, Clarke's fund may have been running a little low, as Nancy Wyse Power later alleged that it was when 'the Volunteer Aid funds ran out' that the merger of the two organisations occurred.[18] Thus, when the Irish American group, Clan na nGael, sent two delegates to Ireland with a substantial sum of money and a merger proposal, the financial position of the IVDF might have been what forced Clarke into negotiations. After the negotiations, in September the Inspector General of the RIC reported the merger of the two groups as follows:

> The Irish National Aid Association and the Irish Volunteer Dependants' Fund were amalgamated during the month at the instigation of two American delegates – J.A. Murphy and J Gill – who brought over a contribution of £5,000 collected under the patronage of Cardinal Farley of New York. The amalgamated fund now amounts to £28,000. The Lord Mayor is a member of the committee but seldom attends. The Joint Secretaries are extremists, so also are three of the four Joint Treasurers. Therefore it may be assumed that it is under Sinn Féin control.[19]

Thus it is quite clear by her own account and that of the Inspector General that the merger occurred on Clarke's terms. There were bound to be a number of parliamentarians still associated with the new organisation, but it was controlled by republicans.[20] The new organisation was called The Irish National Aid and Volunteer Dependants' Fund (INAVDF). Cumann na mBan women were still prominent on the committee, with Louise Gavan Duffy as secretary and Sorcha McMahon as one of four treasurers. Curiously, Kathleen Clarke was relegated to the role of 'committee officer' where she was joined by Padraig Pearse's mother Margaret, and

Michael O'Rahilly's wife Nancy. Clarke's less prominent role may well have been the price she had to pay, or indeed was willing to pay, in order that those she had identified as parliamentarians were removed from the higher echelons of the group. The manoeuvrings before the merger might well have sown the seeds of some personality clashes in the upper ranks of Cumann na mBan. Women like Jennie Wyse Power and Min Ryan had been very much involved in the INAA, while Clarke and Daly were prominent in the IVDF. In later years these women would also find themselves on opposing sides during the Civil War.

But, aside from having members in senior positions on the INAVDF committee, what was Cumann na mBan's relationship with this fundraising body? Why is the story of the INAVDF an integral part of the story of Cumann na mBan?

We have already seen that police reported IVDF activity in three counties where they had not reported the presence of Cumann na mBan. The same was true of the INAA. In Galway East, Louth, Monaghan, Derry, Sligo and Tipperary, INAA branches were reported where Cumann na mBan activity was not. Now the newly amalgamated and expanded body would have a noticeable presence in counties where Cumann na mBan were not present, or at least not active. This had the effect of introducing women to nationalism through the new body. Frequently, where women were initially involved in the organisation of fundraising, they were, soon afterwards, involved in Cumann na mBan. Annie Duffy later recalled that a branch of Cumann na mBan was formed in Ballinalee for the initial purpose of collecting money for the INAA.[21] Likewise in Ballina, May Agnes Bowen's inception into Cumann na mBan occurred when her sister organised a concert 'for the dependants of the men in prison'.[22] Neither the *Kilkenny People* nor the Kilkenny police reported a Cumann na mBan presence in the county in the latter half of 1917. But they did report a strong INAVDF presence and the newspaper made it clear that several women held senior positions in the

INAVDF. They may well have been responsible for the reported emergence of Cumann na mBan in that county in June 1918.

All over Ireland Cumann na mBan members worked hard on behalf of the fundraising bodies. This work involved door to door and public collections for the IVDF, INAA and later the INAVDF. Kathleen Clarke had organised a series of flag days where flags displaying the portraits of the executed leaders would be sold to the public in aid of the IVDF. Under pressure from the authorities, who had threatened to arrest anybody selling these flags, Clarke had called off the operation.[23] Her orders were not carried out in Cork however, and Lil Conlon later wrote that: 'on successive Sundays, flags with photographs of the seven signatories of the republican Proclamation and other executed leaders were … issued.'[24] These images of the men who had died for Ireland must have served to keep their memory alive in many parts of the island. Whether you loved or hated these rebels, Cumann na mBan ensured you could not forget them.

All this fundraising work occasionally brought Cumann na mBan into conflict with the authorities. Essentially they behaved as if the Republic proclaimed during Easter week was already established and thus they frequently refused to recognise the authority of the Crown in Ireland. Firstly they would not bother to ask for collecting permits and, on occasion, when they were fined for collecting without permits, they refused to pay that fine and opted for terms of imprisonment instead. In Cork a Mrs O'Hegarty, who had taken these options, refused to eat prison food and thus it was arranged that Cumann na mBan would feed her.[25] She was only one of several Cumann na mBan members who went to extraordinary lengths to defy the authority of the Crown. Also in Cork, Susan Walsh, Nora Murphy and Josephine O'Sullivan refused to give their names to police when arrested for collecting, whilst in Dublin Maisie O'Loughlin would only give her name in Irish and even directed a kick at the arresting officer.[26] Immediately after the rising the RIC

County Inspector for Galway East was to declare that, 'whatever little attempts there are to spread disloyalty is the work of the young priests and some women at Athenry'.[27] One of those women was Deirdre Lowe who attended a GAA tournament at Athenry to sell badges and collect money for republican funds. Police reported that she 'attempted to cause a Sinn Féin demonstration on the platform' when leaving by train for her native Kilcolgan.[28] Lowe may not have been an Athenry woman, but as a very active branch of Cumann na mBan had been present in Athenry since 1915. It is quite likely that some of the women to whom the Inspector referred were members of same.

On the anniversary of the rising Cumann na mBan were again at the forefront of propagandist nationalist commemoration. In Limerick they organised a mass, celebrated at dawn, but which still drew large numbers, whilst in Cork they went one step further following the mass with a procession, by all major nationalist groups through the city. In the midst of the procession another Cumann na mBan member, Theresa O'Donovan, was arrested for striking a policeman with her umbrella during a scuffle. Her fellow Cumann na mBan members were so impressed with her actions that they presented her with a gold mounted umbrella upon her release from prison![29]

Another aspect of Cumann na mBan's activity in the 1916-18 period which may well have won it, and the wider republican family, many sympathisers was their charity work. When the great flu epidemic struck in the winter of 1918, Cumann na mBan were keen to do what they could to alleviate the suffering of the afflicted. In various parts of the country the women set up bureaus where those families in need of assistance could call upon members who had Red Cross training. Two of these bureaus were set up in Dublin, one on the south side at 6 Harcourt Street and another on the north side at 25 Parnell Square.[30] In Gorey the women opened a milk depot to provide the extra milk being prescribed by a local doctor who had asked them not to engage in home nursing for fear of spreading the virus.[31] The people who were assisted by this republican organisation during their illness must have been grateful to the women and their gratitude may well have made some less hostile to republicanism. Certainly one member later claimed that many of the Jewish families whom the women had assisted during the influenza epidemic later transferred substantial political support and funding to Sinn Féin.[32] Among the other admirers of Cumann na mBan were the Society of St Vincent de Paul for whom the members defied a ban on flag days to collect for the charity on Dublin's north side.[33]

Cumann na mBan's propagandist activities were not confined to Ireland. With US President Wilson having announced the self government of ethnic groups as an important part of his fourteen point peace plan, Irish republicans began to look to America for support and assistance in their campaign. Cumann na mBan members were among the first to do so. Min Ryan was dispatched to meet with John Devoy, the leader of Clan na nGael. She presented him with a report of the rising and also collected funds for the INAA. Nellie Gifford undertook a tour of the US, lecturing on the events of the rising. James Connolly's daughter, Nora, went to the US in order to provide for the Connolly family who found themselves near destitute. However, when she arrived, having travelled under a false name as the British authorities refused to grant her a passport, she was soon involved in republican propaganda work. She even wrote a republican account of the rising entitled *The Unbroken Tradition*, which was published in New York in 1918. Margaret Skinnider also made the journey to the US and was engaged in similar propaganda work. Immediately after the rising Kathleen Keyes McDonnell had travelled to London in order to campaign on behalf of republican prisoners. She was granted an audience with several MPs and succeeded in having the prisoners' issue addressed in the House of Commons.[34]

Even the ordinary members of overseas' branches sometimes found themselves involved in low-level, but memorable, propaganda work. Mrs Sidney Czira later remembered the day she and fellow Cumann na mBan members first flew the Irish tricolour in New York. Among its foremost admirers were members of the New York Police Department (NYPD), an organisation with a large proportion of Irish ex-patriots:

> We introduced the flag to New York by flying it at the top of a Fifth Avenue bus and it was quite something to see that the cops already recognised it, as at every intersection of the streets, they stood to attention in salute.[35]

In October 1916 Hanna Sheehy Skeffington travelled to the US campaigning for justice, after the British officer who had killed her husband, a non-combatant, whilst in military custody during the rising had been found 'guilty but insane'. During her campaign she made four lecture tours of the US. Sheehy Skeffington remained outside Cumann na mBan, but she did agree to deliver a message from the organisation to the American president when she became the first Sinn Féiner to meet with him in January 1918.[36] The message portrayed an organisation that had grown in confidence since the rising. Cumman na mBan not only asserted the right of the Irish people to a Republic but also the right of equality for women within that Republic. Doubtlessly this was part of the reason Sheehy Skeffington became the messenger of the women she had once described as 'slaves'. The message was signed by the Cumann na mBan executive, in absentia by Markievicz who was still in prison, and read as follows:

> We the undersigned, representing a large body of Irish Women whose President was condemned to death for her share in a struggle for the freedom of our country, make an appeal to you, and we base our appeal, first, on the generosity of the American administration on all things affecting women's lives and welfare,

and secondly on your recognition, many times extended, of the justice of Ireland's demand for political freedom.

For many lamentable generations the women of Ireland have had to bring up their children in a country in a perpetual state of economic and political disarray consequent of its being governed in the interest of another country. Your declaration of a war settlement which has called into being and endowed with hope the spirit of democracy in every country has made us feel that a new era is opening for us. Our appeal now is to remind you of a cause which should not be overlooked when so many European nationalities are to be reconstructed in accordance with your declaration. Our country, having behind it twenty generations of repression, has, we believe, a profound claim on those who have declared their will to make the world safe for democracy. We appeal to you to recognise the political independence of Ireland in the form of an Irish Republic.

And encouraged by the knowledge that the States of Wyoming, Colorado, Utah, Idaho, Washington, California, Arizona, Kansas, Nevada, Montana, Oregon, and New York have granted full suffrage to their women, we feel your generous sympathy will be extended to the women of our country in our demand before the world for the recognition of an Irish Republic which, from its inauguration, was prepared to give women their full place in the Councils of their Nation.[37]

Cumann na mBan's appeal to the president to champion Irish republicanism, whilst Britain was an important wartime ally of his, might well have been a little naïve. If it was, then it was a naïvety that was shared by most Irish republican groups. In 1918 there was a very real belief that Wilson would support the cause of Irish self determination at a post-war peace conference and it was a belief which was founded upon what he himself had said regarding the self government of small nations and ethnic minorities.

What was a little more baffling were Cumann na mBan's references to democracy. Although the Irish Republic was theoretically established, nobody had voted for that establishment. Irish republicanism needed a clear democratic mandate from the Irish people in order to make itself more respectable in the eyes of other democratic nations. They had to be able to claim some kind of obscure retrospective mandate for their armed action in 1916. The chance to claim such a mandate, came through another organisation with which Cumann na mBan were to become closely allied – the tiny political party known as Sinn Féin.

Cumann na mBan and Sinn Féin

In the wake of the failure of the Easter rising various separatist groups began to coalesce under the fragile unity of a Sinn Féin umbrella group throughout 1917 and 1918. This coalition radically altered a political party which was not in itself a republican organisation. The Sinn Féin party which emerged in late 1917 was very different to the party which had been formed by Arthur Griffith over a decade previously.

The Sinn Féin movement began in 1905 with the publication of *The Sinn Féin Policy* by Arthur Griffith. This document proposed a dual monarchy for Ireland and Britain, based largely on the Austro-Hungarian model in operation at that time. Essentially, this meant that Ireland and Britain would have two entirely separate and autonomous parliaments but would share a head of state in the form of the king of England. This was a considerably more autonomous arrangement than that contemplated by home rulers, yet it also fell short of the complete independence advocated by republicans. Griffith had urged abstention from Westminster and passive resistance as the methods by which this dual monarchy might be achieved. He was not, in 1905, supportive of violent revolution and he did not plan, or even take part, in hostilities during Easter week. Some of the Easter revolutionaries were Sinn Féin members, most notably W.T. Cosgrave, and others had previously been active in the party. But Sinn Féin had not been responsible for a rebellion which was planned by a small 'military council', consisting mostly of IRB men, and executed by the Irish Volunteers, the Citizen Army and Cumann na mBan.

However, Sinn Féin's lack of culpability did not prevent the press and the authorities assuming that they were responsible. The insurgents were commonly referred to as Sinn Féiners in most mainstream publications and in official documents. Thus, when imprisoned insurgents were released in late 1916 and early 1917, many of them began to flock to a party in which they had demonstrated no previous interest. In a sense the British labelling of the revolutionaries as 'Sinn Féiners' became a self-fulfilling prophesy because, by December 1917, that is what they were.

However, Cumann na mBan's association with Sinn Féin goes back much further than December 1917. As already mentioned, the Inghinidhe Branch shared their HQ with Sinn Féin at 6 Harcourt Street, and as this physical proximity might suggest, they also shared many of their personnel and some of their ideology.

Sinn Féin were a party far ahead of their time in terms of their treatment of women. Indeed Arthur Griffith later wrote that it was a woman (Mary Butler) who had 'christened' his party.[38] From the beginning they made it clear that their ideology welcomed female members on the same basis as men. Jennie Wyse Power, Mary Murphy and May Macken were all members of the Sinn Féin executive in 1907.[39] Wyse Power was a member of Inghinidhe na hÉireann and went on to become a member of Cumann na mBan. And Wyse Power's relationship with Arthur Griffith went back to 1900 when he had founded a loose association of nationalists known as Cumann na nGaedheal. Cumann na nGaedheal had attracted Wyse Power and a number of other Inghinidhe women to its membership. Likewise, when Griffith founded the National Council to protest against the king's Irish visit in 1903, a number of Inghinidhe women were to the forefront of that organisation.

As Sinn Féin re-invented and republicanised itself throughout 1917/18 a number of other Cumann na mBan women became prominent in the higher echelons of the party. The president of Cumann na mBan, Constance Markievicz, was foremost amongst them. She had been a member of the party from its earliest days but had 'stayed in the party after 1910 when others left because it was the only organisation that gave women anything like a fair crack of the whip'.[40] Kathleen Clarke joined the new republican Sinn Féin party although she had been somewhat critical of Griffith's earlier party and resented the assertion that they had planned the rising.[41] Both Jennie Wyse Power and Áine Ceannt became members of the standing committee of Sinn Féin whilst they also served on the executive of Cumann na mBan. However, it should be stated that their presence on the Sinn Féin executive was as much a result of lobbying by feminists as it was a magnanimous gesture towards feminism by Sinn Féin.[42] Nonetheless, all these women were significant Cumann na mBan wheels that attached themselves to the Sinn Féin wagon. Irish separatists were all congregating under the Sinn Féin banner and Cumann na mBan leaders were no different. But what was the reality among the rank and file? Policemen often commented that Sinn Féin and the Volunteers went hand in glove across Ireland. The membership of Sinn Féin clubs and Volunteer companies were often close to identical. But could the same be said of Sinn Féin clubs and Cumann na mBan branches?

As Sinn Féin clubs sprung up all over the island, they did attract some female members. Whilst there is evidence to suggest that in some parts of Ireland every effort was 'made to get not only the men but the girls and women'[43] to join Sinn Féin, the number of women involved in the grassroots of the party was not very large. Thus the proportion of Cumann na mBan joining the party was not substantial. In South Tipperary police reported 47 Sinn Féin clubs with a membership of 3,636. However, only 123 of those members were women.[44] A few months later Cumann na mBan membership is reported as totalling fifteen. Thus we can say that whilst South Tipperary police had noticed 123 female Sinn Féin members, they had only noticed fifteen Cumann na mBan members. Even if all of these identifiable Cumann na mBan women, were also identifiable Sinn Féin members, the proportion of Cumann na mBan members within the Sinn Féin female membership, would have been somewhere in the vicinity of 12 per cent. In Cavan, women accounted for only 114 of the 3,017 members of Sinn Féin. As that county had a reported Cumann na mBan membership of 142, it is quite clear that not all visible Cumann na mBan members involved themselves visibly in Sinn Féin,[45] yet over two-thirds of Sinn Féin's visible female membership might also have been members of Cumann na mBan. Furthermore, if we look at the women contacted by Eithne Coyle and Sighle Humphreys in order to gather information for their proposed histories of Cumann na mBan, the number of those women who referred to a dual membership of Sinn Féin and Cumann na mBan, although they are not specifically asked the question, was negligible.[46] Longford Cumann na mBan pension applicants were similarly lacking in reportage of dual membership.[47] Surprisingly it was not until February 1919 that Cumann na mBan officially urged their membership to join their local Sinn Féin clubs.[48] It was after that date that increasing dual membership was reported in Limerick. By 1921 female membership of Sinn Féin in the treaty city had risen to about 9 per cent.[49] In the Courtbrack (County Cork) Sinn Féin Cumann, approximately 33 per cent of the membership were female and about 22 per cent were Cumann na mBan members. About eight of the Courtbrack Cumman na mBan branch's fourteen members were also members of the local Sinn Féin Cumann.[50] Thus, in some areas, dual membership could be quite high but hardly uniform. The attitude of local male Sinn Féin members with regard to female membership may well have been a key factor in determining levels of dual membership.

Yet, even though Cumann na mBan did not flock to Sinn Féin at the same rate as Volunteers, their lack of participation was not borne of a lack of support. It is quite likely that many people saw party politics as the sole preserve of the male gender and thus women's support for Sinn Féin was primarily reflected through their own organisation. Indeed, there is evidence to suggest that many Cumann na mBan members began to see their organisation as more of an auxiliary to Sinn Féin than to the Volunteers. In 1918 the Cumann na mBan leadership admitted that by February of that year they had felt it necessary to re-emphasise the military purposes of the organisation to a membership that had become somewhat confused:

> It seemed ... that the main reason for which we were established was in danger of being lost sight of. The spread of Sinn Féin clubs and the series of by-elections in which members of Cumann na mBan take a prominent part occasioned an impression that our branches were women's Sinn Féin Clubs. Some confusion may still exist on this point in parts of the country, but things are much clearer than they were at the beginning of the year.[51]

If Cumann na mBan's own membership had begun to see the organisation as a women's Sinn Féin, then it is little wonder that they did not bother to join the political party. And members of Cumann na mBan were not the only people who saw the organisation as the women's section of Sinn Féin. There is also evidence to suggest that this analysis of the organisation was prevalent in wider society. The RIC County Inspector for Longford commented that both the GAA and Cumann na mBan were 'merely auxiliaries of the Sinn Féin association', and a month later he went on to cast the Volunteers in the same auxiliary role.[52] In Fermanagh the organisation was referred to as 'an ambulance corps of women Sinn Féiners'.[53] In Donegal the County Inspector connected Cumann na mBan specifically with Sinn Féin and not with the Volunteers.[54] Even at the very top of the RIC the Inspector General was under the impression that Cumann na mBan were 'women's Sinn Féin clubs.[55] Some Sinn Féin clubs may well have had a similar vision of Cumann na mBan and thus they attempted to divert women away from the political party and into the women's organisation.[56]

Likewise, Count Plunkett had not envisaged a role for women within his 'Liberty Clubs'. These Liberty Clubs had been set up by the Count after his victory in the Roscommon by-election and before the subsequent coalition of abstentionist politicians under the Sinn Féin umbrella. Whilst in theory women could join the clubs, membership of clubs could also be reserved for men, and women could set up corresponding 'circles' of exclusively female membership having 'the same power and the same rights of representation as the Liberty Clubs'. Plunkett wrote to at least one woman encouraging her to start a Liberty Circle and in what seemed like an attempt by the Count to capture the Cumann na mBan movement he instructed that, 'if there is any women's organisation in your district that is pledged to the principles of complete independence for Ireland and abstention from the Westminster Parliament such a society should communicate with my committee'.[57] Until the Sinn Féin convention of October 1917, a power struggle among abstentionists threatened to tear the separatist movement apart and Plunkett sought allies within Cumann na mBan. It was also during this period that serious divisions were reported in Cork where a separate Cumann na mBan branch broke away from the already existing one, and gave itself the unmistakably republican title, 'Craobh Poblachta na hÉireann'.[58]

Cumann na mBan's association with Sinn Féin was a confusing one. Wider Irish society, members of Sinn Féin and members of Cumann na mBan had all begun to see the organisation as a women's section of Sinn Féin. Thus Cumann na mBan members did not generally become members of Sinn Féin but instead they expressed their support for the party through their own organisation. That organisation was the forum which nationalist Ireland deemed most appropriate for women and the women of Cumann na mBan did not disagree. Instead they threw their weight fully behind Sinn Féin and became an intrinsic part of the wider republican movement, a movement within which all the lines of distinction between various nationalist and republican groups were beginning to fade. These fading lines were further blurred when the conscription crisis of 1918 promoted additional anti-British sentiment among the various shades of green in nationalist Ireland.

With the outcome of the First World War still very much in the balance, the British authorities were in dire need of more troops due to the high rate of casualty in all theatres of war. Recruitment in Ireland had been very sluggish since the beginning of the war. Indeed, the British Prime Minister, David Lloyd George, had commented that one county in Wales did more for the British war effort than all of Ireland.[59] With this attitude to Irish recruitment becoming more and more typical in a Britain that had been drained of much of its male population, the British government were coming under increasing pressure to apply conscription in Ireland. Eventually they had to act and thus a new Conscription Bill was passed through the Westminster Parliament on 16 April 1918. The new legislation entitled the government to extend conscription in Britain and to apply it in Ireland should it be deemed necessary. The Irish Party withdrew from Westminster, lending credence to the Sinn Féin claim that attendance at the London Parliament was a waste of time, and nationalist Ireland was united in its burning hostility toward the authority that would force its manhood to fight in Flanders.

The Irish Volunteers declared they would resist conscription by force and thousands of Irishmen flocked to their ranks. Trade Unions organised a one-day strike in opposition to the extension of conscription to Ireland. Sinn Féin and the Irish Party formed a committee to direct opposition in Ireland, whilst the Roman Catholic clergy issued a strong condemnation of the legislation from Maynooth.

Cumann na mBan were, predictably, equal to all other nationalist groups in their opposition to what they later referred to as; 'the proposal to exact the blood tax from Ireland'.[60] In some areas they had already been engaged in a rigorous anti-recruitment campaign, thus their resistance to conscription was always going to be absolute.

With the Volunteers planning a war against conscription, Cumann na mBan were engaged in similar preparations. One member later wrote that, 'all over Ireland our branches prepared for the struggle under directions from Headquarters'.[61] These preparations were pretty typical of the auxiliary role that Cumann na mBan had defined for itself since its earliest years. In Donegal considerable quantities of bandages were openly purchased by the local Cumann na mBan in the week preceding the passing of the Conscription Bill.[62] The first time police reported Cumann na mBan activity in Roscommon was at the end of April. There, it was reported that two branches had been formed in Boyle and Deerpark and were engaged in receiving first-aid instruction.[63] All over Ireland, women were beginning to mobilise themselves against conscription and suddenly the organisation was growing at a phenomenal rate. By July the Inspector General of the RIC was reporting Cumann na mBan activity in the previous month as follows:

> The Cumann na mBan continued to form new Branches. The ostensible reason for this development is that the women may be trained as 'Green Cross' nurses to the wounded should an attempt be made to enforce conscription, but the movement is possibly largely spectacular.

In many areas it is possible that Cumann na mBan were little more than another one of Irish nationalism's range of spectacular demonstrations. They were just another group to participate in anti-conscription marches. But the spectacular element of Cumann na mBan was becoming an important propaganda tool for the anti-conscription movement. The organisation became a vital part of the visible face of a unified anti-conscription effort. All over Ireland

Cumann na mBan began to march publicly in the company of other nationalist organisations.[64] They became a visible symbol of the resistance of Irishwomen to British conscription. Their spectacular effect should not be underestimated.

For all their spectacular value, Cumann na mBan were also lending assistance to Irish republicanism in more clandestine ways. There was at least one policeman who was beginning to see the threat the organisation posed to the security of the state. The County Inspector for Longford gave an eerily accurate report on what he felt the women's organisation was about to become engaged in. In May 1918 he reported that:

> The Sinn Féin association seems lately somewhat keen on establishing branches of the Cumann na mBan about Granard – a fresh branch has been started there. The intention probably is that these women should be able to carry revolvers and chiefly ammunition on account of their immunity from search and also carry secret documents for the use of the Irish Volunteers.

In Cork, Cumann na mBan were already involved in the preparation of violent resistance. There, they collected scrap metal for use in bomb making by the Volunteers.[65]

It was the conscription crisis that drove Cumann na mBan back out into the open. The organisation's rapid expansion and participation in several anti-conscription rallies ensured that the public and the police were much better acquainted with the women's organisation. As early as September 1917 British military intelligence was reporting that a fear of conscription in Connaught and the Midlands, was leading to the formation of what they called 'Women's Clubs':

> Women's Clubs or Societies have been formed in places, and women are unfortunately the most active supporters, if not

> openly, by their home influence, of Sinn Féin, viz., they hate the idea of enforced military service for their male friends.[66]

Yet Cumann na mBan's greatest coup during the crisis was not solely a Cumann na mBan initiative.

Women's day was organised by 'an outside committee'[67] of women who had attended the Mansion House conference in order to determine the national response to the threat of conscription. This outside committee consisted of several capable women and former members of Cumann na mBan. Its chairman was Alice Stopford Green, whilst Agnes O'Farrelly performed secretarial duties. It was decided that on 9 June 1918 women all over the island should sign the following pledge:

> Because the enforcement of conscription on any people without their consent is tyranny, we are resolved to resist the conscription of Irishmen.
>
> We will not fill the places of men deprived of their work through refusing enforced military service.
>
> We will do all in our power to help the families of men who suffer through refusing enforced military service.[68]

At first, some Cumann na mBan branches did not know whether or not they should co-operate with this outside committee. The secretaries of the organisation had to officially state their desire that all branches should take part and do all they could to make the day a success.[69] Once that order was given, however, Cumann na mBan not only participated in Women's day but effectively organised, marshalled and led all other participants. Outside Dublin, the other organisations who had been involved in its conception, simply did not have the all-island presence required to make it work. Women's day should not be seen as a single day when all nationalist women signed an anti-conscription pledge. Rather it was the spectacular event that introduced the pledge to the public and began the process of signature collection. Indeed, the date on the pledge itself was left blank, allowing the signatory to fill it in for herself. In Longford, women's day occurred a week after 9 June when about 120 women signed the pledge and then marched through Granard.[70] Most curious was the time lag between Dublin and Cork, where women's day did not occur until 7 July when Cumann na mBan members 'were at church doors everywhere getting women to sign the pledge'.[71] This Cork pledge included a clause which stated that the women would not even learn to do the work of conscripted men. Cumann na mBan did not choose to parade publicly in Cork, as their organisation had been proclaimed 'dangerous' by the Lord Lieutenant on 3 July. In Donegal the signing of the pledge would appear to have continued throughout the month of June and beyond, with the County Inspector commenting that by the end of the month some 2,700 women had already signed.

In Dublin the pledge was first signed on 9 June in City Hall. The first to sign were 700 uniformed Cumann na mBan members who 'from the spectacular point of view, provided the leading features in the day's proceedings'.[72] Curiously, although Cumann na mBan did lead the procession in Dublin, they were actually outnumbered by some 2,400 women from the Irish Women Workers Union.[73] In rural centres all over southern Ireland, however, Cumann na mBan were both numerically and spectacularly superior to all other organisations. In Caherciveen the precision of the event's organisation was interpreted as 'a credit to the leaders of the Cumann na mBan'.[74] Kilkenny Cumann na mBan made a fine display in leading the procession through the city and creating substantial floral displays of green, white and orange, whilst at Mullinahone 'the Cumann na mBan ladies took charge of affairs in general'.[75] Drogheda Cumann na mBan added a musical dimension to the day by closing proceedings with the singing of Sinn Féin songs, whilst in Waterford the organisation was also to the forefront.[76]

In excess of 100 Monaghan women signed the pledge on 9 June, with some of their number returning to parade through the town to evening prayers at the Cathedral on 16 June.[77] This religious aspect was an important part of the day's visual effect. June 9th was the feast day of St Columcille and it had been recommended that having signed the pledge, 'women should form a procession to some place of veneration or pilgrimage'.[78] Thus when the County Inspector for Tipperary South commented that women's day in his area was in the 'nature of a religious function', he was merely stating that events had occurred as planned.[79]

Women's day, or *Lá na mBan* as Cumann na mBan referred to it, proved Cumann na mBan's worth in terms of visual political propaganda. They were the largest women's organisation on an island where women were about to be substantially empowered with the receipt of the franchise. As such they were becoming an increasingly important part of the Sinn Féin family.

The first opportunity that this newly reinvigorated Sinn Féin movement had to flex their electoral muscle came with a series of by-elections in 1917 and 1918. Those by-elections occurred in Roscommon North, Longford South, Clare East, Kilkenny, Armagh, Waterford, Tyrone and Cavan East. The Sinn Féin party met with mixed success in these campaigns, taking seats in Roscommon, Longford, Kilkenny, Clare and Cavan but losing out in Armagh, Waterford and Tyrone.

Whilst many Cumann na mBan members were doubtlessly present during all these campaigns, the organisation was seldom distinguishable from those female Sinn Féiners who did not belong to it. However, Sinn Féin could and did rely on Cumann na mBan to add a female presence to their election platforms. Mabel Fitzgerald appeared on several such platforms in Longford, whilst Markievicz was also prominent among the speakers in the early days of that campaign.[80] Alice Cashel was present in the Cavan area during the campaign there.[81] In Armagh, 'Cumann na mBan took on duties in connection with the famous South Armagh election when they acted as canvassers and general helpers, and organised food supplies for election workers. They also organised transport and helped bring voters to the polls'.[82]

It was late 1918 when Sinn Féin, now a fully unified group after some internal conflict during the by-election campaigns, finally cranked its electoral machinery into overdrive. The reason was the end of the First World War and the announcement of a general election for 14 December. During the campaign, Cumann na mBan were to become a very effective spoke on the Sinn Féin wheel.

The general election of 1918 was the first in which the franchise was extended to women with property, and over 30 years of age. Reports leading up to the election indicated that women would account for approximately 40 per cent of the total electorate.[83] Indeed, on 2 December the *Freeman's Journal* carried an extensive article on the statistical relevance and 'enormous influence' of the female vote.

Against this background it is not surprising that both the Irish Party and Sinn Féin attempted to secure as much female support as possible. Women regularly marched with supporters on both sides and their presence was acknowledged graciously from election platforms everywhere. In Cork, nationalist women headed the 'band of the discharged soldiers and sailors association' in a march through the city,[84] whilst republican women were clearly visible in a photograph of a Sinn Féin march on 8 December.[85] Even the unionist women of Cork were determined to get their vote out and took the time to explain, through the pages of the *Cork Examiner*, exactly how polling cards should be marked in favour of unionist candidates.[86] Cumann na mBan had beaten them by nearly six months, having placed similar instructions for Sinn Féin supporters in the *Cork Examiner* of 11 June. The final Sinn Féin procession through Cork city took place by torchlight on the eve of polling day, the night of 13 June. The procession was described as 'impressive' by the *Cork Examiner* and J.J. Walsh publicly thanked Cumann na mBan for their part in it.[87] In Dublin, Cumann na mBan had the potential election of their own president to occupy their minds. There, the organisation rallied behind Markievicz and ensured that, 'no public meeting of her election committee was held without speakers from amongst us'.[88] One week before the election the *Waterford News* reported that a feature of a political procession in that county had been, 'the presence of Cumann na mBan those earnest and enthusiastic workers in the grand cause of Irish nationality'.[89] In Donegal, Eithne Coyle later recalled that:

> Our branch canvassed every house in the parish. We helped the local Volunteer company to provide transport and refreshments for old people who came from the mountain districts to vote for our republican candidate, Joe Sweeney, who was elected by a large majority.[90]

Coyle's recollections do not appear in the least exaggerated, and are corroborated by the recollections of many other Cumann na mBan members from all over Ireland. Indeed it would appear that in addition to doorstep canvassing, Cumann na mBan members were engaged in the dissemination of Sinn Féin election propaganda by a variety of other methods, as well as providing meals and refreshments for Volunteers and voters, manning first-aid stations at polling booths, and even providing baby sitting services for the children of female voters.[91]

It has been established that both sides interfered in the democratic process on polling day.[92] Like most other organisations Cumann na mBan were also involved in such anti-democratic activity. Two sisters who were members in Leitrim later claimed that in their area Cumann na mBan had personated extensively on polling day, a process which involved disguising themselves as absentee voters.[93] Likewise, in Dublin Éilis Bean Ui Chonnaill recalled that after the election 'a certain number of dead people were shown to have voted'.[94] This personation was also practiced by women during the 1920 municipal elections.[95]

Getting the Sinn Féin vote to the polls was a task which had occupied the minds of senior Cumann na mBan members for months before the election. For all female voters, this was an entirely new experience and as unionist women in Cork had directed their voters, so too did Cumann na mBan direct theirs. But unlike the unionist women, Cumann na mBan had an extensive national organisation and attempted to use it to full effect in ensuring that every female Sinn Féin vote was recorded. As early as 13 April Cumann na mBan were preparing for the election and issued the following explanatory instructions to their branches through the pages of *Nationality*:

> A woman of thirty years of age or over on 15th April 1918 is entitled to be registered as a voter if she fulfils either of the following conditions: -1. That for the six months prior to the 15th April she herself has occupied in the constituency either a dwelling house or else land or business premises value £5 or over. (If she occupied a dwellinghouse the question of value does not arise). -2. That she is the wife of a man who fulfils the conditions in paragraph 1.
>
> It is sufficient to occupy part of a dwelling house, provided that that part is occupied separately, independently of other people in the house. Lodgers are entitled to vote only if they rent unfurnished rooms.
>
> A woman who resides on premises by reason of her employment is entitled to be registered as a voter if her employer does not reside on the premises. The same applies to the wife of a man who resides on premises by reason of his employment.
>
> Secretaries are directed to prepare lists of all women in their

> districts who possess above qualifications and would be likely to vote for a Sinn Féin candidate.
>
> On or before June 15th the Clerk of the Crown and Peace will publish, either at his own office or at the local Post Office, lists of voters. Secretaries are directed to compare their lists with these official ones, and if there are some names missing from the latter to see that the women claim their votes. Particulars as to making the claims will be published at the same time as the voters' lists. Secretaries must see to it that the claims are properly made …[96]

This notice appeared in Sinn Féin's official organ underneath an appeal for Sinn Féin clubs to claim male votes in a similar fashion, thereby adding some credence to the perception of Cumann na mBan branches as women's Sinn Féin clubs. It is impossible to ascertain to what extent Cumann na mBan engaged themselves in this activity but there is evidence to suggest that some branches took it very seriously.[97]

In the end the 1918 election was an overwhelming victory for Sinn Féin. The winds of change blew to gale force across Ireland and the old Irish Party that had entered the election with 78 MPs sitting in Westminster was able to win only six Irish seats.[98] Of those six, four were the result of an electoral pact with Sinn Féin in Ulster. Sinn Féin took 73 constituencies, 25 of which were uncontested. For Cumann na mBan the major triumph was that their 'president (Markievicz) was the only woman elected in Ireland, England, Scotland or Wales'.[99]

With many women involved in Sinn Féin at all levels and their contrasting and more secondary role in the Irish Party, some historians like Feeney and Murphy have argued that the female vote may have tended to go to Sinn Féin in greater proportion than the Irish Party.[100] It is certainly true that the suffragette activists in Ireland would indeed have reason to dislike the Irish Party. They believed passionately in extending the franchise to women but the Irish Party did not support them. Indeed, its leader, John Dillon (John Redmond died in March 1918), had told a women's deputation that 'women's suffrage will, I believe, be the ruin of our western civilisation. It will destroy the home, challenging the headship of man, laid down by God'.[101] In 1911 the Irish Party voted against a franchise bill fearing that it would bring down the Liberal government whom they had hoped would attempt to grant Home Rule. Some women would undoubtedly have turned away from a party they may have considered old fashioned and supported a Sinn Féin party that espoused the right of suffrage for women, and even had several women in senior positions.

While the contrasting position of the Irish Party would not have endeared them to suffragettes it should be stated that the views of some of them, like Dillon, were not as bizarre in 1918 as they seem today. It is quite conceivable that in 1918 there were women who did not believe in their individual right to vote. And that these more conservative women may well have supported a particular party out of a sense of duty to their husbands or fathers. Thus it is impossible to tell how many women voted independent of male influence. What is very clear though is that any woman who did so must have believed in her right to vote and may have seen the Irish Party as a group who had recently sought to deny her that right. A Sinn Féin party that nominated three women – Winifred Carney, Constance Markievicz and Hanna Sheehy Skeffington who subsequently turned down the nomination – as candidates for the election would have been much more likely to attract the vote of such a woman. Add to this the largest Irish women's group in existence throwing in their lot wholeheartedly with Sinn Féin and it becomes even more likely that nationalist women tended to prefer that party. The influence of Cumann na mBan on the female electorate was undoubtedly enormous but alas it is impossible to accurately state the full extent of its bearing. Nonetheless Lil Conlon's assertion that; 'Cumann na mBan … had rendered invaluable service to Sinn Féin', during the election, would appear to be a fair analysis.[102]

Over the years there has been much debate as to the nature of the mandate bestowed upon Sinn Féin.[103] However, the extent of that republican, or perceived republican, mandate is not relevant to the history of Cumann na mBan. In the story of Cumann na mBan the Sinn Féin victory can only be interpreted in one way, and that is the way in which the organisation itself chose to interpret it. In early 1919 Cumann na mBan sent Louise Gavan Duffy to the American president with another message. This time their previous references to democracy seemed a little less hollow when they asserted that:

> At the general elections which took place recently in Ireland women for the first time in our modern history had the opportunity of declaring the form of government which they desired for their country. An overwhelming majority of the electorate voted for the complete severance of the English connection … The republican candidates fought the election on one issue only, that of complete separation. So much was this felt that other parties such as the Women's Party and the Labour Party, stood aside so that the vote might be clearly recognised as one for self-determination … If the government of a country is to be subject to the consent of the governed, then there is no justification for the continuance of British government in Ireland.[104]

For Cumann na mBan the Republic was a proclaimed and democratically mandated reality, and a reality which they would assert by force of arms. But that had not been the case prior to their participation in the Easter Rising. Cumann na mBan had assisted the Irish Volunteers in striking the first blow for a Republic which had not previously been an official goal of their organisation. Between 1916 and 1918 Cumann na mBan made the attainment of that Republic the primary function of their organisation and reorganised themselves around that declared objective.

Reorganisation and 'Republicanisation'

Immediately after the rising Cumann na mBan's organisation very nearly fell to pieces. The British military had closed down their offices and confiscated all their records, leaving them to start again from scratch. One Cumann na mBan member remembered that; 'Parnell Square in those months was deserted but the members of Cumann na mBan seemed to keep in close contact'.[105] It was through these contacts that the Central branch eventually began to meet again and immerse itself in the administration of the IVDF. One of those first meetings was a divisive one with Kathleen Clarke later remembering that a motion was proposed that those who had not fought in the rising be expelled from the organisation. She spoke against the motion and, pointing to the disorganisation that had prevailed during Easter week, she urged unity.[106] Clarke's argument carried the day and no members were expelled from the organisation. Aside from these clandestine contacts and secretive meetings Cumann na mBan appear to have remained resolutely underground until the autumn of 1916. Of course, we have already seen that many members were immersed in work on behalf of the INAVDF, but Cumann na mBan itself maintained a discreet silence, for a few months at least.

Then, in December, the first efforts at reorganisation came in the form of a small and unrepresentative convention. The convention was held in 6 Harcourt Street, an interesting choice of venue as it was the Sinn Féin and Inghinidhe branch HQ.[107] Whatever this convention was, it was not a large or elaborate affair and few records of its proceedings survive. Nancy Wyse Power later noted that 'there were only fifteen or twenty people present, mostly from Dublin'.[108] A brief account of proceedings in *Leabhar na mBan* seemed to indicate that it was at this convention that 'plans were made to revive our work and get in touch with our branches'.[109] If that is the case, it is safe to assume that few, if any, branches from outside Dublin were represented at the 1916 convention.

Although small, the convention did see the election of some very important figures into senior positions on the executive. Markievicz, although still incarcerated, was elected president while Nancy O'Rahilly remained vice president. Kathleen Clarke maintained her position on the executive committee and was joined by Áine Ceannt, widow of the executed Eamonn. Min Ryan and Mimi Plunkett, sister of the executed Joseph Mary, maintained their positions on the executive and became joint secretaries of the organisation.[110] By 1918 Clarke and Ceannt had been elevated to vice-presidents and had been joined in that role by another of the bereaved, Margaret Pearse, mother of the executed Padraig and Willy.[111]

Some of these women were little more than figureheads used to connect the organisation to the martyrs of the rising, but not nearly as capable as many of the women who served under them. Kathleen Clarke was an extremely effective and hard-working leader, but she herself described Margaret Pearse as being a little lost in the political world.[112] Although Nancy O'Rahilly had been an executive member since 1914, she never took an active part in the organisation.[113] But Áine Ceannt and Mimi Plunkett had both been executive members prior to the rising. They both took their roles seriously and were to engage in substantial recruitment tours on behalf of Cumann na mBan.[114]

The 1916 convention saw Cumann na mBan formally embracing their role in the rising by further connecting themselves with its leaders. But they did not yet commit the organisation to the attainment of an Irish Republic. Instead they merely stated that the organisation had been founded 'to advance the cause of Irish liberty'.[115] Between Easter 1916 and the Sinn Féin Ard Fheis of October 1917, all Irish separatists were reluctant to commit to any specific form of government. In order to unify anti-British sentiment and unite Irish separatists generally, republicans were slow to publicly proclaim their views. The republicans within Cumann na mBan were no different.

The organisation remained committed to arming the Volunteers (who from 1916 onwards began to refer to themselves increasingly as the Irish Republican Army or IRA, but were at odds to point out that they were 'an independent body of nationalist Irishwomen'.[116] The constitution had been significantly altered but it was still curiously at odds with an organisation that had fought for a proclaimed Republic. A clear commitment to that Republic was inserted at a much larger and more formal convention on 2 December 1917.

At that convention the constitution of the organisation was not so much altered as it was completely scrapped and rewritten. The new document began by pledging the organisation and its membership to the Irish Republic as follows:

> Cumann na mBan is an independent body of Irish women pledged to work for the establishment of an Irish Republic, by organising and training the women of Ireland to take their places by the side of those working and fighting for a free Ireland.[117]

Thus from the very beginning of the new document a substantial intellectual shift in the policies of Cumann na mBan was evident. Not only was the organisation now officially a republican one but it was also placing itself by the side of, and not merely in assistance to, the Volunteers. Further evidence of their proclamation of equality with the Volunteers occurred when it was stated that Cumann na mBan would collect for the arming and equipping of both the men and women of Ireland.[118] There is no evidence to suggest that this new-found feminism ever progressed from paper into the reality of Cumann na mBan arming itself. Indeed the very same constitution did not refer to weapons instruction as one of its suggested military activities. Whatever the women of Ireland were to arm and equip themselves with, it was not to be firearms. However, even the placement of such a feminist policy on paper was, for its time, a revolutionary departure.

For Cumann na mBan it was important that the guarantee of gender equality given by the 1916 proclamation was honoured. And there seemed to be a perceptive realisation that if women were to achieve that envisaged equality, they would have to rely on their own determination and intellectual capacity to do so. Thus, it became a policy of Cumann na mBan:

> To follow the policy of the Republican Proclamation by seeing that the women of Ireland take up their proper position in the life of the nation.
>
> Members of Cumann na mBan should participate in the public life of their locality, and assert their rights as citizens to take part in the nomination of candidates for Parliamentary and local elections.
>
> Branches should take steps to educate women by means of lectures, literature, debates and classes in the conduct of public affairs, so that they may be acquainted with the correct forms of procedure to be followed at all meetings in which they take part, and may be fitted to occupy public positions.[119]

The organisation of lectures and provision of a republican education for members became the norm in most urban branches. And in the years that followed an increasing number of Cumann na mBan women did occupy public positions within the republican administration. However, there were still many, of both genders, who simply did not agree with Cumann na mBan's interpretation of a woman's proper position in the life of the nation. The increasing participation of women in public affairs was only ever going to be a gradual one. But, were it not for Cumann na mBan's commitment to it, it is likely that this slowly increasing participation would never have occurred.

The 1917 constitution also envisaged an organisation which would remain rigidly centred in Dublin. The executive would consist of a president and vice presidents with an eighteen member committee, eleven of whom would reside by the banks of the Liffey. Secretaries and treasurers would also be resident in Dublin.[120]

Whilst this over-centralisation may appear odd to the modern reader, a number of conditions prevailing in 1917 made it sensible and perhaps even necessary. Firstly, the only republican military campaign of the twentieth century, the 1916 rising, had occurred primarily in Dublin. Whilst the fighting did move substantially southwards in the coming years, Cumann na mBan could not have known that in 1917. Secondly, communications technology was not what it is today. Cumann na mBan could not avail of electronic fund transfers, video conferencing, e-mail or even a simple telephone call. Thus, as the organisation would have its HQ in Ireland's largest city, the bulk of the administrative work would have to be carried out in that same city. By 1918, however, the need to decentralise some of the power held by Dublin was recognised and thus the representation on the executive was altered to include twelve country women, three from each province. Curiously, the motion for this alteration was proposed, not by a provincial branch, but by the Dublin branch of Ranelagh.[121]

All branches would naturally be entitled to send delegates to the annual convention in proportion to their numbers. From 1916 each branch was entitled to one delegate for the minimum of ten members, and one additional delegate for every subsequent 50 members. In 1918 this clause was temporarily simplified to allow one delegate for the first 50 members or part thereof, and one additional delegate for every subsequent 50 members or part thereof.[122] In 1919, it was again altered so that branches of 25 members or less would have an entitlement of one delegate, branches of between 25 and 70, an entitlement of two, and branches of over 70, three delegates.[123] This system was maintained for the duration of the revolution.

The minimal number to form a branch had been reduced from fifteen to ten in 1916.[124] This reduction may be indicative of a failure to expand into more remote rural areas. However, in terms of affiliation fees the organisation discriminated against smaller branches. In 1917 every branch was expected to forward an affiliation fee of 5s per annum for the first ten members and an extra 5s or each additional 50.[125] Thus branches of ten members were expected to pay 6d per member, whilst branches of 59 members paid approximately 1d and branches of 60 members only paid 2d per member and less than 2d as their membership increased. This billing system may well have been intended as an encouragement for smaller branches to expand. However, if Cumann na mBan had already admitted a difficulty in assembling fifteen members in some rural areas, it is difficult to see how they expected those same branches to assemble 60. Although affiliation fees were amended by subsequent conventions, they always discriminated against smaller branches. Every branch was also expected to collect funds by organising an entertainment each year. This was not such a cumbersome task for urban dwellers, but again the expectation may not have been a reasonable one in smaller rural areas. Even if the smaller branches succeeded in holding such an event, they then had to suffer the embarrassment of having the amount of money raised 'announced' at the next convention.

Another new departure in the 1917 constitution was its commitment to the Irish language, a commitment which was very much in vogue among all republican organisations of the era. The original constitution had not even mentioned the Irish language. However, the 1917 document exhibited the first signs of a lingual obsession which Cumann na mBan would continue well into the future. Irish was an 'essential qualification' for at least one secretary and, among the suggested activities of the new Cumann na mBan, Irish language and history classes were primary.[126] By August of 1918 the leadership had become so infatuated with the promotion of the Irish language that they requested branch secretaries conduct their business with HQ in Irish.[127] In 1921 twice yearly examinations in elementary Irish were adopted,[128] although subsequent examination proposals in 1925 appear to have been greeted with substantial opposition.[129]

Perhaps the most significant element of the 1917 constitution was its adoption of the District Council. District Councils were to be formed in undefined districts where three or more branches existed. A secretary and one other delegate from each branch would form a District Council and work to ensure that the activities of these branches would not clash or overlap.[130]

The establishment of these District Councils does suggest that Cumann na mBan was, in some districts at least, a rapidly expanding organisation. One of those districts was Cork city, where the first District Council was established just two months after the convention. But how rapidly was Cumann na mBan growing? And as the War of Independence loomed, how big was the women's auxiliary?

In answering those difficult questions we have to refer to a number of widely divergent sources: those from within Cumann na mBan and republicanism generally and those from outside of that circle.

Throughout the first half of 1918 Cumann na mBan's primary public utterances came in the form of a number of small columns afforded them in Arthur Griffith's Sinn Féin newspaper, *Nationality*. The appearance of these columns was further testament to the intellectual alignment of Cumann na mBan and Sinn Féin, but more importantly, they occasionally gave an indication as to the extent of the former's expansion. By April 1918, Leinster, not including Dublin, boasted only 26 branches in total.[131] Elsewhere the situation seemed even worse. One month previously it was reported that Connaught had only fourteen branches. Waterford, and at least some counties in the northeast, had none.[132] Even at the beginning of the conscription crisis Cumann na mBan were still a long way behind the Volunteers in terms of their national penetration and found it necessary to appeal for a branch to be formed 'in every parish where there is a corps of Volunteers'.[133] Cumann na mBan still had not captured the imagination of many Irish nationalist women. One former Dundalk member later commented that between the rising and the conscription crisis, the Volunteer movement was 'scarcely respectable'. The leadership of the local branch sought recruits in terms of quality rather than quantity, lest an incautious word be spoken within earshot of the authorities. She went on to claim that 'the Cumann activities were carried out under the cloak of the Gaelic League without the general public – or – more importantly – the authorities being very much the wiser'.[134] With regard to Dundalk she was correct. Cumann na mBan had been present in the town for three years and police were not aware of its existence. Police intelligence of the organisation generally was already lagging behind and was about to get worse.

Of the 26 Leinster branches, RIC County Inspectors were reporting seventeen and of the fourteen Connaught branches they reported only four. As the conscription crisis heightened, Cumann na mBan had already begun a series of recruitment drives, which saw the organisation expand at a phenomenal rate. First on their list was the unionist dominated stronghold of Ulster, where Alice Cashel began her recruitment tour in April. Her efforts met with some success in Donegal, Cavan, Monaghan and Tyrone but not in the loyalist heartlands of the east. Even among the nationalists of east Ulster republicanism was never as strong as it was elsewhere and parliamentarianism remained the dominant nationalist creed. Shortly thereafter she was dispatched to Connaught where, although police 'got on her track', she was able to bring the province into line with the expectations of the Dublin executive.[135] Although Cumann na mBan did not seem to be aware of it at the time, police in Donegal and Fermanagh had also noted Cashel's presence but were not concerned enough to get 'on her track'.[136]

With their full-time paid organiser (Cashel) in Ulster and Connaught, Cumann na mBan reported the dispatch of other high profile organisers as follows:

> Miss Plunkett made a long and exhaustive tour of the Cork County Branches in February; Miss Brennan visited Longford and West Wicklow; Miss Price, West Cork, Miss Ryan, South Wexford and Waterford; Mrs Ceannt, Tralee; Mrs Wyse Power, Kells; and Miss Gavan Duffy, South Armagh.[137]

In most of these areas police were soon reporting increased Cumann na mBan activity. However, they had already underestimated Cumann na mBan's branch strength. And as the conscription crisis came to its height, between April 1918 and the end of the war, they were unable to keep track of Cumann na mBan's rapid expansion. Indeed the organisation itself found it difficult to keep track. So how does the historian best estimate the size of the organisation at that time?

The Cumann na mBan 1918 convention report stated that between the 1917 and 1918 conventions the organisation had grown from 100 to 'considerably over 600' branches. Yet only 'over 150' delegates were present at the 1918 convention. This inconsistency is probably best explained by Lil Conlon's statement that in Cork it was decided a Miss O'Leary would represent smaller branches at the Dublin convention as their financial condition would not permit them to send their own delegates.[138] If 150 delegates represented 600 branches at the 1918 convention, we must assume that at least 450 branches were what Conlon described as 'smaller', and thus were unable to collect enough money for a train ticket to Dublin, could not find a delegate who was willing to go, or were not as active as other branches.

The convention was held at the end of September 1918. If we

take the police reports for that month we see that, outside Dublin, 112 branches of Cumann na mBan had come to the attention of the police, as illustrated by the following table:

RIC REPORTS OF CUMANN NA MBAN MEMBERSHIP IN SEPTEMBER 1918

County	*No of Branches*	*Total Membership*
Armagh	1	20
Cavan	9	261
Donegal	13	396
Down	1	84
Wicklow	3	105
Carlow	1	40
Kilkenny	2	47
Offaly	3	141
Longford	8	269
Laois	1	30
Westmeath	3	62
Wexford	2	75
Galway ER	9	317
Mayo	10	346
Roscommon	3	130
Sligo	7	197
Clare	9	335
Cork WR	3	31
Kerry	11	327
Limerick	8	392
Tipperary SR	2	18
Waterford	3	68
Total	112	3,691

For the purposes of establishing Cumann na mBan's numerical strength police reports, when taken in isolation, are useless. Many

County Inspectors did not bother to tabulate organisational statistics for Cumann na mBan, although we know the group was present in their areas. Indeed, in Cork city (which formed the centre of Cork East), in July 1918, the Inspector reported that uniformed Cumann na mBan had formed part of a Volunteer funeral procession. Yet he never attempted an estimate of the extent of their formal organisational structure. Likewise, the County Inspector for Tyrone reported Cumann na mBan activity in his area in May and July but never tabulated organisational statistics. In West Cork the County Inspector reported only three branches by the end of 1918, although we know that the organisation was significantly larger.[139] Thus, it is quite clear that as the organisation began its rapid expansion during the conscription crisis, branches frequently went unnoticed or unreported by police.

What police reports can shed some light upon, however, is the active membership of reported branches. Police did not have access to Cumann na mBan roll books. Where they noted a branch of Cumann na mBan, the members they noted were the active ones. They noted the women they saw engaged in Cumann na mBan activity, and not those who were merely nominal members. Assuming that the membership numbers tabulated above were indeed numbers of active members, we can see that the average active membership per reported Cumann na mBan branch was approximately 33. Taking that 33 and multiplying it by Cumann na mBan's own reported number of branches, 600, we come to a figure of 19800. This figure might be in need of downward revision as police may have been reporting larger rather than smaller branches. However, there is no way of accurately undertaking such a revision.[140]

This figure may appear small when placed next to the membership estimates of Sinn Féin and the Volunteers.[141] However, when viewed in the context of its time, it was actually quite impressive. We should not forget that Cumann na mBan was a women's organisation and this was a time when women did not tend to get involved in political or militant organisations. We have already seen that the maximum active membership in late 1915/early 1916 was 1,700. Thus, in less than three years, the organisation had grown at an astonishing rate.

By the beginning of 1919 Cumann na mBan was a changed organisation. It had experienced enormous growth, committed itself completely to the republican agenda and become an essential part of the wider republican family. The results of the 1918 election were interpreted by Cumann na mBan as the democratic establishment of the Irish Republic. Cumann na mBan's self confidence was expressed in a number of counties as members began to emerge uniformed and on occasion they even 'marched with Sinn Féiners'.[142] This marching 'in formation to words of command',[143] was a demonstration of Cumann na mBan's militant agenda. As violence gradually gripped the country from mid 1918 onwards, these militant women became a part of that violence. By the beginning of 1919 the Volunteers were at war, and so were Cumann na mBan.

The War of Independence 1918-21

On 9 January 1919, a small group of Volunteers ambushed two policemen escorting dynamite to a quarry in Soloheadbeg, County Tipperary. For two main reasons, this incident is often considered the first engagement of the Irish War of Independence. Firstly, the policemen were both shot dead, which made them the first agents of the crown to suffer that particular fate since 1916. And secondly, the ambush occurred after the 1918 election and on the very day the first Dáil sat, and thus this violence in pursuit of an Irish Republic was lent a certain amount of democratic respectability. That democratic respectability was important to the generation of constitutional politicians who themselves had been Volunteers, and later it was important to those who wished to differentiate between the activities of the 'old' and 'provisional' IRAs.

Democratic respectability aside, Soloheadbeg was not, however, the first time since 1916 that Volunteers had violently confronted police. Throughout the country the Volunteers had been actively arming themselves since the threat of conscription had first raised its head. It seems that arms were surrendered to the Volunteers by some supporters and commandeered/stolen from those who were opposed to their militancy. Nowhere was this activity more in evidence than in the south of the country where the Volunteers went on to wage their most violent campaign against Crown forces. Liam Deasy left this description of Volunteer activity in south-west Cork:

> I arranged at a weekly meeting of the Innishannon company for the collection of shotguns and ammunition from friendly neighbours, and led a party to seize them from those who were unwilling to offer them voluntarily … In all, the arms acquired at this time by all companies of the Bandon Battalion from private holders amounted to 200 shotguns and a limited quantity of ammunition.[1]

Widespread Volunteer arms raiding had one very serious effect. It brought the Volunteers into direct and open confrontation with Crown forces and although this confrontation did not lead to the intentional killing of agents of the Crown until the Soloheadbeg ambush, a growing tension was mounting between the Volunteers and the RIC throughout 1917/18.

Liam Deasy left the following account of an incident involving local Volunteers and RIC men following an eviction in Cork:

> Two armed RIC men arrived on the scene to note what was happening. At a given moment they separated from each other, presumably in an effort to glean as much information as possible about the leaders of the operation, and when this occurred one of them was overpowered and his rifle taken from him.[2]

The national media frequently reported on incidents of this nature ensuring that readers all over Ireland were aware that the Volunteers, although they were seldom identified by the press as such,[3] were arming themselves in preparation for conflict.[4] On the night of 13 April 1918 two Volunteers were killed in a raid for arms at Gortlea barracks in Tralee. During the subsequent coroner's inquest in June 1918 two policemen were shot at in the streets of Tralee. One was wounded. Yet this was not the most serious incident in the period between the 1916 rising and 1918 general election. Even as early as June 1917 Volunteers were involved in violent encounters with police. One of those encounters in Beresford Place in Dublin ended with the first fatality of an agent of the crown since 1916. On 10 June a meeting had been organised to protest against the continued internment of Volunteers who had participated in the Easter rebellion. During the meeting an order to disperse the crowd was given by Major Mills of the Dublin Metropolitan Police. During the melée which followed, Major Mills received fatal head injuries when struck on the head with a hurley.

As the violence escalated throughout 1919 and into 1920 a guerrilla war soon developed across the island. Policemen were regularly threatened and attacked by groups of Volunteers who had now begun to refer to themselves as the IRA. Soon the RIC were resigning in their droves. This shortage of policemen, and an IRA arson campaign directed against rural police barracks, led to a withdrawal of police from most parts of rural Ireland. The overall shortage of police led to the introduction of the infamous 'Black and Tans' and a separate 'Auxiliary' police force in early 1920. These British police were demobilised soldiers and were notoriously ill-disciplined. They had been sent to Ireland to restore law and order yet they often employed the most brutal tactics against the IRA and the civilian population. They burned the houses of suspected IRA sympathisers, they sometimes shot innocent civilians dead, and during two notorious rampages, they burned substantial parts of Cork city centre and Balbriggan County Dublin. Their behaviour only served to turn the Irish people further against the British administration, whilst shocking the general public in Britain and farther a field.

Also in the first half of 1920 new IRA units known as 'flying columns' were formed from IRA members who were already 'on the run' because of their previous participation in IRA attacks. These columns sought to ambush British military or police before withdrawing to isolated areas where they were sheltered by sympathisers. The columns were supported by local IRA and Cumann na mBan units in whatever area they were present.

The war was most violent in Cork with substantial IRA activity all across Munster. Other provinces (particularly Ulster) were less violent but IRA activity was noticeable everywhere.[5] By mid 1921 the spiralling violence in Ireland had become an acute embarrassment to the British government. Some British politicians wanted to send up to 100,000 troops to Ireland in order to re-establish control. But there were no guarantees that even such a large force could serve to do anything other than escalate the conflict. Instead they sought to negotiate a compromise.

The IRA had won a partial victory. They had succeeded in forcing the British government into talks with Sinn Féin representatives. But if the IRA had won a partial victory, had Cumann na mBan assisted them in doing so? What was the relationship between the IRA and its female auxiliary?

Cumann na mBan and the IRA

Cumann na mBan's relationship with the Volunteers was officially amended by the female leadership as the auxiliary group reorganised itself throughout 1917 and 1918. We have already seen that the organisation had committed itself to a firmer feminist stance and to political equality for women. However, that equality did not stretch as far as military operations. The women did not envisage themselves performing a role directly in the firing line and thus they did not participate in violent attacks on the British administration. The organisation never armed itself and it never attacked British military or police. Indeed, as the revolution progressed and the IRA stepped up its military offensive, Cumann na mBan's policy on the military training of its own members became less and less pronounced. From its foundation one of the organisation's suggested activities had been rifle practice.[6] This was dropped from the new constitution in 1917, but firearms training in the form of 'cleaning and unloading of rifles' reappeared as suggested military activity in 1919.[7] Even that slightly watered down 'suggested military activity' was replaced by 'home nursing' in 1920.[8] It was clear that as the War of Independence developed Cumann na mBan's policy on its military activities was changing.

Those changes were dictated by reality. The IRA was the organisation involved in the use of firearms. As Cumann na mBan did not seek to join them in this activity, there was little point in training their members in skills that would be of no use to them. Cumann na mBan's military activities depended on the activities of the IRA. In early 1918 the women's organisation had acknowledged this when they ordered their own branch captains to take their orders on military matters from local Volunteer commanders.[9] Some branches may have been slow to react to this order as it had to be repeated.[10] But at the 1918 convention the phrase that, 'for the purposes of military organisation and operations, captains of branches shall take orders from the local Volunteer Commander', was formally added to the constitution. In 1919 *Leabhar na mBan* outlined the organisation's ideal relationship with the IRA as follows:

> The captain must keep in close touch with the Volunteer battalion or company officer, get his help in organising signalling and other classes, see that he knows how to get in touch quickly with mobilisers, and put herself under his orders in all military operations.

There is evidence to suggest that some Cumann na mBan women encountered difficulty with this subordination. It was a difficulty that seems to have arisen when some local IRA commanders did not understand that Cumann na mBan was an independent organisation and was subordinate to IRA orders only in military matters. Thus there were occasions when IRA officers interfered in internal Cumann na mBan business and their interference was resented. The 1918 convention report reported discussion on IRA interference as follows:

> Miss Cashel asked if it was allowable for a Volunteer captain to give advice with regard to the election of a Cumann na mBan captain, but it was agreed that this was purely a branch matter in which outsiders could have no say. Miss Matthews (Dundalk) gave an instance of a dispute which was caused by a Volunteer interfering in the appointment of officers ... Máire Ní Rían, Miss Price and Niamh Bean Ui Laoghaire ... explained that our military activities were meaningless apart from the Volunteers, and must be organised to fit in with their work.[11]

The fact that the grievance was raised by Cumann na mBan's travelling organiser (Cashel) might indicate that it was something which she had encountered in more than one area. Yet, as the Dundalk representative was the only delegate reported as having provided a specific example of it, it was hardly uniform. What was much more uniform was Cumann na mBan's increasing solidarity with the IRA and Sinn Féin. This was further demonstrated when a motion from the Belfast branch, at the same convention, that Cumann na mBan funds should not be used for providing comforts to Sinn Féin and IRA prisoners, was withdrawn. In any event, as senior members like Ui Laoighre, Ní Rían and Price pointed out, Cumann na mBan depended on the IRA in order to provide it with military work. Indeed in some areas it was local IRA officers who had first organised or requested the organisation of Cumann na mBan branches.[12] If Cumann na mBan wanted to be militarily active, their own constitution made them dependent on the IRA to make them so. If local IRA commanders did not work well with Cumann na mBan branch captains, Cumann na mBan could not be militarily active in that locality. And as the War of Independence developed there was good reason why IRA commanders might not work well with Cumann na mBan branch captains: the issue of trust.

When Máire Comerford was dispatched to Leitrim as an organiser in 1920 she gained first-hand knowledge of the IRA's difficulty in trusting Cumann na mBan. She later recalled that the local IRA commander, John Mitchell, had helped her in her organisational work but his help was given with some reserve:

> Do you expect me to trust these girls with the secrets of the IRA, he asked me one evening. His men, he said, were very carefully sifted before they were accepted, and they took a declaration.
>
> I brought this complaint back to Dublin. At the annual convention that autumn we ordered all members to take a declaration of secrecy regarding IRA affairs. It read: – 'I pledge myself to support and defend to the best of my ability, the Irish Republic, and to uphold the aims and objects of Cumann na mBan, and to keep strictly secret all matters relating to Cumann na mBan and the IRA.[13]

Of course Mitchell's concerns were very practical. Some senior IRA men went to considerable trouble to vet the suitability of their own operatives.[14] It was never likely that they would welcome with open arms, a group of women who had not been subject to the same scrutiny. The introduction of the Cumann na mBan declaration was not likely to put all their minds at ease, but at least it proved that Cumann na mBan were aware of security risks and would select their own operatives accordingly.

Throughout the period of the conscription crisis a certain amount of trust had inevitably evolved between local operatives of both organisations. In some parts of the country the IRA were already familiar with local Cumann na mBan personnel and having worked with them throughout that period, knew they could be trusted. Cumann na mBan had been utilised by the IRA in secret preparations for resistance to conscription in a number of districts. One Mayo IRA Volunteer later recalled that Cumann na mBan had been actively involved in the preparation of food for storage in secret locations and in the organisation of first-aid posts as the Volunteers prepared to resist conscription.[15] But there was one primary reason why the IRA trusted the women of Cumann na mBan in the years ahead: the blood relationship which existed between many members of both organisations. Of the 46 IRA men who formed the famous West Cork Flying Column that engaged the Auxiliaries at Kilmichael in November 1920, at least eight had sisters in Cumann na mBan.[16] The leader of that column, Tom Barry, later described the Cumann na mBan members he had worked with as 'sisters, relatives or friends of the Volunteers'.[17] Margaret Broderick Nicholson later recalled that her organisation of concerts during 1917 and 1918 had made her known to local IRA officers in Galway, a fact which made her suitable for dispatch carrying in the years that followed.[18] Similar friendships appear to have existed between most of the women, who later provided Witness Statements to the Bureau of Military History, and their local IRA officers. Oftentimes those friendships had existed from the very beginning. Madge Daly's recollection of Limerick Cumann na mBan's first meeting is typically demonstrative of the ties between male and female revolutionaries right across the nationalist spectrum:

> The first meeting was held in the Gaelic League Rooms and the majority of those in attendance were members of the Gaelic League, or were girls belonging to families who had carried on the Fenian tradition.[19]

Peter Hart's research on the IRA in Cork revealed similar blood ties between Cumann na mBan and the IRA. Where women were not related to local IRA officers they were often related to other members of the Cumann na mBan branch or to members of Sinn Féin.[20]

Cumann na mBan ... grew along with other Republican

> organisations, its members often being drawn from the same pool of families as the Volunteers. The head of the Cumann na mBan in Macroom was Mary Corkery, wife of Dan Corkery, the battalion commander. Bella O'Connell, the leader of the Beara organisation, was the sister of Christy O'Connell the captain of Eyeries company. Mary MacSwiney and Mrs Seán O'Hegarty were in charge of one of the city factions. In Kilmeen company, again it was the Volunteer officers' sisters who founded the local Cumann na mBan branch. Over half the Courtbrack Cumann na mBan were sisters, all of whom had brothers in the IRA, while the Shandon branch in Cork city was formed and run by the Conlon and Crowley sisters. For women as well as men, Republicanism seemed to run in families.[21]

It was these ties of family and friendship that first established trust between Cumann na mBan and the IRA. It was Cumann na mBan's own record of keeping the IRA's secrets that maintained that trust.

Cumann na mBan had also taken steps to dovetail their own organisation with that of the IRA. At the 1920 convention a formal military structure corresponding to that of the IRA was suggested by Eileen McGrane.[22] McGrane's proposal did become a 'scheme of organisation' for Cumann na mBan but was not incorporated into the organisation's constitution until 1921.[23] The intention was that Cumann na mBan branches, or squads, should correspond to IRA companies, District Councils to battalions and brigade councils should also be formed for each IRA brigade area. However, in reality Cumann na mBan never quite matched the IRA in terms of its organisational structure. Where comparisons can be made, the women's auxiliary falls well short of its male counterpart. In Cork's 3rd brigade, 7th battalion area, the IRA boasted ten companies, whereas Cumann na mBan had only six branches.[24] The Carlow IRA brigade consisted of six battalions of 46 companies. Carlow

Cumann na mBan consisted of one DC and twenty branches.[25] The South Leitrim IRA brigade area consisted of at least three battalions of 26 companies. South Leitrim Cumann na mBan was one DC of sixteen branches.[26] Overall, the IRA boasted at least 294 battalions by the date of ceasefire on 11 July 1921. More than two months later, Cumann na mBan boasted only 85 DCs.[27]

By the beginning of 1919 Cumann na mBan had subordinated itself to the IRA in relation to all military matters. Accordingly their military activities would depend on how often the IRA sought to involve them in the military campaign. Trust between the two organisations was an issue but not for those members who had known each other through kinship or friendship over a period of years. So how effective was Cumann na mBan's military machine?

The Women at War

As the War of Independence was heading towards its most violent phase in late 1919, Cumann na mBan published their military organisational objectives in *Leabhar na mBan*. Perhaps what is most interesting about the article in question is the organisation's presumption that the war had not yet begun. Cumann na mBan seemed to envisage the development of a large-scale conventional war between the IRA and the British army. They did not really consider the 'hit and run' tactics that the IRA were already employing as a part of that war. Indeed in early 1919 some branches were actually less active than they had been during the conscription crisis.[28] *Leabhar na mBan* reminded its readership that:

> Stretcher drill and improvising stretchers is very important. The Volunteers, in case of war, could seldom spare men for the work of bringing the wounded to safety. Semaphore and Morse signalling are of great use to stretcher squads, and in many cases the Volunteer officer will be glad to know there are efficient signallers to be called upon in emergency.

The article also stressed the importance of the organisation of field hospitals in dwelling houses and even the supply of flags to local IRA units. Local branches were again reminded that the practice of drill was the 'only way to ensure good discipline'. All these military activities were to be performed under the command of the branch captain and, in larger branches, her section leaders. Those officers were elected by the branch members based on their proficiency in various military matters.

It is clear the Cumann na mBan leadership did not truly understand that the war was already in progress and was not going to develop into an open confrontation. They were not alone in their innocence, however. Policemen only began to recognise that the IRA was engaged in 'guerrilla warfare' and not mere 'outrages', at the beginning of 1920.[29] The war had developed in such a haphazard fashion that most Volunteers had no idea of what was coming next. Indeed, it was only in January 1920 that IRA GHQ sanctioned Crown forces, and not just their arms and equipment, as legitimate targets for IRA attacks.[30] Newspapers did not refer to a state of war with Britain either.

Cumann na mBan were waiting for a war that would never happen. Yet their proposed military training did include some activities that could be of use to the IRA. Members were to be trained to co-operate with the IRA in areas such as dispatch carrying, cooking, catering and nursing. The importance of dispatch carriers and cyclists who had good geographical knowledge of their own districts was also emphasised, as well the equipping of local IRA units with field dressings.[31]

We have already seen that the branch captain was to take her military orders from the local IRA officer. She was also to ensure that he knew 'how to get in touch quickly with mobilisers'.[32] Thus, in an ideal situation, an IRA officer who needed Cumann na mBan's assistance, could mobilise them through making contact with their branch captain or designated mobilisers. But, as the war developed and the emergence of flying columns, Black and Tans and guerrilla warfare made IRA command structures more complicated and oftentimes haphazard, the mobilisation of Cumann na mBan was not likely to work exactly as planned.

When the IRA needed Cumann na mBan, they made contact with whomever they trusted, whenever they could. They did not worry about the women's chain of command and neither did the women themselves. Cumann na mBan members were often mobilised randomly and by chance. Máire Comerford later recalled her only involvement in an IRA ambush, which occurred when she met an IRA officer she knew on the streets of Dublin. He told her there would be an ambush on Merrion Square within 30 minutes and asked her if she could set up a 'first-aid post somewhere handy'. She mobilised sympathetic friends, not all Cumann na mBan members, who pledged to provide these posts at their residences. However, no IRA casualties were sustained in the action and thus the first-aid posts were not required.[33] Likewise, when Eithne Coyle was asked by the IRA in Longford/Roscommon to provide them with sketches of a local police barracks, she was asked directly by a local IRA officer. She was clearly known to him through her work on behalf of Cumann na mBan and the Gaelic League, he trusted and had confidence in her, and thus his request was informal and did not go through any chain of command.[34] Coyle's experience was mirrored all over the country as IRA men utilised female friends and family regardless of whether or not they were Cumann na mBan members, and certainly regardless of any chain of command. Indeed Brigit Lawlor of the UCD branch, later recalled that when it came to provision of supplies and safe houses, establishment of lines of communication, carrying of dispatches, and help for political prisoners, her activities were usually unofficial and on behalf of friends and acquaintances.[35] Thus a situation developed where small numbers of militarily active members assisted their friends in the IRA and became peripherally involved in combative operations. David

Fitzpatrick's research revealed that the women's assistance to the IRA in Clare was substantially informal, with only eight branches of Cumann na mBan maintaining formal organisation up to the time of the truce.[36] Lil Conlon does reveal that Cork city Cumann na mBan maintained formal organisation throughout. However, this formal organisation was channelled primarily into propaganda and charity work, and not military activities on behalf of the IRA.

So is it fair to say that whilst Cumann na mBan members were useful to the IRA, the organisation itself was not? Would republican women have been able to provide the same level of assistance to the IRA even if Cumann na mBan had never existed? Hardly. What Cumann na mBan provided was a pool of republican women into which the IRA could dip if required. If IRA officers asked a woman known to them for assistance, she could provide it from the reservoir of Cumann na mBan members whom she trusted. On occasion the organisation was mobilised on a large scale. In Carrick-on-Suir, for example, members assisted local IRA men in clearing the streets of the town of mass goers in time for a planned ambush by the local column.[37] Cumann na mBan provided them with a pool of female operatives from which they could choose. Without Cumann na mBan, the women who were not initially known to but wished to assist the IRA would have found it enormously difficult to gain the trust of the male leaders. And those women do appear to have provided invaluable assistance on many occasions.

Aside from the many glowing tributes Cumann na mBan received from IRA leaders, perhaps the most telling recognition of their activities came from the British administration itself.[38] Throughout 1919 the RIC frequently reported Cumann na mBan as 'inactive'. However, as the months progressed, many County Inspectors were to change their assessment to 'secretly active'. Eventually, as the violence intensified in southern areas, there was no denying Cumann na mBan's involvement. The County Inspector for East Cork, who never deemed Cumann na mBan worthy of a place on his table of major political organisations, was forced to concede that Sinn Féin, the Irish Volunteers and Cumann na mBan were, 'directly responsible for the present state of the country'.[39] Five months later his colleague in West Cork welcomed Cumann na mBan into the family of violent republicanism when he wrote that the:

> IRA and Sinn Féin, with Cumann na mBan assistance are the only living political organisations and are extremely active. Their murder campaign has been extremely successful during the month.[40]

Soon the activities of female revolutionaries generally brought some individual women to the attention of the authorities. In Granard, County Longford the famous (because she would later become engaged to Michael Collins) Kitty Kiernan was arrested and questioned regarding the shooting of an RIC District Inspector in her brother's hotel. It was alleged that Kiernan had been one of four people in the company of the District Inspector when the incident occurred.[41] But the arrest which probably drew most attention to Cumann na mBan, and female republicans generally, was that of Linda Kearns in County Sligo in November 1920. The County Inspector reported the incident as follows:

> On 20-11-20 a police and military patrol stopped a motor car driven by nurse Belinda Kearns of 29 Gardiner Place Dublin and found therein ten service rifles, four revolvers, 403 rounds of service rifle ammunition, 23 rounds of revolver ammunition and a quantity of equipment. Two rifles, one revolver and part of the equipment have been identified as the property of the police who were murdered and robbed near Grange on 25-10-20. Three male suspects were being conveyed in the same motor car. All were arrested and will be tried for murder ... It has been ascertained that Miss Kearns has for the past two years been the

> medium of communication between Head Quarters IRA Dublin and County Sligo.[42]

Kearns was not a member of Cumann na mBan. However, her arrest made the British more keenly aware of women's military activities. After Kearns' capture it was clear that women were involved in the carriage of weaponry and dispatches for the IRA. As such Cumann na mBan came under increased scrutiny and raids by British authorities were more frequently targeted at their members.

As Cumann na mBan organisers travelled around the country from HQ in Dublin, some were bound to have assisted in communications work. Indeed in December 1920 police in Fermanagh asserted that the, 'recent capture of seditious literature on a woman shows that orders are being sent to this county from Sinn Féin headquarters'.[43] Leslie Price was dispatched to Cork by the Sinn Féin leadership in July 1921. Price's Cumann na mBan work in Cork had made her known to the local republican community. Thus, when Eamon de Valera needed to know whether a loyalist hostage taken by the IRA in Cork was still alive, he sent her. She was able to locate a column that did not want to be located and report back to de Valera that Lord Bandon was still alive and well.[44] Other senior Cumann na mBan organisers who moved around the country and were likely to have helped in establishing and maintaining republican lines of communication between Dublin and the provinces were; Miss Ring who travelled from Dublin to Waterford and Tipperary; Miss O'Mullane to Down, Derry, Kildare, Louth, Meath and Westmeath; Miss O'Byrne to Laois and Offaly; Miss Deigan to Wexford; Miss Humphreys to Kerry; Mrs Power to Meath; Miss Kennedy to Sligo, Leitrim and Offaly; Mrs Gordon and Miss Ryan to Cork and Limerick; Miss O'Reilly to Kilkenny; Miss McGavock to Antrim, Tyrone and Cork; Miss Plunkett to Roscommon and Miss Hyland to Cavan and Monaghan.[45] These senior and respected members of Cumann na mBan could travel openly in a manner that male leaders could not. This made them more suitable for dispatch carrying. For that very reason Leslie Price had been asked by IRA GHQ to set up specific lines of communication between Dublin and the provincial commands.[46]

At local level too members of Cumann na mBan were found in possession of 'literature of an incriminating nature.[47] Indeed Major Percival, who served with the noted Essex Regiment in Cork from 1919 to 1921, was later to note that republican women had been; employed largely for carrying messages and orders about, and as these (women) could only be searched by women searchers who were not often available when required ... the IRA Lines of communications were not at all vulnerable'.[48] Likewise, the RIC County Inspector for Galway West had expressed concern about his inability to search women whom he suspected of carrying IRA documentation. In January 1921 he reported that:

> Miss Alice Cashel: a well-known Sinn Féiner, and Vice-Chairman of the Galway County Council was arrested here during the month as a result of information received. 2 Women searchers were employed and Miss Cashel was found to be in possession of seditious documents. She is at present awaiting trial.
>
> This incident is mentioned as showing the value of women searchers who it is submitted might often be usefully employed.[49]

From late 1920 the British authorities began employing female searchers and these women sometimes even accompanied British raiding parties to the homes of republican suspects.[50] On occasion, if the authorities' suspicions of resident women were aroused during a raid, they would return to the house accompanied by female searchers.[51] Searches of the residences of Cumann na mBan members became more common from early 1921 and resulted in the discovery of republican literature in Galway, Tyrone and Offaly.[52] By January 1921 these female searchers had become commonplace on the streets of Macroom, County Cork, and by March they were very active in Clonakilty, County Cork.[53] Yet, in less militarily active areas like County Leitrim, whilst female searchers did accompany raiding parties, they were seldom seen on roadway cordons during British roundups.[54] As late as June of 1921 the County Inspector for Meath still complained that he was 'more or less helpless' in attempting to deal with female dispatch carriers.[55] In some areas local tans or auxiliaries may well have overcome their numerical difficulties regarding female searchers by disguising male officers as women. In 1955 two sisters who were former members of Cumann na mBan remained, or had become, convinced that one of them had once been searched by a man disguised as a woman.[56] However, overall the British authorities were comparatively powerless in attempting to deal with female couriers. An interesting comparison can be made from statistics provided by the County Inspector for Laois. In May 1921, his forces managed to conduct 503 searches of male suspects, whilst only nineteen women were searched.[57]

It was not just the carriage of dispatches that worried the British authorities. They had also noted that women were being used to smuggle guns. On 22 January 1921, *The Irish Times* reported an interview given by Major General Strickland to the *Manchester Guardian* as follows:

> In many cases arms would be brought out for use at the scene of an ambush or other attack, by women, who concealed them in their skirts. The army was not making war on women and soldiers never interfered with women unless they had direct evidence against them, so that the difficulty of getting hold of arms which were disposed of in this way could be imagined.[58]

Strickland was obviously engaged in attempting to explain why he had not yet defeated the IRA to a British readership. Yet there is a certain amount of truth in his statement. In Kilkenny the County Inspector was also under the impression that women, specifically Cumann na mBan women, were 'carrying arms and dispatches' for the IRA. He also reported that arms had been posted to women in the county.[59]

Women did carry guns for the IRA but it is impossible to ascertain to what extent they did so. It is equally impossible to distinguish those Cumann na mBan members who did so from non-members like Linda Kearns. The fact that soldiers seldom 'interfered with women', kept the numbers of female arrests for firearm possession artificially low and thus they are of little use in ascertaining the full extent of Cumann na mBan's involvement with firearms. Many ex-Cumann na mBan members later claimed to have handled and stored weaponry on behalf of the IRA. There is no reason to doubt the validity of their claims. The IRA would use whomever they could in order to smuggle armaments from place to place. The sheer volume of women who later reported having done so suggests they were frequently involved in that kind of work. It is most likely that the IRA employed those women whom it trusted, not necessarily Cumann na mBan members, to move guns through crowded areas in broad daylight when men were more prone to search. Máire Comerford's memoir certainly suggests that this was a role in which republican and Cumann na mBan women were heavily engaged:

> Dumps were moved where necessary and I learned from experience that the Lee Enfield service rifle could be carried under my coat without protruding at the bottom if the muzzle was held under my ear. With a concealed rifle each a company of Cumann na mBan could infiltrate from one hiding place to another through the city streets, and in an evening remove a large amount of material from one dump to another. There was at least that much to be said for the longer skirts which were worn to boot-top level in those days.[60]

Other women also reported that the fashions of the day had assisted them in concealing weaponry when in public. Anne, Lilly and Eileen Cooney later recalled that they had carried guns from the scene of an ambush in the Harcourt Street area of Dublin through the city streets to a safe distance from the ambush site. Some women in the Liberties carried guns away from IRA actions in their handbags.[61]

In those isolated rural areas from which police had retreated by mid 1920, the IRA could and did carry its own weapons, particularly under the cover of darkness. But in the cities and towns where the British authorities maintained a presence and men could be searched at any moment, it would have been foolhardy to leave weapons in their hands for any longer than was absolutely necessary. For that reason it would appear likely that women may well have been the dominant gender when it came to the transport of IRA weaponry in urban areas. In Macroom, County Cork, for example, women had to be utilised to carry weapons between the two IRA companies present in the town and past the British sentries at the castle in between. Mollie Cunningham remembered the process as follows:

> At this time there were two companies of the IRA in Macroom town. One A Coy west of the Sullane River … 'B' was based on the portion of the town to the east of the river. Small arms were not too plentiful and the duty of transferring those available from one company area to the other as they were required for operational purposes fell to me. It was nothing unusual for me to take two or three revolvers at a time from one company area to another. In the transfer I had to pass by the sentry at the lower gate of Macroom castle and was liable to be challenged at any moment.[62]

Likewise, in nearby Cork city, Peg Duggan later recalled that the carriage of arms from place to place before and after ambushes became a 'feature of Cumann na mBan activities' as fighting intensified during 1920-21.[63]

Another important part of Cumann na mBan's frontline activity was their participation in the intelligence war. In some senses the organisation had limited its own effectiveness in this area by insisting that no woman who was a member of 'an organisation doing any kind of work for the English enemy' could be a member of Cumann na mBan.[64] Naturally this ruled out all female civil servants, some of whom would undoubtedly have been willing to provide intelligence to republican organisations. But even if Crown agents had been allowed to join the organisation, their usefulness would almost certainly have been negated by the very fact they had identified themselves with a republican organisation. If they were not dismissed for having done so, they certainly would not have been trusted with any useful intelligence. The years that Cumann na mBan had spent openly propagating the Republic had made its members virtually useless when it came to high-level intelligence work. Thus some women were actually asked to disassociate themselves from the organisation before becoming engaged in intelligence work.

Early in 1919 a supervising telephonist in Mallow was instructed by Liam Lynch to disassociate herself from Cumann na mBan. Having done so, she went on to provide the IRA with details of police and military telephone conversations as the war progressed.[65] Austin Stack made a similar request of a female intelligence agent in Kerry.[66] Likewise, it is hardly surprising that some specialist female couriers employed by Michael Collins were not Cumann na mBan members.[67] Collins also appears to have occasionally actively encouraged some members 'not to identify themselves further with Cumann na mBan' in order that their intelligence work might be more effective.[68] In a fashion typical of the man he wrote to one woman asking her to 'stop this blasted forming fours, get out of Cumann na mBan and do some work'.[69] On one significant occasion the 'big fellow' did use Cumann na mBan to supplement his growing intelligence network. He contacted the organisation with a view to finding a 'young and good looking' maid for a member of the British staff in Dublin Castle. The woman selected was not a member of Cumann na mBan, but Cumann na mBan members did call on her. They would call while prisoners were being paraded in order to identify the internees and report on their whereabouts.[70]

Cumann na mBan might not have been overly effective when it came to intelligence gathering in government and military circles on the streets of Dublin but down the country in more rural areas, intelligence provided by Cumann na mBan was often useful to the IRA in the field. Cumann na mBan members became an integral part of an IRA intelligence system which Lieutenant General Percival later described as having 'reached a very high standard of efficiency'.[71] Percival stated that when moving his troops around Cork he found:

> It was fatal to issue orders for any operation more than an hour or two before the troops were due to start, and then the plan should be known only to one or two necessary officers before the troops actually paraded. It is impossible in work of this kind to prevent soldiers and very often even officers, from prejudicing the chances of success of a whole operation by one or two unguarded remarks.[72]

The Lieutenant General was describing a countryside that had ears. Unguarded remarks were overheard by a population which was broadly sympathetic to the IRA. In Tralee the local women were described by Dublin Castle documents as being very inquisitive around British personnel and always forwarding any information they acquired to the rebels.[73] Cumann na mBan simply provided part of the organised network by which wayward remarks and any other indications of British troop movements could be carried back to the IRA. Indeed in some areas the couriering of British troop movements fell almost exclusively to members of Cumann na mBan who, although somewhat inhibited by the presence of female searchers, were still able to move about more freely than male intelligence officers.[74] One former IRA member from Leitrim later commented that women 'could get through where men could not even make the attempt'.[75]

Towards the latter end of the War of Independence the British military formed themselves into small mobile columns designed to scour the countryside for IRA flying columns, and to engage and defeat them where possible. When Percival himself led one of these columns into Macroom the local Cumann na mBan kept track of their movements:

> We were all busily engaged in keeping a record of their movements all around the clock. These records were taken to Battalion Headquarters, which were being moved about the district each night, by me or by some other member of our unit. As curfew was in operation, at this period, we often had to remain in the countryside overnight.[76]

Sometimes reports of enemy movements were of immediate and mortal importance to flying columns who were about to be encircled. When the West Cork Flying Column fought its way out of such an encirclement at Crossbarry in March 1921, Cumann na mBan members later claimed to have carried reports of British troop movements between the various IRA units, deployed in several positions around Crossbarry, sometimes even running in relays through the local fields.[77]

Cumann na mBan also involved themselves in scouting operations on behalf of the IRA. Essentially this activity involved moving around the perimeter of a column, whether at rest or on the move, and reporting any movements of nearby British forces. In that way a column would not be surprised by a British force, could escape encirclement, or could choose to engage crown forces when and where it wished. Scouting for flying columns was primarily a function of local IRA units. However, as women who encountered the tans were less likely to arouse their suspicion, it seems that local IRA sometimes involved local Cumann na mBan in this risky activity.[78]

However, even at local level, Cumann na mBan may well have compromised their own intelligence function in one key way. Members were expressly forbidden from speaking to RIC officers. As the war progressed this boycott was extended to British military and all Irish women were expected to obey. It is common knowledge that the arrival of the infamous 'Black and Tans' and their kindred 'Auxie' police force in Ireland, was one of the reasons for the escalation of hostilities between the IRA and the British authorities in early 1920. These forces were initially sent to Ireland as mass resignations from the RIC had made the country impossible to police. The RIC had been resigning in droves as a result of the direct threat to their lives posed by IRA activities and the boycott of the wider Irish community. This boycott made life very awkward for policemen. In some areas they were denied basic provisions, whilst a general lack of information from the public had made it impossible for them to do their job.

Cumann na mBan had supported the boycott from the very beginning and seemed determined that Irish women would participate as willingly as Irish men. Indeed they had asserted that the responsibility for carrying out the boycott rested 'more on the women than on the men of Ireland'.[79] Louise Gavan Duffy had a leaflet circulated to all branches reminding them that the RIC were, 'the eyes and ears of the enemy. Let those eyes and ears know no friendship the leaflet urged, before making biblical reference to the Lord's marking of Cain.[80] In Leitrim the local Cumann na mBan went as far as discouraging not just their own membership but 'all girls' from associating with the RIC. In addition they reported any businessperson who dealt voluntarily with the RIC to the local

IRA.[81] IRA reprisals for such commercial co-operation were sometimes ugly and drastic. In April 1919 the Inspector General reported Cumann na mBan's participation in the boycott as follows:

> During the past week typed circulars from the Head Quarters of the Cumann na mBan (Women's Branch of Sinn Féin) forbidding members of the Society to hold any conversation, or even to sit in the same pew in Church, with a policeman were distributed through the post.
>
> This organised hostility to the constabulary, besides endangering their lives, renders the ordinary duty of criminal investigation increasingly difficult, and is part of the scheme of making British Government in Ireland impossible.

In addition the members distributed threatening letters to RIC members, a task which required hand delivery and a quick getaway.[82] By early 1920, the boycott, the continuing IRA attacks on RIC personnel (although throughout 1919 the policemen's arms and not the policemen themselves were theoretically the targets of these attacks) and the mass resignations from the force had made policing in Ireland impossible. Enter the Black and Tans. Cumann na mBan had played their part and supported the republican campaign fully, but in doing so had certainly significantly undermined their own intelligence capabilities.

Where the young single women of Cumann na mBan may have been able to obtain information from British officers who might have courted them, their own organisation, and the republican community generally, expressly forbade them from maintaining any kind of relationship with any agent of the crown. The punishment for breaking this boycott was most severe. At least one Cumann na mBan member was court-martialled by her own organisation for this offence. Having been found innocent, she was one of the lucky ones.[83] Elsewhere young women were sometimes beaten and often had their hair shorn off by local IRA men who had spotted them 'walking with soldiers'.[84] In Carlow IRA men embarrassed a local girl who was known to visit soldiers at the barracks. They searched her person so thoroughly and intrusively that she never dared call on soldiers again.[85] But the boycott was not strictly operated in every area. We have already seen that the women of Tralee were quite adept at extracting information from British personnel to whom they spoke. Likewise, a Galway Cumann na mBan member later recalled that the job she had hated most was 'enticing British soldiers down the docks in order to have them relieved of their arms by the Volunteers'.[86]

As the IRA employed themselves in shaving the heads of women whom it considered disloyal, so too did the Black and Tans. Many Cumann na mBan members were to suffer this punishment at the hands of those whom Britain still claimed were maintaining law and order.[87] Indeed one woman was awarded £400 compensation by the British courts after police had shorn her hair and threatened her life.[88] In addition to their forays into hair styling, the Tans also demonstrated a fondness for arson when it came to reprisals against single women and widows.[89] Women were also wounded and even killed, as a direct result of gun fire from ill-disciplined crown forces.[90] However it is worth noting that the IRA's treatment of women whom it considered traitorous was also severe. On one occasion a Fermoy woman was shot dead whilst walking in the company of two soldiers.[91] Another girl appeared to have sacrificed her own life by jumping in front of an IRA bullet intended for her auxiliary sweetheart.[92] In Galway and Tipperary two women were killed, accidentally or otherwise, simply because they were in the company of senior RIC targets.[93] In addition to these unfortunate victims, two other women were shot by the IRA as British spies and some female civilians were accidentally killed or wounded during IRA actions.[94]

Cumann na mBan members also demonstrated a capacity to involve themselves in the administration of IRA punishments. On occasion they were used to search other women suspected of being

British informants and on at least one occasion a member procured the necessary tar for the tarring and feathering of a man who continued his employment as a police driver when he had been warned to cease all such activity.[95] Bridget O'Mullane and a number of her comrades kidnapped a suspected female spy at gunpoint and delivered her to a republican court, where she was ordered to leave the country.[96]

The front line military activities of Cumann na mBan revolved around intelligence work and the carriage of guns and dispatches. Yet the active IRA volunteers were also supported by a sympathetic community that ensured they could survive in the field. Cumann na mBan were an organised part of that community. They helped local IRA units shelter and cater for flying columns. They sheltered men and weapons in their own houses. They nursed wounded republicans. They provided for the needs of republican prisoners and buried republican dead. They maintained an organised and visible feminine resistance to British rule in Ireland. In short, much of Cumann na mBan's war was not fought on the front lines but they performed an equally important support role.

The Support Role

In early twentieth-century Ireland the role of women in society was much more limited than it is today. Women tended to live their lives and perform their societal role primarily within the confines of their own home for the majority of their lifetimes. Thus it is no surprise that much of Cumann na mBan's war was fought within those same confines.

In their own homesteads and various safe houses in any given locality Cumann na mBan members provided shelter for IRA men and columns who were on the run from British authorities. These tasks were never the sole preserve of the women's auxiliary. As an IRA column moved throughout its assigned locality it was supported primarily by local IRA units, who may or may not have sought to involve local Cumann na mBan or local members of Cumann na mBan.[97] In 1920 Cumann na mBan had urged their branch officers to compile a list of safe houses in their area. This list was to be forwarded to the secretary of the District Council, who would in turn forward it to the battalion O/C IRA.[98] There is no evidence of these lists ever having been compiled. However, if they were, it is likely that they were destroyed. But in any event the provision of shelter for men on the run was never really formally structured. Local IRA, Cumann na mBan and republican activists found it whenever and wherever they could among a largely sympathetic population. Again it was a case of the IRA essentially dictating the scope of Cumann na mBan's activities. They would ask the women to provide food and shelter, or they would not. With the movement of the columns subject to the strictest secrecy, it was never likely that entire Cumann na mBan branches would be mobilised to cook or clean for the IRA. However, in some quieter counties entire branches do appear to have operated in catering support of the IRA and even found time to organise dances for the men's entertainment.[99] There is little point in providing the reader with the names and accounts of the women who later claimed to have provided shelter or food for the IRA. It is sufficient to say that there are many such accounts and that they are generally corroborated by the accounts of IRA leaders.

Where there was a good deal of more organised activity was in the provision of food and comforts to those IRA men who were already sheltered in British and Irish prisons. Unsurprisingly this activity first commenced during the post 1916 period when vast numbers of Irish Volunteers were placed in British internment camps. Cumann na mBan set up a prisoners sub-committee in Dublin. This committee included notable Cumann na mBan activists such as Mabel Fitzgerald, Niamh Plunkett and Lily O'Brennan. The committee expressed concerns in relation to the treatment of prisoners in a number of areas. An open letter from Fitzgerald to the relatives of the internees urged them to write to the governors of British prisons and the Home Office in order to enquire whether men could practice their religion and had access to Irish publications. The letter also urged enquiry about various aspects of the men's prison diets.[100] This concern about prisoners' diets was to become an important one for Cumann na mBan.

In its early days, the health of the men interned in England seemed to weigh heavily on the minds of the prisoners committee. This is hardly surprising as many of the committee's membership were married to the internees. Wartime rationing in England led to concerns that the prisoners may be underfed and thus suffer from ill-health. As such, the committee appealed to the public through the columns of the major national press 'for home made bread and cakes, or the materials; butter, eggs, sugar, lard, jam and good flour'. It was also proposed to supply prisoners with comforts such as tobacco, cigarettes, chocolate, sweets, fruit and biscuits.[101] These provisions were sent to the British internment camps until Eamon de Valera halted the initiative. De Valera, who was the most senior republican survivor of the Easter rising, wired Cumann na mBan to express his concern that wartime exports of Irish food to Britain may result in rising prices on the Irish market. As such he stated that he and his fellow prisoners were of the opinion that Ireland should keep as much of its own domestic produce as was possible:

> We are anxious that the attention of the people should be directed to one food question only – that of retaining in Ireland sufficient food for the Irish people … Now is the time for making arrangements for the securing of stocks so that the poor may be able to buy next winter at reasonable prices. All the energy of your food committee will be needed to make a success of any scheme that may be devised, and we shall be happy to put up with our short commons if we feel that it will result in more food for, say some of the little children in Dublin … Conscription is not quite dead yet. England wants the Irish har-

> vest gathered in. A winter campaign might suit the Irish expeditionary force. Cumann na mBan will have its hands full.[102]

With the war ended by Christmas 1918, the women once again organised parcels for the prisoners who were in British custody following the 'German Plot' controversy.[103] In January 1919 Arthur Griffith wrote to *Nationality* on behalf of himself and fellow internees to thank Cumann na mBan for the Christmas parcels they had sent to Gloucester jail.[104]

At local level many Cumann na mBan members were also active in providing comforts to republican prisoners throughout the War of Independence. As IRA activists were imprisoned in various jails and barracks across the island, the women regularly supplemented their prison rations with parcels from the outside. In some localities they arranged that republicans received their full visitation allowances by ensuring that local sympathisers stood in when the prisoner's own family or friends could not make a visit.[105] They also provided information to the prisoners' families as to their whereabouts in the early days of their detention.[106]

Cumann na mBan was to the forefront in the care of wounded men. They became a part of the network that sheltered and cared for these men. In addition they were frequently involved in finding safe hospitals for seriously injured men. As these hospitals were primarily located in urban areas, it was in those urban centres that Cumann na mBan were busiest in their care for the wounded. Men from all over Leinster and even beyond were brought to the Dublin hospitals. Some were wanted men and thus they could not be admitted in the normal way. They were frequently smuggled between safehouses and 'friendly hospitals' when either location was vulnerable to British raids. Eventually this work became so taxing for Cumann na mBan that two of their Dublin members had to devote all their spare time to it and withdraw from all other republican activities.[107] Similar services were provided to IRA wounded in Limerick city.[108]

Likewise in Cork, when Tom Barry became seriously ill in late 1920, it was two members of Cumann na mBan who initially nursed him, along with a qualified nurse and doctor, at a safe house before he was smuggled into a Cork city hospital.[109] Four months later the smuggling was reversed as a few Cumann na mBan women removed the dead body of Barry's friend, Charlie Hurley, from the Bandon morgue. Hurley was engaged to Leslie Price and she had the sad duty of driving her fiancé's body by pony and trap through the night to a small cemetery in Clogagh, County Cork. There, at 2am, they were joined by the now recuperated Barry and the West Cork flying column. Charlie Hurley was laid to rest with full military honours under the blackness of a night sky and Barry presented Price with a part of the tricolour that had draped her fiancé's coffin.[110] Their shared grief at the loss of a close friend undoubtedly did much to foster the relationship that was to result in the marriage of Price and Barry less than six months later.

Where Cumann na mBan were not directly involved with the IRA in either combatant or support roles, they were often in the background providing support of another kind. A key strategy of republicanism during the revolutionary period was the capture of public support. The IRA could not fight the war unless the public were supportive of it. Cumann na mBan were very active in attempting to swing public opinion away from the British administration and towards the fledgling republican one.

We have already seen that Cumann na mBan's propagandist activities were a primary function of the organisation from its inception, through 1916, and up to the conscription crisis. Although they had gone underground in the wake of the 1916 rebellion, they had continued to propagate the Republic until the conscription crisis brought them back out into the open as the visible face of feminine republicanism. However, with the declaration of the organisation as 'dangerous' in July 1918 and its complete suppression in parts of Munster in July, August and September

1919, followed by its suppression across the island in November 1919, the organisation was once again forced partially underground. They still conducted their propaganda war; they simply ceased to identify themselves as Cumann na mBan.

Throughout the War of Independence women continued to distribute republican propaganda on behalf of Sinn Féin and the IRA. Whilst few women were arrested for the possession of what the British authorities called 'seditious literature', their virtual immunity from search until the introduction of female searchers in late 1920 definitely kept arrests to a minimum. However, whilst policemen may not have been able to search female suspects, they could, and did, search their houses and places of business.

In Dundalk one police search seemed intentionally targeted at prominent local Cumann na mBan members. The search of their houses and places of business and employment yielded a quantity of Sinn Féin literature.[111] Dundalk Cumann na mBan had avoided police attention for some time. They had even been the source of considerable embarrassment to local police, who had had to admit that they had been unaware of the organisation's presence in the town until they found Cumann na mBan literature on a republican suspect. The women themselves were so amused at the police's ignorance that they committed their considerable glee to satirical verse:

> There's myself and Sergeant Sheridan, near wore upon our feet,
> Since the Sunday after Easter, we've been absent from our beat,
> On bicycles we scorch along, from dewy eve 'til dawn,
> For this most elusive runaire, of Dundalk Cumann na mBan.[112]

Elsewhere, other Cumann na mBan propagandists might have been happy if their activities had aroused as little suspicion as in Dundalk. Throughout the War of Independence, particularly in 1919, female shopkeepers were continually raided by British police and military and quantities of 'seditious literature' were frequently found on their premises. In Killarney, Cumann na mBan member, Miss Gleason, eventually had her shop closed for continually re-offending.[113]

Much of Cumann na mBan's own propaganda was aimed at a female audience. As an all-female organisation they were probably best placed to identify the most effective methods of gaining the support of women for the republican movement. One leaflet asked, 'Irish Mothers do you want your children kidnapped?' Another went on to explain the alleged mistreatment of those mothers' sons who had been imprisoned by the British authorities.[114] At the height of hostilities, Cumann na mBan bill posters in several counties, urged Irish women to stand by the IRA.[115] This 'Standfast leaflet' was issued by Cumann na mBan HQ in January 1921 in poster and hand-bill form. Many branches requested the draft text only and then organised their own printing. 50,000 of these leaflets were distributed in Dublin alone, whilst in the environs of Cork city nineteen branches distributed them outside of twenty churches.[116]

In Limerick city Cumann na mBan were engaged in distributing vast amounts of propaganda throughout the Anglo Irish war. One of their members later recalled:

> During the years of the campaign we regularly got bundles of posters, leaflets and other literature from Headquarters. These parcels generally arrived by rail … and were later distributed amongst the members of each district. They were then posted on walls or otherwise by night. We often went into the country and put posters on chapel gates.[117]

In Cork city Cumann na mBan had been regularly standing outside Roman Catholic churches distributing propaganda since 1919.[118] Up to ten Cork women served one month in prison, having been arrested for this activity.[119] In Fermanagh Bridget O'Mullane was arrested for a similar offence.[120]

Cumann na mBan maintained a visible presence on the streets

of Irish cities. Whenever organised groups of republican women appeared on city streets there was little doubt that they were Cumann na mBan members, even if they no longer had the banners to proclaim it. Nancy Wyse Power later explained that this visible presence was an important gesture of defiance for many members, particularly as practical experience had taught them that it would take a change in British policy for this public activity to result in widespread arrests of the membership:

> The policy throughout was to keep the organisation an open one, as it was felt that open activity on the part of women would help maintain public morale. I recall an argument on this point at the height of the Black and Tan activity in the early part of 1921, when the Hon. Mary Spring Rice pleaded that it would be preferable to have in each district a few reliable girls or women who could be counted on to carry out all necessary work and orders and to drop general activities of a semi public nature ... but the general opinion was that to follow such a policy would amount to a confession of defeat. Besides it was evident that the Government did not wish to make large-scale arrests of women. A very small number, in fact, were ever made.[121]

This open defiance was evident in different towns and manifested itself in different ways all over Ireland. In rural areas members sometimes provided the visible face of militant republicanism at the funerals of those IRA members who had been killed in action.[122] Meanwhile, in the larger urban centres more prominent public displays were possible. When republican prisoners demanding political status began a hunger strike in Mountjoy Jail in April 1920, Cumann na mBan were to the forefront of the public manifestation of outrage and grief. They stood outside the walls of the prison in military ranks, sometimes kneeling to pray the rosary.[123] During their protest, emotions ran so high that some women forced their way through the main gate and insisted on seeing the prisoners.[124] On 12 April labour leaders called a general strike and the population of Dublin descended on Mountjoy Street. Cumann na mBan helped to form the cordons and organise the public protest outside the jail.[125] When the youthful Kevin Barry was executed the women again provided a public demonstration of their grief by marching to Mountjoy and kneeling in prayer outside.[126] Cumann na mBan continued to organise similar protests outside of Irish prisons for subsequent executions.[127]

In one of the more ceremonially important public demonstrations of the period, five members of Cumann na mBan were the only republicans to make the journey to Bodenstown in 1921. After a close encounter with the British authorities in 1920 it had been deemed too dangerous to send any men to the Kildare cemetery the following year. Thus, in 'the smallest Bodenstown on record', Máire Comerford, Éilis Ní Rian, Fiona Plunkett, Emily Valentine and Margaret McElroy laid the customary wreath on Wolfe Tone's grave. Details of their guarding of the sacred republican tradition were circulated to the press by Seán O'Muirthile.[128]

On other occasions Cumann na mBan's public defiance led them into violent confrontation with those expressing alternative political viewpoints. In Monaghan a woman was stabbed and beaten with sticks and stones because she had waved a tricolour out her window during a parade by the Ancient Order of Hibernians.[129] When the British authorities decided to proclaim 20 July 1919 'Victory Day' in recognition of their victory in the First World War, a parade of recently demobilised Irish soldiers was scheduled for every major urban centre. Trouble flared in Limerick and Dublin, but it was only in Cork that Cumann na mBan appear to have been involved in physical confrontation with loyalist women. *The Irish Times* left the following account:

The soldiers were waylaid and beaten whenever they were found

> in small groups or alone, and chased off the streets for no other apparent reason than that they were in uniform. Their female companions were in many cases hustled and their loyal badges torn from them by women wearing Sinn Féin emblems.[130]

The pro-unionist *Cork County Eagle and Munster Advertiser* described the violence between the Cork women in more dramatic terms:

> Amongst the first indications of the temper of some of those who paraded the streets early in the night was the behaviour of a number of young girls, some of whom wore Sinn Féin, and some red white and blue, favours. These, after an interchange of 'compliments', fought in Patrick Street as fiercely as they could, and it was with no little difficulty that a party of men separated them.[131]

Whilst the unionist press probably over dramatised the events in Cork, it does appear that republican and loyalist women did clash violently on the city's main thoroughfare. The *Cork Examiner* had reported similar clashes between republican women and 'separation women' on 26, 27, 28 June and 12 July 1917.[132] Such unladylike behaviour was bound to have been frowned upon by the society of the time.

On occasion the women were publicly criticised by the Roman Catholic hierarchy. During a confirmation sermon in Westport the Archbishop of Tuam described republican women who had been active in the area as, 'thoughtless girls who … are ready to fling themselves at anybody who takes them up.'[133] After a particularly violent period in Cork, Bishop Cohalan declared that, 'anyone who shall within the Diocese of Cork, organise or take part in an ambush or in kidnapping, or otherwise shall be guilty of murder or attempt at murder, shall incur by the very fact the censure of excommunication'.[134] Although Cohalan's sermon of the previous Sunday seemed to point the finger at 'boys and men' who were involved in such things, his subsequent decree applied to republican women and men, and could even be interpreted as applying to crown forces. Cohalan had certainly been critical of the British reprisal policy and in that he was not alone among his clerical colleagues.[135] In October 1920 the Catholic hierarchy had expressed concern about cases where Crown forces had torn young women 'undressed from their mothers care in the darkness of night'.[136]

Throughout the period Cumann na mBan also grabbed occasional newspaper headlines when its members continued to defy the authority of the crown in Ireland. Documents captured on the person of Lillian Hawes in Cork, proved that on 10 November 1919 the organisation formally instructed its members that upon arrest they should behave as follows:

1. Speak Irish only if you know it well.
2. Refuse to recognise the court.
3. Give no bail.
4. Demand the rights of political prisoners.

(a). Insist on wearing your own clothes. Prisoners are entitled to this, and should be searched only by one officer appointed for the purpose.
(b) See that you get rights in regard to parcels, letters, visits, intercourse. Every untried prisoner is entitled to write and receive one letter per day.
(c) If you cannot eat prison food, refuse it.
(d) Refuse to see prisoners through cage.
(e) Refuse to do menial work.[137]

Some women did give their names in Irish when arrested, others refused to eat prison food and others refused to recognise British courts.[138] Hawes herself was one of them. She stated, to the press and not the court, that the only laws she would recognise were those laid down by the Irish Republic.[139] Eithne Coyle later claimed that she had read a newspaper throughout her trial, which she considered a 'farce'.[140] However, there were other women accused of republican activities who did co-operate with the British courts and attempted to mount defences.[141] Whether or not they were members of Cumann na mBan is difficult to say.

In addition to their work on the home front Cumann na mBan were also of key importance in winning the propaganda war abroad. Senior members from the organisation travelled to the US and Europe in order to highlight the increasingly desperate conditions in Ireland. Nancy Wyse Power was involved in the embryonic Republican Foreign Service in Berlin whilst Mary and Muriel MacSwiney toured America in 1920-21. The MacSwineys tour was not a Cumann na mBan initiative. It was to be part funded by the fledgling republican government and by royalties from the now deceased Terence MacSwiney's writings. In the end, Mary MacSwiney paid considerable expenses out of her own pocket.[142] Nonetheless, she brought the republican message to a mass American audience and even succeeded in speaking in the legislatures of five States. Thousands of people greeted her in many towns and cities right across the country, whilst the tour also received widespread coverage in the US media.[143] In addition, MacSwiney became the first woman to be granted the freedom of New York City.[144] There was never any chance that a Cumann na mBan member would be granted speaking rights in the British legislature. However, the organisation spoke to MPs by forwarding them all a leaflet entitled 'The Irish Woman and the IRA', in late 1920. In addition the leaflet was forwarded to a 'large number of foreign journalists'.[145]

Mabel Fitzgerald was central to all this propaganda work. Her husband, Desmond, was responsible for the issuance of republican propaganda to foreign journalists and other interested parties. In order for him to perform this role to the best of his ability he needed accounts of alleged British atrocities from all over the island.

These accounts were placed in the *Irish Bulletin*, which first appeared in November 1919 and was regularly forwarded by Fitzgerald to his contacts abroad. Mabel became one of Cumann na mBan's propaganda directors, a role which dovetailed nicely with that of her husband. It is probably no coincidence that the women of Cumann na mBan were then utilised in order to collect details of British atrocities at local level. The Dáil Éireann publicity department was particularly interested in details of British 'murders, floggings, and attacks on women'.[146] Limerick Cumann na mBan collected details of alleged atrocities for a list of foreign contacts provided to them by Desmond Fitzgerald.[147] Whilst in Wexford members were responsible for a copy of the bulletin being posted through the letterboxes of the town.[148]

Yet there were limitations to the extent that Cumann na mBan could involve themselves in the support role. Some were tied by domestic duties and others, perhaps, by the rigidly defined role of women in the early twentieth century. Thus when Máire Comerford suggested that the Sinn Féin offices at 6 Harcourt Street be reopened and staffed by Cumann na mBan after the authorities had closed them, she was biting off more than her organisation could chew. Comerford later explained she had not appreciated the full extent of the domestic and political responsibilities of the other members and her superiors had had to explain that the organisation was already fully engaged.[149]

Cumann na mBan also maintained a charitable dimension(although they would not have described it as charity) to their work through their alliance with the Irish White Cross. The White Cross was established in January 1921 in order to distribute funds raised in America by the American Committee for Relief in Ireland. Although the senior and parish councils of the organisation were dominated by clerics and many lay men, and the organisation received backing from groups as diverse as Sinn Féin, local councils and local Farmers' organisations, the White Cross organisation also contained a number of key Cumann na mBan personnel. Mary Spring Rice, Kathleen Clarke and Nancy O'Rahilly served on the executive committee, whilst Áine Ceannt was a member of its general council.[150] The White Cross HQ was situated next door to the Cumann na mBan offices on Dawson Street.[151] As such the two organisations were bound to have developed a relationship of some sort.

At local level Cumann na mBan members were well placed to assess the families most in need of aid due to the devastation caused by the war. Thus, Cumann na mBan members became involved in White Cross parish committees.[152] Further evidence of the close connection between the two organisations was the White Cross contribution of £10,000 to the Irish Republican Prisoners Dependants' Fund (IRPDF). This fund had been founded in 1917 in order to raise funds and distribute aid to the families of imprisoned republicans. Theoretically the IRPDF was a separate organisation with its own HQ and not a part of Cumann na mBan. Its first president and vice-president were Eamon de Valera and Count Plunkett respectively, whilst several men served on its committee. At local level, places on battalion committees were reserved for IRA adjutants. However, in reality it was administered by executive members of Cumann na mBan and fundraising work on its behalf became a regular activity for members of the women's auxiliary. By the time of the truce the IRPDF had distributed £17,260 in aid and dealt with 861 cases. As it is commonly estimated that approximately 4,000 republicans were imprisoned during the War of Independence, it is clear that the fund was hardly sufficient for its purpose and that the White Cross' £10,000 contribution accounted for a huge proportion of what the IRPDF itself had raised.[153] The White Cross contribution to the IRPDF was the source of some controversy. Nonetheless, the former organisation endorsed the wisdom of this contribution to an organisation that had 'co-operated with the Irish White Cross during the whole period of relief'. Whilst the White Cross never officially thanked a combatant organisation like

Cumann na mBan for their assistance, they did express their gratitude for 'the unselfish labours of the many women throughout Ireland'.[154]

Throughout the period of the War of Independence Cumann na mBan women from overseas were also engaged in the republican struggle. In Glasgow Jean Quinn was sentenced to twelve months for carrying explosives.[155] Another member in Britain later recalled running guns through London and onwards to Ireland:

> I can remember another occasion when with some Volunteers and other Cumann na mBan members I went to Tilbury Docks to collect guns and ammunition off a boat from America. These were Thomson guns and we brought them to London station and then by taxi to a flat in Waverly mansions.[156]

The above mentioned flat was occupied by a member of Cumann na mBan and it is presumed that the guns were to find their way to Ireland from there. On some occasions members were used to smuggle these guns across the Irish Sea and the member quoted above was involved in trips of that nature. She also claimed to have been involved with the IRA in the intimidation of relatives of Black and Tans in Britain. From 1920 Cumann na mBan's public operations in London were carried out under the cover name of the 'Ladies Distress Committee'. This was a necessity for a minority group on the British mainland if they wished to undertake fundraising activities in the public sphere.[157]

Although we have seen that Cumann na mBan were publicly defiant in most areas it would be erroneous to assume that their activities were uniform across the island. We have already seen that Dundalk Cumann na mBan were active in propaganda work in 1919, yet one member in Dundalk later commented that 'as after 1919 most of the fighting veered southwards there was not so much organised activity for the Cumann'.[158] Nancy Wyse Power later recalled that from 1920:

> It became increasingly difficult to hold the organisation to fixed lines of activity, although the membership continued to grow. In the fighting areas, such as West Cork where Cumann na mBan was particularly well organised, the members worked in direct contact with the flying columns, providing shelter, catering, carrying messages, hiding arms, doing most of the work of the Volunteers Dependants' Association and so on, but in general the Branches devoted themselves to whatever activity seemed most suitable to the needs of the particular area in which they were situated. Strict supervision or control from headquarters was impossible ...[159]

As with other republican organisations, the level and nature of Cumann na mBan's activity often depended on local conditions and was intrinsically linked with the geography of the revolution. In those areas where the IRA was most active, Cumann na mBan were active too. They were active in both clandestine military work and in gestures of open defiance. Where the IRA were less active, so were Cumann na mBan. Without IRA activity they could not be militarily active. Nonetheless even in those areas where the IRA's military campaign was less successful, Cumann na mBan did occasionally organise republican demonstrations as gestures of solidarity with comrades elsewhere in the country.[160]

Numerical Contraction and Geographical Penetration

Cumann na mBan's branch network continued to expand for the duration of the War of Independence. However, like other republican organisations its membership declined significantly from the peak experienced during the conscription crisis.

The following table represents police reportage of the organisation's strength in January and November of 1919 and in September of 1921.

RIC ESTIMATES OF CUMANN NA MBAN'S STRENGTH IN JANUARY AND NOVEMBER 1919 AND SEPTEMBER 1921

County	*Jan 1919 Branches*	*Jan 1919 Membership*	*Nov 1919 Branches*	*Nov 1919 Membership*	*Sept 1921 Branches*	*Sept 1921 Membership*
Armagh	2	190	2	190	2	190
Cavan	11	313	12	343	12	343
Donegal	14	415	19	606	19	606
Down	1	84	1	84	1	84
Wicklow	3	88	3	85	-	-
Carlow	1	40	-	-	-	-
Dublin Co.	1	30	1	30	1	30
Kilkenny	2	47	3	70	3	75
Offaly	3	140	4	187	-	-
Longford	2	299	11	384	10	350
Laois	1	30	1	30	1	30
Westmeath	3	62	4	92	5	112
Wexford	2	75	2	75	2	75
Galway East	9	316	9	316	9	316
Mayo	10	346	11	384	11	343
Roscommon	3	130	5	185	5	185
Sligo	7	197	7	167	8	277
Clare	9	339	9	339	9	399
Cork West	3	31	3	31	-	-
Kerry	11	327	11	157	12	351
Limerick	8	840	8	450	10	344
Tipperary S.	2	18	2	18	2	18
Waterford	3	68	3	68	1	68
Monaghan	-	-	-	-	3	49
Fermanagh	-	-	-	-	2	40
Louth	-	-	-	-	6	264

From the above it is immediately apparent that police did not report a uniform expansion in branch or membership numbers across the island. In Cork East, Tipperary North, Meath, Kildare, Antrim, Tyrone, Derry, Galway West and Leitrim, throughout the period of the War of Independence police never attempted to tabulate statistics for Cumann na mBan, although some of these County Inspectors did mention Cumann na mBan activity.

It is also apparent that by September 1921, in Monaghan, Fermanagh and Louth, police had attempted to estimate Cumann na mBan's strength where they had made no such attempts in January 1919. Furthermore, we see that in Wicklow, Carlow, Offaly and West Cork the County Inspectors had ceased to tabulate Cumann na mBan statistics by September 1921. In Wicklow and Carlow this lack of tabulation would seem to stem from frequent changes of police personnel and organisation in both counties. As County Inspectors changed so did their attitude to Cumann na mBan and by September 1921 the men who held the position in both of these counties did not attempt to estimate Cumann na mBan's strength where previous inspectors had. In West Cork the County Inspector stopped submitting numerical data on all political organisations in November 1920. However, up until that date his estimates were never altered from three branches of 31 members. The omission of Cumann na mBan from the latter reports in Offaly is a little more curious. The last tabulation of statistics for the organisation in that county occurred in October 1920 when it was estimated that Cumann na mBan had four branches of 177 members.

In the period tabulated, the only other counties which show significant alterations in Cumann na mBan statistical estimates are Cavan, Donegal, Kilkenny, Longford, Westmeath, Mayo, Roscommon, Sligo, Kerry and Limerick. These were the counties where police noticed changes in Cumann na mBan and tried to report same. They attempted to keep track of the organisation where many others merely clung to the same old estimates throughout the period. With the notable exceptions of Limerick and Mayo, in all these counties police reported substantial increases in Cumann na mBan's strength. Indeed in Mayo's case the organisation was reported as maintaining its overall membership numbers whilst gaining a branch. In Limerick they gained two branches but lost more than half their membership. This would tend to indicate that in these two counties some women were becoming less active in Cumann na mBan. Thus in those counties, whilst the branch numbers increased, the average number of active members per branch declined.

Much of the police reportage depended on the nature of Cumann na mBan's activities in their area. The organisation was frequently prominent in various republican demonstrations but such demonstrations could not be relied upon for organisational statistics. If numbers of Cumann na mBan were present at a funeral or protest, there was still no way of telling how many branches were present or precisely where they were from. In some counties they could be more openly active and thus changes were more easily tracked. In others they became completely inactive and thus no real change in police reportage occurred. In those counties where they worked mostly in secret with the IRA changes in their numerical strength were unnoticeable to police.

A number of British initiatives also served to drive Cumann na mBan's formal organisation increasingly underground in various counties. The first of these was the declaration of the organisation as 'dangerous' by the Lord Lieutenant in July 1918. Although the secretaries of Kerry Cumann na mBan may have been practicing a little sarcasm when they expressed surprise at the proclamation of 'a purely women's organisation', worse was to follow.[161] In July 1919 Cumann na mBan were suppressed in Tipperary, where the first of 1919's violence had occurred. In August and September that suppression was extended into Counties Clare and Cork, until in late November Cumann na mBan were declared illegal across the island. Thus from the above table it is noticeable that even those County

Inspectors who did report substantial changes in Cumann na mBan's strength tended to do so before November 1919. The only administrative areas (aside from West Cork, Wicklow, Carlow and Offaly, where tabulation had ceased) where police still reported substantial alterations in Cumann na mBan's strength after November 1919 were Longford, Westmeath, Sligo, Kerry, Limerick and Waterford. The decrease in Longford branch numbers and corresponding increase in Westmeath's branch numbers are explained by a portion of the former county being inserted into the latter for administrative purposes in August 1920. Sligo's reports fluctuated until February of 1920 when they settled on eight branches of 277 or 278 members. By January of 1920 estimates in Kerry had settled on twelve branches of 351 members. The membership estimate was extended to 357 in February 1920 and there it remained until September 1921. It took the Limerick inspector a full twelve months of fluctuation until he settled on ten branches of 344 members in November 1920. And in Waterford the organisation was reported as having dropped two branches but maintained its membership in August 1920. Presumably the Inspector there must have been reporting what he interpreted as an organisational change.

It is clear, therefore, that as soon as Cumann na mBan's formal organisation was driven underground in November 1919 police reports which were never very accurate to begin with, became almost entirely useless in attempting to analyse the numerical strength of the group. The only other source from which we can attempt to extract an estimate of Cumann na mBan's size are the statistics provided by the organisation itself in the 1921 convention report.

The 1921 convention report is different from the other convention reports of the period in that it is precise in its statistical breakdown of the organisation's numerical strength. No vague estimates were provided. The organisation did not claim to have 'over x branches' or 'more than y' members as it had on previous occasions.

Instead it broke down its membership and branch numbers precisely. The 1921 convention was attended by over 400 delegates from all over the country. This ensured that the numbers would have to be pretty accurate, or at least accurate enough to satisfy the women who knew the situation on the ground. The report gave the organisation's strength in the various provinces as follows:

CUMANN NA MBAN'S PROVINCIAL STRENGTH

Province	*District Councils*	*Branches*	*Branches/DC*	*Head of Pop./1 Branch*
Munster	51	375	7.4	2,761
Leinster	18	188	10.4	6,181
Connaught	12	93	7.8	6,569
Ulster	4	46	11.5	34,385

Looking at the above, it is obvious that the organisation was stronger in Munster than in the other three provinces. Even in terms of the organisation of its branches into District Councils, Munster fared best with Connaught coming a close second. Thus, although the organisation's branch network was small in Connaught, the province's organisation of branches into District Councils was comparatively efficient.

Adjusting the above figures to take in the population statistics of the 1911 census we find that Munster had one branch for every 2,761 of its population, Leinster one for every 6,181 and Connaught had one for every 6,569. However Ulster, primarily because of its large unionist population, lags a long way behind the other three with only 1 branch per 34,385 head of population.

Peter Hart's work has demonstrated that the War of Independence was more violent in Munster than in any other province.[162] Is there, therefore, a correlation between Cumann na mBan's geographical strength and the geography of violent revolution? If we break down the above table further, there would appear to be. The following is the breakdown of the 51 District Councils in Munster on a county by county basis. A column for head of population per one District Council has also been inserted.

County	*District Councils*	*Heads of Population/DC*
Cork	22	17,823
Kerry	10	15,969
Tipperary	6	25,406
Waterford	6	13,994
Limerick	5	28,614
Clare	2	52,116

Again Hart's work concludes that Cork was the most violent county during the revolution. Kerry, Clare, Tipperary and Limerick were also violently republican strongholds but Waterford was considerably more peaceful than its Munster neighbours.[163] The above table demonstrates that Cork also led the way in terms of its number of District Councils. Waterford fares best in terms of the number of DCs per head of population. However, as the organisation of DCs was intended to co-ordinate the work of branches, and not members, or the general population, the number of DCs per head of population is not nearly as telling as the number of branches per head of population. Unfortunately, the data provided by the 1921 convention report is not sufficient to enable the calculation of the latter number on a county by county basis.

This correlation between republican violence and Cumann na mBan organisation is broadly reflected in two other key ways. Firstly the delegate attendances at the 1921 convention demonstrated the same broad provincial breakdown. The Munster branches sent 158 delegates to the convention. Leinster, although obviously closer to the Dublin venue, was represented by 123 women, Ulster by 46 and Connaught by only twenty. These were the branches that were sufficiently financially solvent to send a delegate to Dublin, or the branches with women desirous or capable of representing their branch at the convention. Again most were from the southern province. Breaking that Munster figure of 158 down into its constituent counties, we find once again that Cork and Kerry are dominant with a representation of 50 delegates each, Tipperary was represented by 34 women, Waterford by eleven, Limerick by ten and Clare by only three.[164]

There are a few peculiarities in the lists of names and branches attached to the convention report. The names of the Cappoquin, Ballygran and Effin delegates appear among the names of delegates from County Cork. Cappoquin is in County Waterford but not far from County Cork. However, as the branch was quite close to a number of other West Waterford branches in attendance, the only logical reason for its inclusion among the list of Cork attendees, is that of clerical error.[165] Effin and Ballygran are both located in South Limerick close to the Cork border. The only other Limerick attendees (with the exception of the Drumcollogher delegate) came from branches located considerable distances from County Cork.[166] Thus, it might be that due to a lack of local branches in their own county, the branches at Effin and Ballygran had affiliated themselves with District Councils that were primarily located in Cork. In what they considered a national struggle it was never likely that Cumann na mBan were going to pay any attention to county boundaries. They had been urging branches to affiliate themselves with District Councils since early 1919. Where no District Councils existed, branch secretaries were to communicate with HQ for further instructions.[167] It is plausible that on some occasions those instructions, understandably, ignored county boundaries.

Finally in terms of the financial contributions of the various provinces to Cumann na mBan's organisational fund, Munster again leads the way. Of course. this is to be expected, as we have already seen that branch numbers in the southern province were larger than elsewhere. The total amount raised for Cumann na mBan's organisational fund in 1920-21 was £679-5-0. £201-0-0 of that total came from branches in Great Britain, £253-15-0 from the Munster branches, £128-0-0 from Leinster, £69-10-0 from Ulster and £26-10-0 from Connaught. However, when we adjust these figures for the branch numbers already tabulated we find that Munster contributed an average of £0.677 per branch, Leinster £0.684 per branch, Connaught £0.285 per branch and Ulster £1.51. Thus, whilst Munster was foremost in terms of its organisation, it was beaten into third place in terms of its fundraising effectiveness. The province that shines in that regard is Ulster. As Ulster, particularly its northeast corner, was comparatively quiet in terms of IRA violence, it seems the Ulster women were able to divert most of their energies into fundraising and did so most effectively. Meanwhile, in Munster the women's attention was more focused on the violence that raged around them. Connaught fared particularly badly when it came to fundraising, yet there are plausible explanations for its poor performance. It was the least populated and poorest province and thus did not provide the same pool of wealth as other provinces.

By the time Cumann na mBan held their convention on 22 and 23 October 1921 they boasted 702 branches across Ireland. Some had only become affiliated in the wake of the truce in July of that year. We cannot say with certainty how many of the 702 Branches were affiliated or formed post truce, but there were enough of them to prompt the Shandon branch to propose a motion that they not be allowed to vote at the convention. That motion was ruled out of order.[168] Certainly Cumann na mBan had taken advantage of the truce in order to extend their organisation into some rural areas where it had not yet established a presence.[169]

Despite a few larger estimates drawn from the reminiscences of some members it is safe to assume that Cumann na mBan's own convention report is correct and that the organisation had exactly 702 branches in Ireland in October 1921. The detail of this convention report makes it far more reliable than any that came before it.

Although a blatant contradiction occurred within the report when the secretary referred to the organisation having 'over 800' branches, we must assume that the remainder of the branches to which she referred were located overseas. It is also possible that she was counting squads as branches. The squad had been established in 1920 in order that areas that could not raise the minimum of ten members required for a branch might still be allowed to participate in Cumann na mBan.[170] However, there seems to have been a tendency among the organisation's membership to refer to what were really squads, as branches. Although there are some lists where 'branches' contained less than ten members, they were never referred to as squads.

Attempting to extrapolate a membership number from this information is a difficult task. Any meaningful estimate of active membership is impossible. Police reports are almost useless from November 1919 as even active Cumann na mBan members could not be easily counted. Unlike some IRA officers, Cumann na mBan personnel did not frequently leave lists of branch members. Where records of pension applications are available they must be treated with caution.[171] As the monetary amount of a military service pension might depend on the number of personnel an applicant commanded, the imprecise and rounded estimates found among these retrospective accounts are more likely to reflect the maximum (or even exaggerated) numerical strength of the branches during the period under examination.[172]

Estimates of Cumann na mBan's branch strengths are reasonably plentiful within the witness statements and the Coyle and Humphreys surveys. However, these estimates are often very rounded and do not commit to any clear date. As these estimates were written many years after the revolutionary period, often as pension applications were still being made, their accuracy is questionable. However, two estimates taken from two large brigade areas, stand out in terms of their likelihood of accuracy, due to their less rounded figures. Those estimates come from the Carlow and North

Wexford brigade areas. In July 1921, the Carlow brigade area contained twenty branches of Cumann na mBan with a combined membership of 384.[173] In 1920/21, after the organisation of the North Wexford brigade area, Cumann na mBan totalled 27 branches of 396 members.[174] Combining these two areas for a branch membership average we arrive at 16.6. Adjusting that figure for the 702 Irish branches reported by the convention, we can estimate that the organisation had some 11,650 members in mid to late 1921. This estimate is reasonably close to Aideen Sheehan's estimate of approximately 9,000 members and is almost identical to another estimate derived by an alternative method and reproduced in Appendix.[175]

Thus, two very different methods arrive at two remarkably similar conclusions. It appears therefore, that by the end of the War of Independence, Cumann na mBan had somewhere between 11,000 and 12,000 members of varying levels of engagement.[176] Their membership abroad is likely to have been reasonably substantial. The organisation was fairly widespread in urban Scotland, for example.[177] However, as no meaningful data for foreign branches exists, Cumann na mBan's strength outside Ireland remains inestimable.

In relation to the age profile of Cumann na mBan's more active members it is also worth noting one final feature of the 1921 convention report. As with the participants in the 1916 rising, the great bulk of attendees at the 1921 convention were unmarried and thus quite likely to have been under thirty years of age. Of the 46 Ulster delegates at least 39 were unmarried, of the twenty Connaught delegates at least fifteen were single and of 123 Leinster delegates at least 82 were single.[178]

The explanation for the marital status of the 1921 delegates being overwhelmingly single is an obvious one. In an era where a married woman's primary responsibilities were considered those of her home and family it was always less likely that married women would leave their husbands or children for a two-day convention in Dublin. That proportionately more married Leinster women attended the convention is likely to have been a result of their proximity to the venue. However, even with that proximity, it is quite clear that more single Leinster women were able to partake in this essential Cumann na mBan activity. For the very same reasons it is much more likely that the Cumann na mBan women who participated most actively in the revolution were overwhelmingly young and unmarried women without the duties expected of a wife. The vast majority of Cumann na mBan Witness Statements filed at the Bureau of Military History are written by women who were single at the beginning, or for the duration of the revolution. Likewise, lists of Cumann na mBan personnel from various branches in rural Cork indicate that the overwhelming majority of the organisation's grass roots personnel were single.[179] Indeed in some areas newly married women resigned from more challenging positions and there were, 'many changes in the officers of the branches as time went on owing to marriages and other reasons'.[180] Even the most active members like Sorcha McMahon were to curtail their activities after their marriages.[181]

The members of Cumann na mBan were mostly young, unmarried women. But what do we know of their social status?

Social Status

In attempting to establish the social structure of Cumann na mBan a number of difficulties present themselves. Firstly, we simply do not have the long lists of personnel that are available for the IRA. Secondly where names of personnel do appear, they are not often in conjunction with addresses and may also be the married, as opposed to maiden, names of the women concerned. Finally, as the British authorities paid comparatively (with the IRA and Sinn Féin) little attention to the women's organisation, they seldom commented on its social structure.

For all these difficulties some work has been done in establishing an idea of the social stratification of Cumann na mBan.

Matthews has used a survey of prisoners undertaken by a Cumann na mBan member imprisoned in the North Dublin Union internment camp during the Civil War, to construct a sample of the prisoner's occupations. The total number of women surveyed was 80. Their occupations were broken down into the following categories:

At home: 19
Secretary: 1
Sewing: 4
Printing: 10
Medical student: 1
Nurse: 2
Typist: 7
Clerk: 7
Dressmaker: 4
Packer in Jacob's: 11
Ladies tailor: 1
Box-maker: 2
Shop assistant: 8
Teacher: 1
Cup-maker: 1
Housekeeper: 1[182]

Aideen Sheehan reports a similar breakdown of the women's occupations, most likely drawn from the same, or at least a similar, source.[183] Whilst these figures certainly suggest a group of women who had made very different lives for themselves, they can only hint at the social background of the women involved. The number of women employed by Jacob's factory also suggests that the sample was significantly biased towards the Dublin membership. In addition, historians should be careful when using prison records to analyse the social structure of Cumann na mBan. Until a reliable social profile of the organisation is available there is simply no reason to assume that the social strata of those who were imprisoned were identical to those of the women who were not. Indeed there are many conceivable reasons why those members who were interned might have been generally of different social backgrounds to those who were not.

Unfortunately, where names and addresses of Cumann na mBan membership can be attained, they are significantly biased towards the Cork membership. Through the years, local historians in Cork have provided limited lists of Cumann na mBan personnel who were active in their areas. Fortunately they have also provided some addresses that enable a check of the occupation of each woman's father on the 1911 census. The lists are provided by Duggan, Browne and Ó Ríordáin in their local histories of revolutionary activity in Courtbrack, Macroom and Kiskeam.[184] As the author of this text was born in the mid Cork area, and resident there for part of the research on this text, it was possible to ascertain the occupations of those fathers who could not be located on the 1911 census, via various local sources. Using the occupations of the fathers of Cumann na mBan members from Clondrohid, Kilmurry, Toames, Courtbrack, Macroom and Kiskeam the following table has been constructed:

OCCUPATIONS OF MEMBERS'S FATHERS

Fathers Occupation	*Number of Members*
Farmer	52
Farm labourer	11
Un/semi-skilled	2
Skilled	16
Shop assistant/clerk	4
Professional	2
Merchant	13
Other[185]	7
Total Sample Size	107

Thus, it is clear that in rural Cork, a massive proportion of Cumann na mBan's membership were farmers' daughters. Indeed, if the Macroom branch is removed from the sample farmers daughters account for 40 of the remaining 58 women. No other single category stands out as being particularly large or small.

It is difficult to speculate as to why so many farmers' daughters belonged to the organisation. Farmers' sons were also common in the IRA.[186] The only reasonable explanation may be the comparative wealth of the agricultural class and the formal education that bought for their children. It took a certain amount of self-confidence and strong political opinion for any youth, and particularly young women, to become involved in a political organisation. That self-confidence might well have been provided by formal education and the wealthier classes were better able to afford that privilege. The merchant and skilled classes were also reasonably prevalent in Cork Cumann na mBan. Merchants and skilled workers were also more likely to have been able to meet the costs associated with educating their daughters.

Unfortunately this is as far as analysis of Cumann na mBan's social composition can go. The limited data makes any breakdown of rank meaningless. Likewise, as we do not know when these women became active in the movement, we cannot say whether the composition changed as the revolution progressed. As so many women worked in the home, both before and after marriage, analysis of their own occupations tells us little about their social class. Even if it did, such data is unobtainable via the 1926 census, by which time many members were married, and is also difficult to gather via local sources.

By the end of 1921 Cumann na mBan were a substantial body of women who had provided useful but immeasurable assistance to the IRA in their war with crown forces. The IRA was certainly appreciative enough to express their gratitude to the convention and many senior officers did so. The commandant for Longford was explicit in his praise of the women's auxiliary. He had written to Cumann na mBan in his own area as follows:

> I assure you that if it were not for Cumann na mBan things would have been very unpleasant for us here on various occasions. You came to the rescue individually and collectively and it is only those of us who have been through it that can fully

> appreciate the value of such splendid work. My only hope now, and I am expressing the sentiments of everyone who has served under me, is that you continue on in the future as you did in the past and that our officers and yours who know each other so well and have worked so harmoniously together in the past, will always assist each other in the same spirit. Let us be prepared to face with full determination and bright hopes of the final victory for which so many Noble Ones have failed.[187]

Cumann na mBan were active in the Longford area. The authorities were so aware of their activity that during the height of hostilities the organisation was forced to meet under the cover of the woods outside the town.[188] In Clare the local IRA commandant heaped similar praise on the women 'both organised and unorganised'.[189] Clearly Cumann na mBan were not the only republican women in Ireland and the IRA was also grateful for the assistance of those republican women who were not members of the organisation.

The praise of the Longford and Clare commandants was evidence of a growing IRA respect for their Cumann na mBan comrades. Indeed, the convention report boasts that the tributes of these two quoted officers were only a sample of the vast praise the organisation had received from the male combatants.[190] The women's auxiliary had come a long way from the days of the courteous but half-hearted IRA tributes of 1915.[191]

There were still problems within their ranks and it seemed that the secretary was concerned that in some areas women ignored the orders of HQ in fear of enemy reprisals, whilst in other districts local members did not trust messengers dispatched from HQ.[192] Internal disputes sometimes occurred between and within branches and the secretary asked the membership to put their work for Ireland ahead of such 'side issues'. A particularly divisive dispute in London was actually discussed at the convention.[193]

Markievicz also asked the membership to put themselves in touch with local Volunteers and avoid quarrelling. Internal strife was a feature of Cumann na mBan's war. Markievicz's caution regarding quarrelling certainly implies but does not explicitly state that a certain amount of tension may have existed between some Cumann na mBan branches and local IRA volunteers. Some of Kerry Cumann na mBan had encountered what they deemed 'male chauvinism' in an IRA organiser, Andy Cooney, dispatched from Dublin. However, local IRA personnel had also had difficulties with Cooney.[194] Much of this squabbling was no more than one would expect in an organisation of Cumann na mBan's size. Personality clashes within the organisation or with local IRA officers were bound to occur from time to time. There is no evidence of any serious disputes, with the IRA or otherwise, having emerged prior to the Anglo-Irish Treaty. Yet some of the personality clashes were about to add fuel to the fire of serious political division. Cumann na mBan had reached the pinnacle of its success. Now it was about to tear itself asunder.

Division and Civil War 1921-23

The truce came into effect on 11 July 1921. Under its provisions both sides were to retain their arms and all attacks on each others force's were to cease. The IRA was effectively on ceasefire and, as such, so was Cumann na mBan.

De Valera made the journey to London and began negotiations with the British prime minister, David Lloyd George, in mid July. There, he was informed that the British government would not contemplate an independent Republic on its doorstep and were only willing to offer southern Ireland a limited form of independence known as dominion status. The status of the British dominions, i.e., Australia, Canada, New Zealand, and South Africa, on the world stage was gradually changing in the aftermath of the First World War. However, in theory at least, they were still bound by British foreign policy and the British parliament could still recommend that the king veto the legislation of their national parliaments in his capacity as head of State. As the king remained their head of state, all dominion MPs were obliged to swear an oath to him. As far as the British were concerned Ireland had already been partitioned by the Government of Ireland Act 1920, and that partition would remain in place for the immediate future. Thus two separate parliaments would govern northern and southern Irish states. De Valera rejected these terms and returned to Ireland where the cabinet and the Dáil supported that rejection.

Negotiations continued via an exchange of letters throughout

August and September 1921, until eventually in October it was decided that Irish representatives should return to London for further face-to-face dialogue. These delegates were chosen by the Dáil from among its own members and were known as 'plenipotentiaries'. This meant that they had the power to sign a Treaty with Britain. However, they had been instructed to refer any such document back to Dublin before signing. The six members of Cumann na mBan who were also sitting TDs were eligible for selection as plenipotentiaries. Indeed, it appears that Mary MacSwiney was considered for the role, but subsequently ruled out, probably due to her intransigent republican views.[1] De Valera himself was not part of the delegation and remained in Dublin.

In the early hours of 6 December 1921 the Irish delegates signed the 'Articles of Agreement for a treaty between Great Britain and Ireland' at Downing Street. They had been threatened with 'immediate and terrible' war by a British Prime Minister who had insisted that he had to let Ulster unionists know the result of the negotiations before the northern parliament met the following day, and hence they did not have time to refer the articles back to Dublin for agreement.

In terms of independence the Treaty offered southern Ireland much more than Home Rule, yet considerably less than a Republic. The island was to remain partitioned by the Government of Ireland Act, with a 'Boundary Commission' to determine the exact location of the border. Southern Ireland was to be known as the Irish Free State with dominion status, whilst 'Northern Ireland' would remain a part of the United Kingdom of Great Britain and Northern Ireland with a devolved parliament and senate of its own. All members of both Irish parliaments would take an oath of allegiance to the British king who would remain their head of state and be represented in the Free State by a 'Governor General' and in Northern Ireland by the 'Governor of Northern Ireland'. The strategic naval installations at Cork harbour, Berehaven and Lough Swilly would remain in the hands of the British navy. However, all these restrictions on Irish independence could not satisfy puritanical republicans. They argued that the Republic had been established by the Irish people in 1918 and that the plenipotentiaries had had no right to disestablish it. Supporters of the Treaty argued that it was the best that the British would offer and could be used as a stepping stone towards full independence. The stage was set for political division within the ranks of Sinn Féin, the IRA and Cumann na mBan.

De Valera issued a statement outlining his opposition to the Treaty on 9 December. Dáil Éireann began debating the Treaty in secret session on 14 December. During this session de Valera proposed an alternative treaty known as 'Document No. 2'. This document proposed an external association with the British Empire, whereby the king would not be the head of state and thus no oath of allegiance would be required of Irish MPs. The proposal met with little support from republicans who saw it as an unnecessary compromise. Neither was it endorsed by those supportive of the Treaty, who pointed out that the British had already ruled out such a proposal during the London negotiations. Document No 2 was withdrawn and when the Dáil met in public session on 19 December it was to debate acceptance or rejection of the Treaty as it stood.

The debate was a long drawn out, bitter and hostile affair. It revolved mostly around the hated oath of allegiance, which neither side liked but, the pro-Treaty faction argued, was a necessary evil. Eventually on 7 January, the Dáil voted by 64 votes to 57 to accept the Treaty. Two days later, having resigned as president and failed in his bid for re-election, de Valera led his 56 anti-Treaty deputies from the Dáil. Of those 56, six – Kathleen Clarke, Kate O'Callaghan, Countess Markievicz, Margaret Pearse, Ada English and Mary MacSwiney – were senior members of Cumann na mBan. As the only female members of the Dáil they were soon to continue their opposition to the Treaty via the women's organisation.

Griffith was elected president of the Dáil and, subsequently, appointed a cabinet of pro-Treaty TDs. Under the terms of the Treaty a provisional government also had to be formed in order to facilitate the hand over of power from the British authorities, which was to take place gradually over the twelve-month period following the signing of the document. This dual administration was kept in place in order to placate republicans who may have been distressed at the sudden disappearance of the Dáil. As no female TD was in favour of the Treaty, no member of Cumann na mBan served in either the cabinet or the provisional government.

Meanwhile, de Valera led his supporters back into the Dáil, as efforts at a compromise between him and Collins continued. The two men decided to postpone elections until June and in May they worked out the details of a pact. Essentially this pact would have entitled each side to the same amount of Dáil seats that they had had before the election, thus ensuring that the pro- and anti-Treaty proportions of a post election coalition government would have remained identical to those that prevailed in the pre-election (second) Dáil. In the end the pact broke down as the British government forced Collins to include the oath of allegiance in the new Free State constitution. De Valera and Collins had hoped to avoid the mention of the oath in order that the new constitution would suit both parties. At the subsequent elections pro-Treaty candidates trounced their anti-Treaty opponents with 239,193 first preference votes cast for them, and only 133,864 cast for anti-treatyites. Constance Markievicz, Kathleen Clarke, Ada English and Margaret Pearse all lost their seats. The pro-Treaty (Free State) faction claimed that the election mandated their position. The anti-Treaty (republican) faction claimed that as the new Free State constitution had only been published on the morning of polling day, and Collins had broken the electoral pact at the last minute, the election was null and void.

Meanwhile the IRA had also split into pro- and anti-Treaty factions. On 14 April the anti-Treaty IRA seized control of the Four Courts and several other strong points around Dublin city centre.

Clashes between the pro- and anti-Treaty IRA had already occurred in Limerick and Kilkenny as both sides sought to take control of army barracks being handed over by the British authorities.

In the new northern state clashes between unionists and nationalists had become increasingly violent in the aftermath of the Treaty. Sir Henry Wilson had retired as commander of the British army and was appointed military advisor in Northern Ireland. Wilson increased the British military's presence in the north and enrolled more Special Constables, many of whom were former Ulster Volunteers. The result was a distinct bias in the policing of Northern Ireland where it became increasingly apparent that Wilson's forces of law and order were being used almost exclusively against the nationalist community. Wilson was blamed for this bias and on 22 June he was shot dead by two IRA men in London. Although it now appears that Collins ordered the assassination, the anti-Treaty IRA were blamed for Wilson's death and the British government insisted that Free State forces remove them from the Four Courts. British artillery was lent to the Free State army for the assault.

Thus began the Irish Civil War. Having successfully dislodged the IRA from the Four Courts, the Free State army had dislodged all IRA garrisons from other major cities and towns by the end of July 1922. From July a desperate guerrilla war was fought with much of the fighting occurring in the so-called 'Munster Republic'. The IRA began randomly assassinating Free State supporters and the Free State government executed many of its republican prisoners. By May 1923 republicans realised the hopelessness of their situation. Frank Aiken ordered the IRA to dump their arms and de Valera made his famous 'legion of the rearguard' speech, in which he asserted that military methods would have to be temporarily abandoned and other means found to safeguard the Republic. The Civil War was over, but what side had Cumann na mBan taken?

The Special Convention

The public opposition of the female TDs during the Treaty debates might have been perceived as an indicator of what would happen within Cumann na mBan. These few TDs did claim to speak on behalf of Irishwomen and all were opposed to the Treaty. Among the bitter exchanges between all deputies of both genders some pro-Treaty delegates had even raised doubts about the mental stability of some recently bereaved female deputies.[2] A fear of the reaction of the wider female population to the Treaty certainly developed within Free State mindsets as the political division drifted towards Civil War. That fear may well have begun to assert itself during the Treaty debates and Cumann na mBan's subsequent public utterances and actions cannot have done anything to allay it.

During the Dáil debate on the Treaty, members of Cumann na mBan protested outside the Mansion House. They were the only body to do so, and throughout the debates they 'resorted to some outrageous stunts' to demonstrate their opposition to the Treaty.[3] Jennie Wyse Power expressed her annoyance that the Dublin branches had been posting anti-Treaty bills around the city even before the organisation had arrived at any official position on the Treaty.[4] Not only had they posted bills but in mid January they had written an avowedly anti-Treaty memo to all branches regarding the forthcoming Sinn Féin Ard Fheis. Members were plainly told to 'try and secure the help and adherence of every Sinn Féin Cumann and Chomhairle Ceanntair for the Irish Republic.' Such 'help and adherence' was to be secured as follows:

> In the Cumann and Chomhairle Ceanntair area where you live you should endeavour to influence these bodies to send, where Republicans form the majority, delegates who can be relied upon to support the existing Republic by every possible means. If the majority of any Cumann Chomhairle Ceanntair should prove to be on the side which seeks to subvert the Republic, the

> names of the Republican members of those bodies should be noted and meetings held and the names of such members forwarded at once to Headquarters, Cumann na mBan, 6 Harcourt Street, and we shall forward same to the Republican Headquarters.[5]

In short, Cumann na mBan's leadership had taken sides and were ordering their membership to assist the anti-Treaty faction in winning the support of the Sinn Féin Ard Fheis. They were not waiting for any Cumann na mBan convention to decide on policy and the very announcement of the special convention had made that even clearer, when it first pledged allegiance to the Irish Republic and only then announced that a special convention would be held on 28 January 1922.[6] HQ was reaffirming their anti-Treaty stance before inviting the branches to participate in a convention which was supposed to decide on the organisation's official position. They followed this in mid January when the executive publicly announced their own rejection of the Treaty as follows:

> This Executive of Cumann na mBan reaffirms their allegiance to the Irish Republic and therefore cannot support the Articles of Treaty signed in London.[7]

Clearly, the executive was not waiting for the views of their membership before publicly announcing their own view. They were telling their own organisation that the Dublin leadership were anti Treaty regardless of the views of the rank and file. In addition, 'before the Convention members of the Executive were sent to various parts of the country to counteract pro-Treaty influences that were at work'.[8] In late February Jennie Wyse Power claimed that Markievicz had misappropriated some £200 of the organisation's funds in order to finance the activities of these anti-Treaty organisers. She also alleged that the Countess drafted her own circular to the branches and sent it out without the approval of the executive.[9] Thus, from the date that the executive announced its rejection of the Treaty, anti-Treaty executive members were actually touring the country spreading their own gospel to those pro-Treaty women that disagreed and, quite possibly, telling them that there was no longer any room for pro-Treaty views in Cumann na mBan.

With such avowedly anti-Treaty messages coming from HQ it was little wonder that the pro-Treaty *Freeman's Journal* was under the impression that the convention was summoned 'for the purpose of re-affirming allegiance to the Irish Republic and pledging the Cumann to support only republican candidates in the forthcoming elections'.[10] Anti-Treaty executive member Bridget O'Mullane also stated (some 30 years later) that the purpose of the Mansion House convention had been to ratify the executive's resolution.[11] It is quite likely that pro-Treaty members of Cumann na mBan were under the exact same impression and thus many of them never bothered to attend this perceived anti-Treaty gathering. Those pro-Treaty and undecided delegates who did attend were wined and dined by the overwhelmingly republican executive on the previous evening. Jennie Wyse Power was aggrieved that Markievicz had told the Saturday night gathering to 'lead for the rep[ublic]'.[12]

The special convention of Cumann na mBan was convened in the Mansion House Dublin on Sunday 5 February 1922.[13] Two motions were put to the attendees. Mary MacSwiney's motion was essentially an attempt to have the convention re-affirm the executive's rejection of the Treaty:

> That the Convention of Cumann na mBan reaffirms its allegiance to the Republic of Ireland, and therefore cannot support the articles of agreement signed in London on December 6th 1921.[14]

An amendment suggested by Jennie Wyse Power was not overtly pro-Treaty but effectively suggested a compromise which would have allowed the women reserve judgement on the Treaty until the Irish electorate had been allowed to decide:

> That we reaffirm our allegiance to the Republic, but realising that the treaty signed in London will, if accepted by the Irish people, be a big step along the road to that end, we declare that we will not work obstructively against those who support the treaty (1) either in their putting the treaty before the people or (2) in their subsequent working of it should the majority of the people accept the treaty at a general election. And we also declare that in such an election this organisation shall not take a party side as between men who have worked so nobly and given such proof of their loyalty to the Republic.[15]

Wyse Power also argued that the women's auxiliary should, at the very least, reserve judgement on the Treaty until the organisation to which they were auxiliary had made its own declaration. The IRA had not yet officially rejected the Treaty, therefore Wyse Power argued that Cumann na mBan, 'would be in a very curious position if they decided on a policy that would be different from the policy of the IRA'. Her amendment, she argued, would leave them in the same position regarding the Republic as they had been since 1917, but would save the group from division and keep it out of 'dirty election work in Ireland'. However, in supporting Wyse Power's amendment, Mrs Richard Mulcahy (Min Ryan) did directly ask delegates to 'support the Treaty'.[16]

Mary MacSwiney's reply was uncompromising and portrayed a growing self-confidence within the women's auxiliary. They were not going to wait for the men to make up their minds for them. They might have been the Volunteer's auxiliary but, at the 1922 convention, many Cumann na mBan delegates clearly displayed a willingness to step outside that role:

> Winding up the debate on the resolution, Miss MacSwiney paid a tribute to Mrs Wyse Power's work in the cause of Irish freedom, but she added she was intensely surprised to hear her advocate that they should wait for the men. For she was fighting, when many of them were in their cradles, for women's right to take their places in the councils of the nation. If the IRA became a Free State army were they going to work for them? (Cries of 'No'). Therefore why wait for the men? Rather let it be their place to give them a lead if they needed it.[17]

Speaking in favour of Wyse Power's amendment a Dublin delegate had also asserted Cumann na mBan's right to act independently of the Volunteers.[18] Delegates on both sides of the divide spoke passionately and forcefully, but concisely. Cumann na mBan had been an underground organisation since 1919. They had been forced to conduct their conventions in the shadows but now the women were back out in the open, and for one journalist the effect was clearly impressive. Comparing the convention to the Dáil debates, he commented on the capability of the women on the platform and the speeches of the delegates declaring that they, 'were brief, concise and to the point. The women were much less talkative than the men – much abler I would nearly say'.[19]

In the end it was the republican delegates who carried the day and won an overwhelming victory. Wyse Power's amendment was rejected by 419 delegates with only 63 votes recorded in favour of it. One journalist speculated that the scale of the victory had shocked even the republican delegates judging 'from the prolonged wave of enthusiasm that greeted the results'.[20] Jennie Wyse Power, on the other hand, claimed surprise that she had secured the support of as many as 62 delegates.[21]

Having decided that their position was definitively anti-Treaty, one further important motion was proposed by Margaret Pearse and adopted by the convention. The organisation's constitution was to be amended in order that paragraph five of the Cumann na mBan policy for 1922 read as follows:

> To organise the women of Ireland to support at the forthcoming elections only those candidates who stand true to the existing Republic proclaimed in Easter Week, 1916, and established as a functionary Government in 1918, and that no Branch of Cumann na mBan and no member of Cumann na mBan can give any help to a candidate standing for the Free State.[22]

One of Cumann na mBan's primary functions now became the assistance of anti-Treaty election candidates, something which could not possibly be reconciled with the position Wyse Power and her supporters had taken. In response to a question from a delegate, Markievicz made it clear that no member who was in disagreement with the constitution could possibly remain within the group.[23] For Wyse Power and her small group of supporters the die was cast. They couldn't possibly remain within a group that was so fundamentally opposed to their position and even if they did wish to remain, the president had made it clear that she did not want them. Wyse Power, Mulcahy, and Misses O'Reilly and Mullen resigned from the organisation. Áine Ní Rían later recalled that 'there was an awful bitterness – I remember them when they were going out passing bitter remarks'.[24] It appears that Ní Rían remembered the Wyse Power group walking out after the convention was concluded, as the newspapers do not refer to any walk out during the gathering.

But how representative of the organisation was the vote taken at the convention? The answer to this question is not easily provided, but it is best attempted by first placing the vote in its correct context.

Firstly, it should be remembered that the vote was taken five months before the first shots of the Civil War were fired. It was not apparent in February that war would break out in July. Indeed negotiations were underway regarding an electoral pact that, it was hoped, would prevent any violence. The women at the convention voted to actively oppose the Treaty, but could they really have foreseen that this active opposition might mean taking up arms against their former comrades? Had they realised that possibility, would they have been as hostile to the Treaty? We cannot know for sure. But it is likely that many of those who voted against the Treaty were not yet aware of where their opposition would lead them.

Secondly, not all branches were represented at the convention. Although 419 delegates voted against the Treaty, they represented only 327 branches. Of those 327 only 312 were Irish branches.[25] We have already seen that the 1921 convention report recorded 702 Irish branches. It is clear therefore, that at least 390 Irish branches did not vote against the Treaty. The newspapers reported that approximately 600 delegates attended the convention; accordingly we can assume that there were approximately 100 abstentions. Thus, almost 300 of the branches who did not vote against the Treaty were not even present at the convention. A railway strike had left 33 Cork and Kerry branch delegates, whom it was claimed would have voted against the Treaty, unable to travel to the convention. However, as that claim was made by an executive that had already declared a substantial bias it must be treated with caution. In addition, only one of the 327 branches that voted down the Treaty was divided on the issue. The Conaghy Branch sent two delegates to the convention, one voted against the Treaty, the other for Wyse Power's amendment. This is certainly a suspicious rate of unanimity.

Looking at the division on a provincial basis, we also see some interesting patterns emerging. The 1921 convention report claimed that Connaught had 93 branches, yet at the special convention only 26 of them voted against the Treaty. Of Munster's 375 Branches, only 80 voted against the Treaty with the possibility that a railway strike had prevented another 33 from doing likewise. In Leinster 144 branches voted against the Treaty, where 188 had been reported in existence in 1921. Ulster, part of which the Treaty would separate from the rest of Ireland, was quite unanimous in its rejection. 62 Ulster branches rejected the Treaty, where only 46 had been reported in 1921. It is clear that the organisation had grown in Ulster. If this rate of growth had been replicated in the other provinces, it is quite likely that the number of branches who did not attend the special convention was even larger than our previous estimate of, 'almost 300'.[26]

It is also apparent that most of the branches that had sent delegates to the 1921 convention did not send a delegate to vote down the Treaty in 1922. The following table illustrates the number of branches that were represented at the 1921 convention (Column A) and the number of those same branches that were represented by an anti-Treaty delegate in 1922 (Column B).[27] In addition, it represents the latter figure as a percentage of the former. It is broken down by geographical area, as far as is definitively possible:

Area	*A*	*B*	*C*
Clare	3	1	33%
Cork	45	12	27%
Kerry	45	16	36%
Tipperary	31	4	13%
Waterford	10	2	20%
Limerick	7	2	29%
Connaught	19	8	42%
Leinster	109	58	53%
Ulster	39	22	56%
Totals	308	125	41%

Thus only 41 per cent of those branches represented at the 1921 convention were represented by an anti-Treaty delegate in 1922. The remaining 59 per cent had either voted for Wyse Power's amendment, abstained from voting, or were absent from the convention. Unsurprisingly, Ulster sent a greater proportion of its 1921 delegates back to Dublin with an anti-Treaty stance than any other province. Northern nationalists were fundamentally opposed to a Treaty which would see the island partitioned and their isolation in a state which would be governed by Ulster unionists. Of the seventeen Ulster branches represented in 1921 which did not dispatch anti-Treaty delegates in 1922, ten were located in the Counties Monaghan, Donegal, Cavan, Tyrone and Fermanagh. All these counties had nationalist majorities. Although the Government of Ireland Act had included Fermanagh and Tyrone with the northern state, it was hoped, although it was far from certain, that they would be included with the southern state by the boundary commission.

So why were so many branches absent from such an important convention? We have already seen that when the executive declared in favour of the Irish Volunteers during the Volunteer split of 1914, some Redmondite branches immediately left the organisation and thus the subsequent convention was a majority republican gathering.[28] Although there were clearly Free State women present at the special convention, their tiny numbers tend to suggest that something similar had again occurred. At least one contemporary female commentator was of the opinion that the pro-Treaty (minority) faction within Cumann na mBan was much larger than it appeared:

> Cumann na mBan is not very representative of Irishwomen in general … There were a number of women in the organisation who would now at any rate swell the minority of opinion in that body but recently, during differences within it, they dropped out of its membership one by one.[29]

In addition it was subsequently claimed that at least one known Free State delegate was refused admission to the convention on the grounds that she was not a resident member of the branch she purported to represent, and that the convention had been 'rigged from stem to stern'.[30] For their part republican women subsequently claimed that members of their branches who had supported Wyse Power, were 'self appointed'.[31] However, whilst Wyse Power did express her annoyance at the executive 'warming' the delegates up at the Saturday night dinner, she did consider that the convention itself was 'conducted to the outside world on impartial lines'.[32]

On 18 February Wyse Power wrote to the *Freeman's Journal*, instructing pro-Treaty branches to ignore an order issued by the executive on 14 February that their funds should be returned to HQ. In addition she asked those branches 'not represented at the convention and who may feel as the minority did' to send to her their secretaries names and addresses. Although the convention had appeared almost unanimous in its opposition to the Treaty, Wyse Power clearly felt that there may have been a significant (significant enough to warrant a letter to the press at least) number of pro-Treaty branches who were not in attendance. For their part, the executive conceded that a number of their branches were majority pro-Treaty when they ordered republican members of such branches to elect their own officials and secure the branch funding for themselves.[33]

Perhaps the most striking evidence of the unrepresentative nature of the special convention is gathered by examining the actions of the Free State women and the support those actions gained them.

Cumann na Saoirse

The Cumann na mBan convention's rejection of the Treaty had certainly generated waves within pro-Treaty circles. The largest women's group in Ireland appeared to have rejected the Treaty and the only female TDs had also voted against it. Pro-Treaty politicians were more than a little worried about the support of the female electorate. Even before the convention the anti-Treaty propaganda sheet, *Poblacht na hÉireann*, had published a number of articles claiming that Irish women did not support the Treaty. Throughout March and April and into early May the republican propaganda sheet continued to claim the support of Irish women and even began to assert their right to equality of suffrage.[34] As the equality issue had never figured prominently in republican thinking before this time, it seems likely that they were now bargaining on the votes of young women to torpedo the Treaty. In addition, a number of male and female correspondents with the *Irish Independent* had been arguing that women would vote en masse, for or against the Treaty, whilst the newspaper itself had given a prominent headline to the united anti-Treaty stance of all the female TDs.[35]

During Dáil debates in March 1922 the anti-Treaty women had argued that all women over 21, and not just those over 30, should be allowed to vote in the forthcoming elections. Rosemary Cullen Owens has summarised the situation as follows:

> Until the provisions of the proposed constitution became law, only women of 30 years could vote. Both pro- and anti-treaty sides claimed the support of the majority of Irish women, yet it would appear that as in 1918 when John Redmond's party had feared the effect of a new female electorate, now the pro-treaty side feared the effect of granting adult suffrage to all citizens over 21 years. The vociferous anti-treaty rejections of many women within the nationalist movement … did little to reassure them in this regard.[36]

The Dáil debate on equality of suffrage had been somewhat bitter. Griffith argued that a new register could not be drawn up in time for the proposed election. In addition he reminded republicans that seeking an amendment of a British franchise act that they professed not to recognise was hypocritical and that the Dáil did not have the power to amend British legislation. He assured the Dáil however, that equality of suffrage would be a feature of the Free State's constitution from its inception and reminded anti-treatyites that he had been a campaigner for women's suffrage long before many of them had so suddenly converted to the cause. On the anti-Treaty side, deputies argued that the election should be run along the lines envisioned by the revolutionaries of 1916 and be as representative of the Irish people as possible.[37]

There was a certain validity to both arguments. However, what is most interesting, from the historian's point of view, is that there may have been an assumption on both sides that young women would vote against the Treaty. Both sides seemed convinced that Cumann na mBan's convention was representative not only of that organisation but of young Irish women generally. Cathal Brugha paid tribute to Cumann na mBan whilst Markievicz declared it would be up to them to torpedo the Treaty whether young women got the vote or not. Of course, neither side would admit that their arguments were based around the assumption that young women were predominantly anti-Treaty. However, two peculiarities seem to build a case for this argument. Firstly, there were many on the anti-Treaty side, de Valera foremost among them, that seemed rather recent additions to the campaign for equality of suffrage. Secondly, on the pro-Treaty side, an established suffragette campaigner like Jennie Wyse Power refused to join in this call for equality of suffrage.[38] In Ireland, one of the great political debates of the early twentieth century was, temporally at least, breaking down along pro- and anti-Treaty lines. It was against this background that Cumann na Saoirse came into being.

A little over a month after the special convention, and just a week after the above debate, an advertisement appeared in the nationalist press announcing the inaugural public meeting of a new women's group, supportive of the Treaty. The number of pro-Treaty names received by Wyse Power following her February appeal may well have been a deciding factor in the foundation of the new women's group. The new groups name was Cumann na Saoirse (Council of the Free) and it identified its immediate policy as assisting 'in the return of pro-Treaty candidates at the forthcoming elections'. Jennie Wyse Power was announced as the chairman of the forthcoming inaugural meeting whilst the speakers were to include Mrs Stopford Green, Mrs Seán Connolly, Mrs Mulcahy, Mrs Gavan Duffy, Máire Ní Chinnéide and Mrs O'Shea Leamy.[39]

The meeting itself was held in the supper room of the Mansion House, a smaller room than the round room that had hosted Cumann na mBan's special convention. Nonetheless, the attendance at this meeting was very large, with over 700 thronging the room and hundreds of others unable to gain access and 'overflowing into the Mansion House gardens and Dawson Street'.[40] Indeed the press's description of this meeting indicates that its attendance was in fact larger, than the attendance at the Cumann na mBan convention where the number of visitors in the galleries of the round room had been described as sparse.[41]

The meeting, which was attended by many 'who formerly belonged to the Cumann na mBan', consisted of avowedly pro-Treaty speeches by the previously mentioned speakers. Mrs Seán Connolly told the audience that this was their chance to repudiate 'the statement made by certain members of the Dáil that the women of Ireland were against the Treaty'. Her comments were greeted with vociferous applause.[42] This was the first opportunity for pro-Treaty women to demonstrate that the Cumann na mBan convention and the female TDs did not speak for them.

The new organisation introduced its constitution, which described its character and immediate policy as follows:

> An independent body of Irish women, pledged to work for the securing and maintaining of Ireland's right as an autonomous and sovereign State to determine freely her form of Government. The immediate policy is to assist in the return at the forthcoming election of candidates who accept the treaty as a step towards the complete independence of Ireland.[43]

After the Collins/de Valera pact, the organisation's 'immediate policy' became somewhat fudged. Members were then 'to go on working for the return of pro-Treaty candidates, but were not debarred from working for other panel candidates'.[44]

By early 1923 electoral work was redundant, the Civil War was well underway and Cumann na Saoirse were ready to place their organisation on a more formal footing. The minimum number of women required to form a branch was eight. This, in itself, may be evidence that the leadership of the organisation thought it unlikely that ten members could be secured in some areas. The new organisation was only to exist for as long as it took the Free State authorities to win the Civil War or as long as it took the members to complete the work they had taken on in connection with that conflict. Thus its structure was a little less formal than Cumann na mBan's. There were no District Councils, although inter branch meetings were considered 'desirable'. Although secretaries and treasurers were compulsory, the election of presidents and vice presidents was to left to the discretion of individual branches. The central executive was again heavily centred in Dublin with sixteen of its twenty members resident in the capital. The executive was also given the authority to alter the rules of the organisation without the formality of a convention, provided that such alterations were made in conformity with 'the principles on which the organisation was founded'. Seven key activities were encouraged by the executive:

1. Providing comforts for wounded soldiers, visiting them in hospital and looking after their interests.
2. Facilitating the troops in every way possible.
3. Intelligence work.
4. Destroying and counteracting irregular propaganda.
5. Organising *Ceilidhes*, dances, concerts etc, entertainments which the local troops could attend proceeds could go to the wounded soldiers' fund.
6. Arranging for the starting of temperance canteens for the

troops throughout the country.
7. Irish classes.[45]

In theory at least, Cumann na Saoirse would be engaged in similar activities to those of Cumann na mBan. The endorsement of temperance canteens was certainly a new departure for organised nationalist women. This new policy was most likely the product of growing concerns regarding the sobriety of combatants on both sides.[46]

Cumann na Saoirse's usefulness as an auxiliary to a conventional army is certainly debatable. Yet there is evidence of a sustained Civil War campaign by the organisation. They continued to distribute propaganda, this time on behalf of the Free State. They provided women searchers for Free State forces, both inside and outside prisons. Women searchers now became much more prominent than they had been during the War of Independence. Indeed, the Cumann na Saoirse organisation was soon to earn itself the disparaging nickname of 'Cumann na Searchers' from some of their former comrades in Cumann na mBan. Kilkenny Cumann na mBan described their members as 'constantly watched by Cumann na Searchers'.[47] Worried about this phenomenon, the IRA had asked some Cumann na mBan members to memorise the contents of any dispatches they carried before destroying them. 'Remember that the Free Staters are utilising women as searchers,' they had reminded Eithne Coyle.[48] During the Civil War it became common for these women searchers to accompany Free State forces during 'sit-down raids'. The sit-down raid was a new tactic whereby the raiders would occupy the house of a republican suspect for a period of time. During that period they would search and possibly arrest all visitors to the house.

Cumann na Saoirse's intelligence gathering activities also worried the republican community. The new women's organisation gathered an amount of intelligence for Free State troops via a network of 'call houses'. These were houses where information on IRA personnel and movements was compiled via a network of 'callers' to the house and later transmitted to Free State authorities. As a rule these houses were associated with Free State organisations like the army reserve and Cumann na Saoirse. The call house network caused enough concern for IRA GHQ to warn the various commands of their existence and of Cumann na Saoirse's connection with them.[49]

The IRA watched Cumann na Saoirse carefully and even compiled lists of women connected with the organisation.[50] Some lists compiled by the IRA identified Free State women by name and address as well as providing little synopses of their alleged activities. A female employee at Jennie Wyse Powers' restaurant on Henry Street was identified as 'Mrs Jennie's special tout'.[51] The IRA attempted to burn the restaurant in February 1923.[52] They had already burned Wyse Power's house in December 1922.[53] Eventually the IRA took their war directly to Cumann na Saoirse when they bombed the organisation's offices on Rutland Square, although the guard of Free State troops in the building may have been the intended target of the attack.[54] The following month they were responsible for a series of arson attacks in Cork city aimed at the dwelling houses of female Free State supporters. Where they did not burn houses they resorted to the older tactic of cutting hair.[55] A few weeks after the cessation of hostilities, two Kerry sisters suffered a savage attack perpetrated by republican men. One of them was beaten with a Sam Browne belt whilst her sister was prevented from assisting her. Motor oil 'mixed with other ingredients' was then poured over both of their heads, whilst they were asked, 'now will you be a Free Stater?'[56] From the very beginning of the Civil War, Free State female propagandists were allegedly threatened and assaulted by republican forces.[57] Free state officers in Kerry had complained to HQ about their powerlessness to prevent assaults on female Free State supporters.[58] Thus, their gender did not protect all

Free State women from the wrath of the IRA and being a known Cumann na Saoirse member or Free State supporter could be risky for some women.

But overall Cumann na Saoirse never had to provide the same level of support to Free State forces that many of their membership had once provided for the IRA. All over Ireland, they returned to the kind of function Cumann na mBan had had in its earliest days. Having been requested by the Free State army to supply wounded soldiers with comforts, they organised the 'Central Comforts Committee' for that purpose. Between July 1922 and February 1923 that fund raised £1,100, and expended £800. Money was also raised by local branches for activities in their own areas. In addition Cumann na Saoirse members paid hospital visits to wounded Free State soldiers. They provided entertainments, organised comforts, quarters and sometimes even cooked for Free State troops stationed in temporary posts.[59] Their entertainments were, according to Conlon, still well patronised by the general public, unlike entertainments organised by Kilkenny's republican Cumann na mBan who complained that it was, 'impossible to get up anything in the city as such things as sales, dances etc, would be boycotted'.[60]

It is difficult to tell how big the Cumann na Saoirse organisation became. However, by February 1923, they did boast that branches had been organised in every electoral constituency.[61] As that claim was part of an official report circulated to the newspapers, it is most likely the most optimistic estimate possible. As such, the organisation was never as large as Cumann na mBan had been. But one distinction Cumann na Saoirse did obtain, was an official representation on the organising body of the new pro-Treaty party, Cumann na nGaedheal.[62] Although Cumann na mBan women had been in place on the Sinn Féin executive, they were not there as representatives of the women's auxiliary. In addition, all Cumann na Saoirse members were 'advised' to join Cumann na nGaedheal and the organisation itself was not to engage in any 'purely political activities'.[63]

Not every member of Free State Cumann na mBan rushed to join the ranks of Cumann na Saoirse. Lil Conlon made it clear that the retention of the Cumann na mBan title became an important point of principle for the Cork District Council (or at least, the Free State portion of it). Delegates at that DC had voted to support the Treaty and thus they ignored all further instructions from the Dublin executive. Mary MacSwiney, of Cork's *Poblachta na hEireann* branch remained a member of the Dublin executive but, as she had never been a member of the Cork DC, Conlon claimed that she had no authority to attend their meetings. The Free State portion of the DC even went to the extreme of locking MacSwiney out of one such meeting. Referring to MacSwiney's lengthy contributions to the Treaty debates, Conlon wrote that they, 'were not anxious to be subjected to a two and a half hours harangue of invective such as was delivered in the Dáil'.[64] MacSwiney's reaction was to call her own 'general meeting of all the branches in the city and neighbourhood … to place before the members the future policy of Cumann na mBan as outlined at the Convention held on the 5th February'. In an adjoining column Cork District Council proclaimed MacSwiney's meeting 'irregular and unauthorised', before declaring that branches 'need not attend'.[65] MacSwiney's invitation made it clear that the meeting was for those who had already accepted the convention's anti-Treaty stance. Nonetheless. it appears that some pro-Treaty women did attend only to walk out when it became clear they were in a definite minority.[66] In Cork two opposing groups now claimed to be the real Cumann na mBan. Each had disguised their stance with a veneer of democracy but neither were truly representative of the members they purported to represent. No such representation was possible. All over Ireland Cumann na mBan was dividing on pro- and anti-Treaty lines. The only members that any governing body could claim to represent were members that fell definitively into one or the other of those categories.

Some branches were majority pro-Treaty, others were majority anti-Treaty but few, if any, were entirely unified on their Treaty position. Even in Cork, where Conlon was later at pains to point out the District Council's pro-Treaty stance, the *Cork Examiner* was under the impression that the bulk of the rank and file were anti-Treaty.[67] Branches fell apart, became dormant, or entered Cumann na Saoirse. Cumann na mBan was an organisation that was very definitely divided and in decline. Whilst the huge anti-Treaty majority at the extraordinary convention disguised this fact, it only succeeded in doing so because the convention itself was unrepresentative of the organisation. The only way of gauging the extent of the division within Cumann na mBan is to move our study away from the elite of the convention and into the grass roots of the organisation.

Branch Division and War

We have already seen that even before the convention occurred the executive were dispatching members down the country preaching the anti-Treaty gospel. On the ground, the split was a serious one and the republican faction had to work hard to hold what they could of the organisation together. Éilis Aughney and Sighle Humphreys were the secretaries during this period. Aughney later described the seriously fragmented nature of the organisation and the executive's attempts to preserve unity where possible:

> I think it was at that stage that each member of the executive went down to various places in the country to contact the district councils with a view to pulling the branches together where defections had taken place. I went to Carlow and met the district council there … This work went on until the Four Courts and Sheila and I spent all our free time in the office trying to keep the organisation together and to counteract the discouragement caused by the split.[68]

As the Civil War became increasingly violent it was clear that all was not well within Cumann na mBan. Although the Leinster branches had voted overwhelmingly against the Treaty, there is further evidence to suggest that the reality on the ground was somewhat different. In Cumann na mBan documents captured in a 'baby club'[69] at 21 Werburgh Street, Dublin on 7 February 1923, reports from various parts of Leinster portrayed an organisation in serious decline.[70]

On 8 November 1922, Kilkenny Cumann na mBan reported an active membership of only nine to the Dublin executive. In a large population centre like Kilkenny this was surely considerably below the levels of active membership during the War of Independence. Kilkenny's active membership was now below the minimum nominal membership that had been required to form a branch since 1916. The Kilkenny branch had voted against the Treaty at the special convention but, given the state of their health just nine months later, it is questionable as to whether their delegates' votes were truly representative of their membership's state of mind. Kilkenny county reported similar anomalies. Although the Grange branch had voted down the Treaty, by November 1922 it was just a squad of two members. The health of Cumann na mBan in northern Kilkenny was described as 'very bad'. However, unlike the situation in Grange and Kilkenny city, this would appear consistent with voting patterns at the special convention, where only four of Kilkenny county's 28 anti-Treaty delegates came from the north of the county.[71]

Elsewhere in Leinster, documents captured during the raid at Werburgh Street continually highlighted inconsistencies between voting patterns at the special convention and anti-Treaty strength at grass roots level. Wexford DC had ceased to exist by 21 December 1922 and only a 'small Branch' existed in the town. Enniscorthy DC had also disappeared and only 'a few girls were left working' in that area. All the branches in Gorey DC had 'turned Free State' and only two republican girls remained in the town branch. Delegates from the Gorey, Enniscorthy and Wexford branches had all rejected the

Treaty at the special convention.

Perhaps the most striking evidence of Cumann na mBan's deterioration in one single county comes from a report of a meeting of the Offaly DC, captured during the Werburgh Street raid. Unfortunately the date of this meeting is not recorded. However, as the Werburgh Street raid occurred on 7 February 1923, the meeting clearly occurred before that date. Represented at the meeting were the four branches of Birr, Cloghan, Kilcoleman and Rath. It was reported that membership in these branches had fallen well below the minimum of ten required to constitute a branch. Birr had only eight members, Cloghan only seven, Kilcoleman eight whilst Rath retained only four members. In addition the branches of Kinnity, Kilcormack, Carrick, Rathcablin and Belmont were not even represented. Kinnity, Kilcormack, Belmont and Carrick each had only one remaining member, whilst Rathcablin had retained only three of its original membership. Of the above mentioned branches delegates from Birr, Cloghan, Kilcoleman, Rathcablin and Belmont had all voted against the Treaty at the special convention.

Excluding the 21 Dublin branches, 123 Leinster branches had theoretically opposed the Treaty.[72] Yet by the middle of the Civil War, a list compiled by Cumann na mBan of contacts for branches in those same eleven counties listed only 104 names.[73] A group numbering ten was not required in order to make this list. All that was required was one reliable name. Yet, in a province where 123 branches of at least ten members each were theoretically opposed to the Treaty, only 104 branch areas could produce one name for the list. Throughout late 1922 and early 1923 large numbers of prominent Cumann na mBan members were being imprisoned.[74] However, as the number detained is not likely to have greatly exceeded 600, and in late 1922 had come nowhere near that figure, imprisonment alone cannot explain the absence of contact names in so many areas where the organisation was supposed to have opposed the Treaty. Longford serves as the most dramatic example of this anomaly.

Delegates from ten Longford branches had opposed the Treaty at the February convention, yet once hostilities had commenced, only one of those branch districts (Esker) produced a contact name.

It is also worth noting that 67 branch areas who had voted against the Treaty did not have a name on the contact list and 48 who had not voted against the Treaty did. This means that only 56 of the 123 Leinster branches whose delegates had voted against the Treaty could provide the name of a contact in their areas. The remaining 67 were unable to do so, suggesting that those branches had ceased to exist. The emergence of 48 names from areas that did not have branches that had voted against the Treaty suggests significant reorganisation in Leinster. It is quite likely that any remaining republican members of the 67 lapsed branches were now part of new branches in these 48 areas. In Carlow, for example, the two branches of Tullow and Kildavin had voted against the Treaty. Yet, by May 1922, neither of those branches existed. Instead the Carlow DC was composed of the four branches of Carlow, Killeshin, Bagenalstown and Bilboa. Of those four, Bagenalstown was in particularly bad health and it was not even certain that a squad could be maintained in the area.[75] In July 1921, Carlow DC had consisted of twenty branches.[76]

Thus it is clear that many of the branches, whose delegates voted against the Treaty, lost substantial membership and even ceased to exist as the Civil War began and progressed. It is likely that the Free State women of these branches simply terminated their membership as it became apparent that the Cumann na mBan organisation had declared itself anti Treaty. They may or may not have joined Cumann na Saoirse. In addition there were women who might have wished to remain neutral and thus did not take any part in hostilities. There were also bound to have been women who were anti Treaty but also anti Civil War and they too would have dropped out of Cumann na mBan. It should be stated that the Werburgh Street papers also refer to a few branches (Kildare, Tullamore, Carlow town, Thomastown and Dundalk) that voted against the

Treaty and continued to thrive in terms of their membership numbers and their efficiency. However, for the purposes of this text the papers are used to demonstrate that the uncompromisingly anti-Treaty stance of the special convention was not representative of the organisation as a whole.

The staunchly republican Madge Daly later admitted that Limerick Cumann na mBan had lost 'some of its members' in the aftermath of the Treaty, although she also claimed that 'the majority remained loyal to the Republic'.[77] It is worth noting that Daly does not describe the anti-Treaty faction as anything other than a majority. Had the anti-Treaty proportion in Limerick Cumann na mBan mirrored the anti-Treaty proportion of convention attendees, it is unlikely that the republican Daly could have resisted describing the extent of the majority. Likewise, the republican Éilis Aughney described the proportion of anti-Treaty delegates remaining in her branch after pro-Treaty defections merely as, 'the majority'.[78] After the Treaty, in Donegal, Derry and parts of Tyrone, Eithne Coyle found the branches demoralised and disorganised. She recalled scrapping many existing branches and forming new ones.[79]

Even the Columcille and Fairview branches, two of the oldest and numerically strongest, were reported as having had active memberships of just six in the opening months of the Civil War. It should be stated, however, that although Cumann na mBan were losing vast numbers of members and many branches, they do seem to have been making some progress on the organisational front. Where the 1921 convention report had recorded the existence of 85 DCs in Ireland, by 5 September 1922 the number of District Councils had increased to 100.[80]

Whatever the proportions of the women who stood on either side of the Treaty debate, there is little doubt that many fought the Civil War with the same level of commitment that they had fought the British. By and large the republican women's function remained identical to what it had been during the Black and Tan period.

However, there is evidence of some women expanding their activities into areas that were traditionally the preserve of the male Volunteer. Indeed, this expansion of the female role seems to have caused some concern for IRA HQ who wrote to their counterparts in Cumann na mBan in order to remind them of the role that the IRA had in mind for the women's auxiliary:

> C/S would like to have a memo from you specifying active operations in which your members are asked to take part from time to time. The conditions in this guerrilla war are so different to those of ordinary warfare that we do not wish women to take an active part in hostilities.[81]

The IRA's reminder to Cumann na mBan may have been a reaction to the increasingly militant activity of a few republican women. Towards the end of the War of Independence, police suspected that a Longford woman had fired a shot at one of their colleagues in the town.[82] Even before the first shots of the Civil War, Eithne Coyle's activities in Donegal had caused a stir in the local media. She was broadening her horizons significantly and when the IRA seemed uninterested in enforcing a boycott of Belfast goods, which had been put in place in protest at violence directed against Catholics in Northern Ireland, she took it upon herself to ensure its enforcement.[83] The *Belfast Telegram* left the following account of Coyle and her Cumann na mBan comrades' activities:

> The now customary burning of Belfast newspapers was again carried out, at Creeslaugh on the Derry and Lough Swilly line, on the arrival of the evening train. Three women, one of them armed with a revolver, removed all the papers from the guards van and set them alight on the platform.[84]

Less than a week later, the *Derry Sentinel* described how the 'slim, neatly dressed' Coyle had once again raided a train on the Lough Swilly line, and in 'cool decided tones' demanded access to the Belfast newspapers which she burnt on the platform as the train pulled away.[85] Cumann na mBan had ordered their branches to enforce the Belfast boycott by refusing to 'purchase goods coming from the affected areas of Ulster and by endeavouring to prevent Ulster commercial travellers from securing orders in Irish towns'.[86] They had not officially ordered women to involve themselves in activities like Coyle's. She acted outside the chain of command.

Likewise, in Cork, it was alleged that young women had thrown bombs at a Free State patrol. This allegation was subsequently denied by republican propagandists.[87] In Kerry too, republican women seemed to be partaking in more traditionally masculine activities. Free State officers in Tralee commented that local Cumann na mBan were 'known even to carry and use arms'. They were also allegedly responsible for attempting to disarm wounded Free State soldiers following an IRA ambush at Blennerville Bridge.[88]

As the republican campaign grew more and more desperate, republican Cumann na mBan expanded their activities in other key ways. The death of Harry Boland at the hands of Free State forces saw the women's auxiliary providing the military honours at his funeral in August 1922. Eileen McGrane later remembered the occasion as follows:

> At the funeral Cumann na mBan took charge as the men did not appear. Sighle Humphreys and I were in charge and walked at the head of the cortege to Glasnevin. There were several bands playing the dead march on the route. It was very solemn and sad and left on me an unforgettable impression.[89]

Likewise, members of Cumann na mBan had provided the guard of honour at Cathal Brugha's funeral. Brugha's widow had specifically requested that the women's auxiliary provide these honours. In addition she requested the non-attendance of all pro-treatyites and Cumann na mBan members distributed a typewritten notice of her wishes to those Free State supporters who dared to attend the funeral.[90] The IRA was already stretched to capacity fighting a losing battle against an ever expanding Free State army and a general public that were increasingly less interested in assisting them to sustain their campaign. They could not spare men (that might well be arrested) to provide military honours at funerals, and thus, in some areas, this task became the sole preserve of Cumann na mBan.[91]

Intelligence gathering was also falling increasingly on the shoulders of Cumann na mBan. With the IRA reminding them that, 'girls can get any amount of information from most men', some Cumann na mBan branches found that they were the only local intelligence units available to the IRA.[92] Certainly, as the war moved into its guerrilla phase in Munster, women were the only operatives that were still able to move between the Free State garrison towns and the countryside from where the increasingly smaller IRA columns operated. Nora Cunningham later recalled the situation in Macroom, County Cork, where she and her comrades would move through Free State cordons around the town in order to make contact with the IRA in the surrounding countryside:

> The IRA columns were now moving around the outskirts of Macroom and with other members of Cumann na mBan I was engaged in maintaining contact with them and reporting on the activities and movements of the Free State forces in the town … I managed to get through on a few occasions as I had disguised myself by wearing a Macroom hooded cloak, but eventually some local officers of the Free State forces, who had been in the IRA before the truce, suspected me and I was informed that I would not be allowed to leave Macroom town.[93]

Cunningham ignored the order and continued to leave the town by wading through the river or walking along the railway line. In using the latter route she was forced to crawl along two suspension bridges which may have made her visible to Free State troops. On 28 November 1922, the Free State authorities changed tack, this time ordering her out of the town of her birth. Again she defied the order, by first leaving, but then returning to reconnoitre the town every week and reporting back to IRA forces in the hills to the north of Macroom. On one occasion, Free State troops who had recognised her escorted her to the outer cordons with drawn revolvers.[94] In a town that the *Irish Independent* described as a 'storm centre' of the Civil War, Cunningham and her Cumann na mBan colleagues were an essential communications link between the town and local IRA forces who attacked the Free State garrison in Macroom on several occasions.[95] Eventually, on 20 March 1923 Free State troops attempted to break this link by arresting eleven members of Macroom Cumann na mBan.[96] Likewise in Bantry, Free State officers were aware of increased Cumann na mBan activity. They noted that, 'movements of our troops are regularly and quickly reported through this channel'.[97] In late March/early April 1923, ten Bantry women were arrested.[98] Although the Cumann na mBan intelligence department had advised that any woman involved in intelligence work should not be involved in any other work 'which would identify herself too prominently with the organisation', the members simply could not hide their activities from an enemy who knew them personally.[99]

Where British troops had sometimes been inclined to ignore women, Free State forces were well aware of the security threat that they posed. Where Cumann na mBan had not sustained any casualties during the War of Independence, at least two of its members were killed during the Civil War. A Mrs Hartney, the mother of two small children, was shot dead whilst on duty with the IRA in Adare,

County Limerick.[100] And Margaret Duggan was shot dead by a Free State officer in west Cork. Whilst Cumann na mBan had been involved in firing volleys over the graves of other rebel dead, it was the IRA who fired the last salute over Duggan.[101]

With the increased risk of search, often by members of Cumann na Saoirse, and subsequent arrest and imprisonment, the appetite of some Cumann na mBan members for the continuation of the war waned considerably. Women from Ballina, County Mayo, wrote to HQ to inform them that propaganda work was no longer possible due to the presence of Free Staters in the town. They had already been 'marked for doing despatches' they wrote, and did not want to do anything else to that would bring them to the attention of a group that they alleged were; 'only awaiting a chance or an excuse to put us in trouble'.[102] Another member in Athlone made it quite clear that she wanted nothing further to do with Cumann na mBan. The organisation seemed to have hoped to involve her in propaganda work, but she insisted that she had no intention of assisting them further. 'I would also feel very much obliged if you would not send any more letters to the covering address,' she wrote, before making what was either a concerned plea or a veiled threat. 'They might be likely to go astray,' she warned.[103]

Cumann na mBan considered that in the light of what they called 'the lying Free State Press', the need for propaganda was almost as urgent as the need for guns.[104] With so many male revolutionaries in prison or on the run, the propaganda war was waged almost entirely by Cumann na mBan. For a time they issued propaganda bulletins from a little room in Clare Street, Dublin, with equipment that Bridget O'Mullane had commandeered at gunpoint.[105] The Cumann na mBan bulletin eventually came in for some criticism from the editor of *An Poblacht*, who felt that Cumann na mBan were intruding on her territory. In addition, the publicity department were frustrated by the lack of a printing press and the repetition of stories that had already appeared in *An*

Poblacht days before they went to press. By early December 1922 they had come to see the bulletin as being 'of very small account' as a propaganda organ.[106]

Anxious to improve on their efforts, in January 1923 Cumann na mBan were centrally involved in the publication of a new republican propaganda sheet, *Eire: The Irish Nation.* This newspaper was printed in Scotland, partly edited by Markievicz, and proof read by the Ann Devlin (Glasgow) branch. It was distributed almost exclusively by Cumann na mBan members throughout the length and breath of Ireland.[107] *Eire* became so successful at highlighting the alleged maltreatment of republican detainees in Free State prisons that the Free State authorities eventually had to act 'to offset the women's campaign'. This they did by intercepting any prisoner's letters which presented the jails in a positive light, and publishing them.[108]

Cumann na mBan continued the old reliable acts of bill posting and street stencilling in urban areas during the Civil War. However, as the war dragged on these activities were less successful than they had been, with members of the public and Cumann na Saoirse (described by Cumann na mBan as 'women of low character') tearing their efforts from the walls. In addition Free State authorities began arresting women involved in these activities where the British had seldom done so.[109] In late October 1922 an intensive Free State campaign against Cumann na mBan bill posters in Tralee resulted in the arrests of ten women.[110] The Tralee branches reaction was the posting of a notice urging women to 'stand fast' and not allow the arrests deter them.[111] By early November, seventeen women were detained in the Kerry town.[112]

Overall the organisation became so synonymous with republican propaganda that one Free State officer in Cork could only surmise that Cumann na mBan had 'lost heart' when he found it difficult to find such propaganda.[113] However, the Cork Cumann na mBan had not lost heart. No propaganda was found in the county simply because a mix up in Dublin, combined with logistical difficulties in the more war-torn regions, meant that no such literature reached southern counties between early October and mid December 1922. The problem was addressed by sending single sheets southwards in order that they be copied and distributed by local branches.[114]

The women that took the republican side obviously had many former friends who had taken the Free State side. We have already seen that it was this familiarity that led to Nora Cunningham's being ordered from the town of Macroom. It was also undoubtedly a huge factor in the large-scale arrest of the republican membership in the latter stages of the Civil War. However, it also had its unlikely advantages. From the beginning, some women were able to cajole or purchase ammunition for the IRA from their former comrades in the Free State army. One girl carried ammunition into the Four Courts which she had obtained from Free State soldiers on the streets outside.[115] Ammunition was purchased from Free State troops in Limerick and Carlow.[116] Elsewhere, members were able to buy weaponry from departing British troops, something which had also occurred during the War of Independence.[117] Some members were even able to obtain useful information from Free State soldiers and then pass it on to IRA intelligence officers.[118]

Cumann na mBan's increasing militancy strengthened the perception among many of its members they were equal combatants in a war, and thus deserved to be treated equally with their male counterparts. When rumours of a peace agreement began to circulate in September 1922, the executive expressed its disapproval of any settlement short of the Free State army pledging its allegiance to the Republic, and wrote to the IRA requesting representation for the women 'on any committee formed to discuss peace terms with the enemy'.[119]

In the end, however, the Free State army did not have to discuss any terms for the IRA's surrender. Day by day the IRA was falling apart and the Free State army was growing ever larger. The Irish public were tired of warfare and their support of the IRA was consequently affected. Even Cumann na mBan's own HQ had expressed its concern to the IRA regarding the destruction of bridges and other communications links.[120] We have already seen, that in many branches membership had dwindled almost to the point of extinction and that some women had expressed no interest in the maintenance of the struggle.

One final key factor in the defeat of republican Cumann na mBan remains to be examined, however. That factor was the large-scale imprisonment of its most active members.

Women Behind the Wire

Cumann na mBan had not suffered from large-scale imprisonment of its members during the War of Independence. The 1921 convention report estimated that in that year 'more than 50 women' had served prison sentences.[121] Obviously this was only a tiny proportion of an organisation with a membership of 11-12,000. The sentences varied in length from just a few weeks to four years in the case of Eileen McGrane, or even penal servitude for life in the cases of three Cork women: Kate Crowley and Madge and Lily Cotter.[122] It was later alleged that the only offence the Cotter sisters and their cousin Crowley were guilty of was being in a nearby field during an IRA action.[123] The numbers of women imprisoned certainly increased in 1921, so much so that some newspapers began to highlight the number of female captives.[124] However, overall the British had been rather lenient when it came to the imprisonment of women. Male householders were sometimes arrested and convicted of harbouring rebels or weaponry whilst their female relatives or co-accused were allowed to go free.[125] Questions about the imprisonment of Mairín Cregan, the mother of an eight month old child, had been asked in the House of Commons and such negative publicity appears to have been generally avoided by the British.[126]

All that was to change with the installation of a new Free State regime, a regime that was more conscious of the security threat these women represented.

At first, Free State authorities were reluctant to imprison women. Whilst they were conscious of the threat that Cumann na mBan posed, they were also fearful of the propaganda implications of the large-scale arrests of women. On 18 March 1922, the Free State's self-titled propaganda organ had published an article allegedly written by a woman which stated that the mass of Irish womanhood stood for the Treaty. In addition, by way of attempting to explain the anti-Treaty tendencies of most of Cumann na mBan's leadership, it went on to say that the majority of Irish women were 'inclined to view political matters from somewhat the same angle as father husband or brother'.

From the very beginning of the Civil War, the Free State's propaganda organ directed a campaign against Cumann na mBan. On 5 July the *Free State* alleged that:

> The Red Cross is being abused by elements who are working to defeat the National Troops ... Motors flying the Red Cross but carrying armed Irregulars have been used to loot food stuffs and other goods from Dublin Traders. Girls wearing Red Cross Armlets have served threatening notices on Dublin newspapers.

Another article in the same edition went on to connect the Cumann na nBan organisation directly with the alleged abuse of the Red Cross flag by republican belligerents. It also claimed that whilst Cumann na mBan propagandists had not been interfered with, the IRA had threatened female Free Sate propagandists.

Still not convinced that the public would support them in any large-scale imprisonment of women, the *Free State* stepped up the campaign a week later. A new column entitled 'A Woman's View on the Present Situation' began to appear in the newspaper. This column was allegedly written by an anonymous woman and conducted much of the Free State's public relations campaign with regard to the arrest of women.[127] Its first installment was an attack on republican women that questioned their intellectual independence. It claimed that it wanted to look at the Civil War from the perspective of an 'independent woman', and then went on to define precisely what an independent woman was:

> The mothers, sweethearts and wives of the men who are fighting under Rory O'Connor are insensibly affected by the position of their boys and are unable to express an unbiased opinion. I was speaking to one ardent Free State lady yesterday, for instance, who had suddenly changed to the other side because of the capture of her eldest son in action … No handful of gunmen or gunwomen can be allowed to run the country.[128]

Of course, there was a certain truth in the article. Overall, republican and Free State loyalties did tend to break down along family lines.[129] However, the suggestion that women would blindly follow the men in their lives must have been a particularly offensive one for republican feminists as it did not suggest that men would equally follow women.

Finally, on 5 August the *Free State* suggested that female combatants should be imprisoned for their activities:

> The working women whom I know are emphatically of the opinion that women captured in combatant service should be treated exactly the same as men. It is well known that women are giving active assistance to the Irregulars. They are both fighting and carrying despatches. Now to be killed by a woman's gun is just the same as to be killed by a man's, to be hungry because a woman loots your goods is as bad if not worse than to suffer because a man loots them.

> Why then should women Irregulars when once captured, be allowed to go free again to offend against the Nation a second time?...It would be a good deal better for the Nation if women were accepted and punished as regular combatants when they chose to be combatants rather than allow them to be protected by their sex and stab the Nation in the back.

This was a peculiar endorsement of gender equality from a newspaper that had, just a few weeks earlier, suggested that women were intellectually bound to the men in their lives. Indeed the article went on to suggest that both male and female combatants wearing the Red Cross were engaged in the only crime deserving of flogging. In an attempt to justify the imprisonment of female republicans, the Free State's propaganda organ had taken an unlikely feminist turning.

With the opening salvos of the propaganda war now fired, in late September the round up of Cumann na mBan's most active members began with the arrest of Eithne Coyle in Donegal. Coyle had been one of those who was arrested and subsequently released prior to September and later commented that this had happened so many times she had begun to think that the Free State authorities would not imprison women.[130] She was held in Ballyshannon and Buncrana, before being transferred to Mountjoy Jail on a cattle boat. By the time she arrived there, some eight weeks after her initial arrest, she was in time to join the swelling numbers of Cumann na mBan detainees.[131] Coyle had also set a precedent by becoming the first Cumann na mBan hunger striker. She had endured a seven-day fast in Ballyshannon in protest at the lack of a female warder.[132]

As the Dublin prisons of Mountjoy and Kilmainham began to fill with women from all over Ireland, several protests at the level of overcrowding were organised by the prisoners. In Mountjoy, Coyle was once again to the forefront of these activities. She and her cell mates threw their beds out into the corridor to protest at the over-crowding. The beds were removed by the deputy governor and the women slept on the floor for six weeks, until they undertook another hunger strike.[133]

The deputy governor of Mountjoy was Paudeen O'Keefe. He was responsible for the female inmates and became a particularly hated figure among Cumann na mBan veterans. He was even accused of firing live ammunition into the cell of female prisoners engaged in a protest. O'Keefe claimed that the rounds had been blank.[134] Live ammunition was definitely fired in the air, in order to frighten uncooperative prisoners in the North Dublin Union (NDU) in May 1923.[135] And, on at least one occasion live rounds were fired at the women in Mountjoy. Máire Comerford was the unfortunate casualty. She claimed that she had been merely 'waving at other female prisoners'.[136] Such gestures had been strictly forbidden as the Free State authorities claimed that they had had difficulties with prisoners signalling prior to escape attempts.[137]

Cumann na mBan themselves were not entirely without experience when it came to prison escapes. During the truce, on Halloween night 1921, Eithne Coyle, Linda Kearns, Eileen Keogh and May Burke climbed over Mountjoy's walls to freedom. Their escape was almost the subject of a Cumann na mBan court martial as claims were made that they had not received approval for their plan from the Cumann na mBan authorities within the prison.[138] This is evidence that a pretty rigid command structure existed among the female internees. Cumann na mBan officers decided on protest and escape policies and all members were expected to obey. During the Civil War the women in Kilmainham, Mountjoy and the NDU organised themselves along the following lines:

> The highest ranking Cumann na mBan officers drew up a set of rules and these were read to the prisoners. A Prisoners' Council was formed. Commanding Officers and Quartermasters and Adjutants were appointed. These were usually the older women such as Nell Humphreys, Margaret Buckley and Catherine

> Wilson. Tasks of the Quartermaster included the distribution of food, candles, soap and notepaper. An adjutant was in charge of the collection and distribution of post. The highest ranking officers made representations to the Governor … The Prisoners Council kept in touch by letter with their comrades in Cumann na mBan outside the jail. Messages were smuggled in, along with daily bulletins that gave them information on the political situation from the Republican standpoint … One of the secret dispatches sent from Kilmainham Gaol refers to a certain prisoner 'continually trying to stir up a mutiny against the Council, and encouraging irresponsible girls to escape by means which the Council knew to be unsafe. Very often we have to keep watch all night to prevent some of the youngsters from being led into a trap'.[139]

Trouble also occurred in Mountjoy where Cumann na mBan were divided into two camps. The more moderate women occupied the downstairs landing, whilst extremists were incarcerated upstairs. The upstairs group included those women who had been captured during a Free State raid on the Sinn Féin offices at Suffolk Street. These women believed that the war should be carried on within the prison and accordingly engaged in various protests whenever the opportunity presented itself. The women on the downstairs landings often grew weary of suffering punishments for the actions of the Suffolk Street faction. This led to continuing tension and a power struggle for control of the prisoners' council in Mountjoy.[140] From May 1923, similar disputes were frequent during meetings of the NDU prisoners' council.[141]

Nonetheless, there were some Civil War escape attempts of which the councils did not disapprove. On 6 May 1923, Máire Comerford, Maura Deegan and Aoife Taffe escaped over the walls of the NDU.[142] The following night twenty two other women escaped via the same route. The escapees were not overly familiar with the railway yard outside the walls and so sixteen of them were recaptured by morning.[143] Among those who were recaptured was Eithne Coyle, a member of the prisoners' council in the NDU.[144] Other women had attempted to dig tunnels out of both the NDU and Kilmainham, however their plans were discovered.[145]

The NDU had created one on the biggest controversies of the period when women from Mountjoy and Kilmainham were moved into it in March, April and May 1923. The controversy began in Mountjoy on 26 March when trouble flared as female inmates resisted searches before their departure for the Union. Nora Spillane wrote the following account of the incident:

> Maire Comerford was so badly beaten about the head that she had to have three stitches by the medical officer. Maire Deegan received a black eye. Sheila Gaughran and Peg Delanaey [*sic*] were flung down the stairs. Eileen Barry's (Kevin's sister) clothes were dragged off her and she was treated very roughly. Rose Killen's (London deportee) dress was cut off her and she was subjected to great indignities. Sorcha MacDermott (London deportee) was knocked on the floor by five Cumann na Saoirse women and stripped of her shoes and stockings and dress; held down by Harry Mangan (prison adjutant) who knelt on her while the women beat her with her own shoes. Two other military men … then took her in a corner, forced her to her knees while they twisted her wrists til she fainted. When she recovered consciousness she was out in the passage, lying on the floor partially dressed, and her clothes were saturated with water which they had flung on her. Her face is bruised and her lip cut, and her body covered with bruises. Her wrist is badly sprained, her arm in a sling, and she is in bed in a helpless condition suffering severely from the strain and shock.[146]

Similar resistance occurred in Kilmainham when prisoners there were told they would be moved to the NDU on the night of 30 April. In the wake of the difficulties with the move from Mountjoy, the prison authorities attempted to compromise with the Kilmainham women. The inmates had expressed the wish to remain in the prison while Kate O'Callaghan and Mary MacSwiney continued a hunger strike they had begun in protest at their detention without trial. O'Callaghan was released and the prisoners were told that only 81 of them would be removed and no further transfers to the NDU would occur until the MacSwiney strike was over. The Kilmainham prisoners still refused to transfer without resistance and thus similar scenes to those described in Mountjoy ensued.

These were some of the most active republican women in Ireland. They could not continue the fight on the outside, and thus they decided they would continue it inside prison walls. Margaret Buckley recorded that whilst some women preferred a more passive approach, there were just as many advocates of the 'perpetual row' and the maintenance of a 'state of war'.[147] In what must be considered a determination to maintain this state of war, one woman being transferred from Kilmainham to the NDU even carried weapons on her person.[148] Writing in May Bowen's autograph book, on the very day of the first transfers from Kilmainham to the NDU, one inmate declared that there would not be 'law or order, but a great deal of disorder, when we start for the Union in the morning'.[149] More prisoners were moved on 1 May, but theirs was 'a peaceful departure'.[150] In the end these futile and courageous protests, during the moves to the NDU gained little mainstream publicity for republicanism and multiple injuries to the women themselves. The republican propaganda sheet, *Eire: The Irish Nation*, ran continual stories about the alleged abuse of women in Free State prisons throughout May and June. However, the mainstream nationalist press did not report the incidents. Curiously *The Irish Times* did publish some small accounts of these protests. In one, Jennie Wyse Power is reported as having doubted the accuracy of the stories that had emerged from the prisons.[151] British MPs had become concerned about the treatment of deportees during the riots and they intended raising the matter in parliament unless a satisfactory explanation by the Home Secretary was forthcoming.[152]

The various Civil War hunger strikes by male and female prisoners received wider press coverage but did little to sway the war weary public to the republican side. Mary MacSwiney was amongst the first republicans to initiate a hunger strike. Her first strike was the subject of widespread publicity at home and abroad. This publicity was generated in no small measure by the constant protest maintained by Cumann na mBan at the gates of Mountjoy.[153] The hunger strikes of Mary and Annie MacSwiney, Kate O'Callaghan and Máire Comerford had secured their release at various stages. In the early days the Free State authorities had been fearful of the death of a woman, particularly women as well known as MacSwiney and O'Callaghan, on hunger strike. But as the war dragged on public sympathy for republicans declined and hunger strikes began breaking down as republicans realised that death was an increasingly likely outcome. The final republican hunger strike occurred in October 1923, long after the final shots of the Civil War. Republicans began the strike in protest at their continued detention by Free State authorities. At its height the strike involved 7,033 prisoners, about 50 of whom were women.[154] As the weeks went by the numbers maintaining the strike dwindled and after the deaths of two male prisoners – Dennis Barry and Andrew Mallow – the republican leadership in Mountjoy called off the strike.

Of all the unpleasantness encountered by the women in Free State prisons, perhaps the punishment that affected them more than any other was not administered by Free State authorities but rather by the Roman Catholic hierarchy. As devout Catholics, most of the imprisoned women would have sought to receive the sacraments of the church on a regular basis. However when the hierarchy condemned republicans for 'carrying on a system of murder', excommunication became a reality for many republican prisoners. In Kilmainham, prisoners were refused confession whilst in Mountjoy they could not receive Communion when attending mass.[155] On the outside several women had allegedly been turned away by priests when they sought the last rites for dying republican Volunteers.[156] Although some of the hierarchy appeared to have turned their back on them, most republican women remained devout. Margaret Buckley later wrote:

> … our religion was our bulwark, our food and our stay. We never confused the Creator with his creatures. Though denied the holy sacraments by human agency we were in close communion with God; nobody could deny us access to him.[157]

Sinéad McCoole's meticulous research has uncovered the names of 563 women who served varying sentences in Mountjoy, Kilmainham and the North Dublin Union during the Civil War. McCoole's list is compiled from various primary sources.[158] It does not specify how many of its names were Cumann na mBan members – indeed such specification would undoubtedly have been impossible – but it is safe to assume that the majority were. The list does not move beyond the Dublin prisons into country jails where other Cumann na mBan members undoubtedly served shorter sentences.[159] Nonetheless, there does seem to have been a Free State policy to move all the more serious female republican offenders to Dublin. In Tralee, for example, following arrests of Cumann na mBan members in late October 1922, the first detachment of female prisoners was sent to Dublin in late November.[160] McCoole's list contains names from all over Ireland, implying that this policy was coming to fruition.

The last imprisoned members of Cumann na mBan were released from Free State jails in December 1923. The Civil War had been over for more than six months and republicans had accepted that the Republic declared in 1916, would not be attained by military means in the near future. The members of Cumann na mBan and Cumann na Saoirse had given up the way of the gun with slightly different agendas. Whilst their organisation quickly fell apart, the Cumann na Saoirse women would continue to lend their support to the Cosgrave government and his new political party, Cumann na nGaedheal. Republican Cumann na mBan would not pledge allegiance to any political party that would enter the Free State Parliament. With the new Ireland a hopeless disappointment to those who maintained their membership of the puritanical republican organisation, Cumann na mBan would remain a fading voice crying from an increasingly irrelevant political wilderness.

Conclusion

Cumann na mBan's impact upon the Irish revolution should be neither underestimated nor overstated. No study of the revolution can be considered complete without reference to the activities of the women's auxiliary organisation. However, the organisation should not be used as a convenient gender balancing tool in Irish historiography. Cumann na mBan never accounted for more than a small proportion of the female nationalist population and were but a tiny proportion of the overall female population.

Throughout the period Cumann na mBan provided significant military assistance to the Volunteers/IRA in their violent campaign against the Crown. But would the end result of that campaign have been significantly different even if the women's auxiliary had never existed? Of course, we can only speculate as to the answer. However, it is quite plausible that even if the Cumann na mBan organisation had not existed, the IRA would still have met with the partial military success symbolised by the Anglo-Irish Treaty.

With regard to the 1916 rebellion, we have already seen that with or without Cumann na mBan's disorganised and courageous assistance, the rebellion would have occurred and failed in more or less the same disorganised manner.

During the War of Independence, in order to sustain its campaign the IRA depended on widespread support from the general population. It also came to depend significantly upon the female proportion of that population to carry out tasks such as spying, scouting, carrying dispatches and handling weaponry. The women the IRA chose to perform these tasks were often, but by no means always, members of Cumann na mBan. However, more significantly, they were known to and trusted by the IRA men who chose to involve them in such activities.

Cumann na mBan certainly brought more separatist women into this inner circle of trust. From its earliest days it had indoctrinated its members with an intense desire for some form of Irish independence. Predominantly young unmarried women met other women of similar political viewpoints and such interaction can only have reinforced the separatist, and later republican, opinions that they themselves held. Over time Cumann na mBan became a very large reservoir of feminine republicanism from which the IRA could draw assistance. Yet even if that reservoir had never existed, Irish republican women would still have been determined to lend whatever military assistance they could to the IRA. The IRA would still have been able to secure the assistance of these women through the normal channels of communication between families and friends. However, it is fair to say that the existence of the Cumann na mBan organisation must have made the IRA more aware that there were women who wished to assist them in their campaign. Had Cumann na mBan not existed there might have been a tendency among some to overlook the huge assistance women could provide. In addition the emergence of so many politically active women in such a vibrant and visible organisation undoubtedly led to other women challenging their own preconceptions regarding the participation of women in politics or revolution.

The role in which Cumann na mBan excelled during the revolutionary years was in the creation and dissemination of republican and separatist propaganda. Throughout the period the organisation produced its own pamphlets, bills and posters which were distributed all over Ireland by the members. In addition they gathered information for Sinn Féin's publications and bulletins to foreign media and governments. Cumann na mBan also lent a feminine presence to Irish republicanism's spectacular demonstrations between 1917 and 1923. They were present at many funerals, election rallies and anti-conscription marches. Their presence, as women, presented the British administration with a united front of Irish opposition composed of both genders. In addition it can certainly be said that whilst reorganising in the guise of the INAA and IVDF in the aftermath of 1916, the women's auxiliary were largely responsible for keeping the memory of the 1916 'martyrs' alive. That martyr image was at least partially responsible for the growing popularity of republicanism in the years after 1916.

In terms of the politics of the revolution, Cumann na mBan's impact was minimal. This is hardly surprising as they were not a political party. They were of some assistance to Sinn Féin in securing the landslide victory in 1918. As the largest visible women's group involved in that election they would undoubtedly have swayed some of the newly-enfranchised female voters to Sinn Féin. But in reality the overwhelming forces that swung almost all of Ireland to the Sinn Féin banner were the British mishandling of the conscription crisis and Sinn Féin's very careful presentation of itself as a catch-all (and not always overtly republican) party. Sinn Féin would have secured a vast proportion of the votes of female nationalists with or without Cumann na mBan.

More significantly for Irish women, Cumann na mBan did keep gender equality on the agenda of the fledgling republican administration. Much of the literature generated by Cumann na mBan reminded its readership not only of the republican agenda but also of the feminist one. Although the Free State government did not accede to the requests of senior Cumann na mBan TDs to grant women over 21 the franchise for the 1922 Treaty elections, they did adopt equality of suffrage as a part of the new Free State constitution. Whilst few within the second Sinn Féin party would have sought to deny women equality of suffrage, equally few would have granted it were it not for the pressure exerted by female suffrage campaigners. All over the world, equality of suffrage only became an issue when vocal groups of women made it an issue. In Ireland the largest and most vocal of all the women's groups was Cumann na mBan. Their literature and their leadership continually asserted women's right to to equality of suffrage in any new Ireland. The assistance of their members in creating that new Ireland made it impossible for anybody to claim that Irish women could not be as politically active, capable and competent as Irish men.

The Civil War effectively terminated any real influence that Cumann na mBan had had in Irish politics. The republican portion of the group fought the war with as much commitment as they had fought the British. However, the war weariness of the Irish public meant that they could never win. With or without Cumann na mBan the Civil War would have occurred. With or without Cumann na mBan the republicans would have lost. The Free State victory did have one very significant effect on Cumann na mBan in that it placed most of the old leadership on the losing side and consequently placed some of Ireland's most politically experienced and capable women in the political wilderness. Although some veterans had achieved high status within the Free State – Jennie Wyse Power was a senator and Dr Brighid Lyons Thornton was the first female commissioned officer in the Free State army – in the years that followed the new Ireland seemed happy to ignore the equality issue. But that is another story.

In the end there is no simple way of quickly summarising the part an organisation as complex as Cumann na mBan had in the Irish revolution. Nearly 100 years on, all that can be said is that this collection of individuals did what they did for various reasons and with various motives. It can be accepted that they were courageous, ruthless, murderous and patriotic. But perhaps what is best said is in the tongue the organisation professed to be its national language, and it reflects the Christian faith of its members.

Ar dheis Dé go raibh a n-anamacha.

Appendix

The convention of 1920, which was held in the Carmelite friary in White Friar Street Dublin, had amended the delegate entitlements of Cumann na mBan branches at future conventions.[1] Branches of 25 members or less were to be allowed one delegate. Branches of 26 to 70 were entitled to two and branches of more than 70 could send three delegates to a convention.[2] Only the branches of James Street, Dunboyne, Drumcondra, Cloghan, Mountrath, Longford, Colmcille, Dun Laoghaire, Ranelagh, Ard Craobh, University, Windgap, Dundalk, Canlough, Middlechapel, Monaghan, Mohill, Kilbrittain, Clonakilty, Curaichlin, Cloughjordan, Waterford, Kildimo and London sent two delegates to the convention. The only branches represented by three delegates were Inghinidhe, Belfast Central, Tralee, Roscrea and Limerick. As we already know that only 347 delegates from the four Irish provinces attended, we can now state that they represented only 314 of Cumann na mBan's 702 Irish branches. If we apply the ratio of 314:702 to the numbers of two- and three-delegate branches that attended the convention, we arrive at an estimate of the total number of branches that may have been of a similar size. Then, taking estimated memberships for these branches, we can estimate the overall membership of the organisation. The information is tabulated as follows:

1. BMH, Eilis Bean Ui Chonaill Witness Statement, WS568.
2. NLI, Cumann na mBan Constitution 1920, LOLB162.

Delegate Entitlement	Delegates Sent	Branches Represented	Branches in Existence	Median membership per branch	Total Membership Estimate
2	46	23	51	48	2448
3	15	5	11	100	1100
1	286	286	639	12	7668
Totals	347	314	701[3]		11216

Thus one estimate of Cumann na mBan's total membership in late 1921 is 11,216. However, that estimate is based on the reasonable, but hardly watertight, assumption that the branches not represented at the convention were proportionately the same size as those who were represented. Nonetheless, it is reasonably close to Aideen Sheehan's estimate of approximately 9,000 members. Sheehan decided that the best average membership that could be attributed to a branch was twelve.[4]

---

3. Total altered from 702 due to the rounding of decimals.

4. Aideen Sheehan, Cumann na mBan-Policies and Activities in David Fitzpatrick (ed), *Revolution? Ireland 1917-1923*, Trinity History Workshop, Dublin 1990, p89.

Endnotes

Introduction

1. Cliona Murphy, 'A Problematic Relationship: European Women and Nationalism 1870-1915' in Maryann Gialanella Valiulis and Mary O'Dowd (eds), *Women and Irish History – Essays in Honour of Margaret McCurtain*, Wolfhound Press, Dublin, 1997, p. 149 and Ann Matthews, 'Cumann na mBan 1913-1926 – Redressing the Balance', MA Thesis, NUI Maynooth, 1995, pxii.
2. Lil Conlon, *Cumann na mBan and the Women of Ireland 1913-1925*, *Kilkenny People*, Kilkenny, 1969, p2.
3. For a complete guide to further reading see Bibliography.
4. Matthews, *Cumann na mBan*, p78.
5. National Archives of Ireland (NAI), Department of the Taoiseach Files, S9243. Verifying Officers were required to testify, before State appointees, as to the active service of pension applicants.

Historical Background, Origins and Foundation

1. Margaret Ward, *Unmanageable Revolutionaries – Women and Irish Nationalism*, Pluto Press, London, 1995, p90.
2. *The Irish Times*, 26 November 1913.
3. National Library of Ireland (NLI), Bulmer Hobson Papers, MS12177 and *The Irish Times*, 26 November 1913.
4. *The Irish Times*, 26 November 1913.
5. University College Dublin Archives (UCDA), Eithne Coyle O'Donnell Papers, P61/4.
6. Ruth Taillon, *When History Was Made – The Women of 1916*, Beyond the Pale Publications, Belfast, 1999, p7. Keyes McDonnell never identified herself as a Volunteer. However, another member of her husbands Castlelack Company did and McDonnell published his list in her book (Kathleen Keyes McDonnell, *There is a Bridge at Bandon*, Mercier Press, Cork and

Dublin, 1972, p15).
7. See p38-9.
8. On 24 October 1914, Francis Sheehy Skeffington wrote to both Bulmer Hobson and Thomas MacDonagh urging them to amend the Volunteer constitution at the forthcoming convention. Since the definition of 'people' was open to interpretation as to whether or not it included women he urged them to add the words; 'without distinction of sex, class or creed', to the word people, or at least publicly proclaim that their definition of the term included women (NLI, Sheehy Skeffington Papers, MS22259). Thomas MacDonagh made that public declaration at the 1914 convention. The *Irish Citizen* welcomed McDonagh's declaration but continued to press the Volunteers for constitutional amendment (*Irish Citizen*, 7 November 1914).
9. *Irish Volunteer*, 7 March 1914. (Italics are my own)
10. Ward, *Unmanageable Revolutionaries*, p91.
11. UCDA, Sighle Humphreys' Papers, P106/1395.
12. Ibid, P106/1404.
13. Bureau of Military History (BMH), Miss Molly Reynolds' Witness Statement, WS195.
14. *Irish Citizen*, 13 December 1913.
15. NLI, Leabhar na mBan, 3B2531.
16. BMH, Miss Molly Reynolds Witness Statement, WS195.
17. Irish Volunteer, 18 April 1914.
18. BMH, Miss Elizabeth Bloxham Witness Statement, WS632.
19. *Irish Citizen*, 28 March 1914. The *Irish Citizen* is quoting from the *Irish Volunteer* of 21 May. Alas, as that edition of the *Irish Volunteer* is no longer available, we can only assume that the quotation is correct and not taken out of context.
20. Ibid.
21. *The Irish Times*, *Irish Independent* and *Freeman's Journal*, 3 April 1914.
22. *The Irish Times*, 26 November 1913.
23. NLI, Mary Colum, The Volunteers, Women and the Nation, Dublin, 1914, LOLB 161.
24. *Irish Volunteer*, 18 April 1914.
25. BMH, Miss Molly Reynolds Witness Statement, WS195.
26. *The Irish Times*, *Freeman's Journal* and *Irish Independent*, 3 April 1914.
27. NLI, Cumann na mBan Constitution 1914, LOLB 161. The documents referred to as constitutions throughout this text were those documents that contained the constitution, policy, rules and suggested activities of Cumann na mBan. The particular convention that produced those documents is

given by referring to the first year mentioned in the policy heading. Although the documents were not titled 'Constitution' that was the name by which the organisation referred to them.

28. *The Irish Times*, 3 April 1914.

29. Ward, *Unmanageable Revolutionaries*, p93.

30. *Freeman's Journal*, 3 April 1914. Questions as to whether or not Markievicz was a Countess have been raised. When contacted by the British authorities after the 1916 rising, the Polish Consul stated that they knew of no Polish Count Markievicz. They did trace a Dumi Markievicz, who had been Russian before the First World War. He refused to give details of his marriage abroad (See Brian Barton, *From Behind a Closed Door: Secret Court Martial Records of the Easter Rising*, Blackstaff Press, Belfast 2002, p78). As Markievicz called herself a countess, and as most of her contemporaries knew her as such, she is occasionally referred to by that name (for we cannot say whether or not it was a title) within this text.

31. *The Irish Times*, 3 April 1914.

32. NLI, Bulmer Hobson Papers, MS12177.

33. *Freeman's Journal*, 3 April 1914.

34. See p25.

35. Sean O'Casey, *The Story of the Irish Citizen Army*, The Journeyman Press, London, 1980, p45. Markievicz's central role in an organisation allied with a Volunteer group who co-opted Redmondite parliamentarians on to its executive, was the source of some conflict between O'Casey and Markievicz. At an Citizen Army Council meeting he moved a motion that she be asked to sever her connection with the Citizen Army or with the Volunteers (and thus with Cumann na mBan). O'Casey's motion was defeated and he subsequently resigned from the Citizen Army. See also, Ann Marreco, *The Rebel Countess – The Life and Times of Constance Markievicz*, Wiedenfield and Nicolson, London, 1967, p181.

CONSOLIDATION, EXPANSION AND THE PRESERVATION OF UNITY 1914-1916

1. Sinéad McCoole, *No Ordinary Women - Irish Female Activists in the Revolutionary Years 1900-1923*, The O'Brien Press, Dublin, 2004, p208.

2. Maria Luddy, *Women in Ireland 1800-1918 – A Documentary History*, Cork University Press, 1999, pp301-304. For a brief explanation of what 'Inghinidhe na hÉireann' was see p25.

3. *Irish Volunteer*, 9 May 1918.

4. *Irish Citizen*, April and May 1914. See also, Margaret Ward, *In Their Own Voice*, Attic Press, Dublin, 1995, pp39-53.

5. BMH, Miss Molly Reynolds Witness Statement, WS195.

6. McCoole, *No Ordinary Women*, pp170 and 212.
7. Luddy, *Women in Ireland 1800-1918*, p300.
8. UCDA, Sighle Humpreys' Papers, P106/1436.
9. Ibid, P106/1404.
10. BMH, Mrs Martin Murphy Witness Statement, WS480. Murphy states that Cumann na mBan rented the Inghinidhe rooms at Harcourt Street for a small charge. See also, Rosemary Cullen Owens, *A Social History of Irish Women 1870- 1970*, Gill and Macmillan, Dublin, 2005, p117 for evidence of Inghinidhe's post 1914 activities.
11. *Irish Volunteer*, 23 May 1914.
12. UCDA, Mary MacSwiney Papers, Mother Margaret MacSwiney's unpublished biography of Mary MacSwiney, P48a/462. See also, BMH, Alice Cashel Witness Statement, WS366.
13. BMH, Miss Bridget O'Mullane Witness Statement, WS450.
14. An appeal to join Cumann na mBan with its HQ at Great Brunswick Street (the organisation's address in the early months) is housed in the National Library of Ireland (NLI/LOLB161).
15. *Irish Volunteer,* 11 April 1916. The Killarney and Enniscorthy branches may have only discontinued activities for the winter period. However branches which took winter holidays could hardly be described as flourishing.
16. *Irish Volunteer*, 12 February 1916.
17. BMH, Miss Elizabeth Bloxham Witness Statement, WS632.
18. BMH, Miss Mollie Cunningham, Miss Elizabeth Bloxham and Mrs Bridget Doherty Witness Statements, WS1681, WS632 and WS1193. See also, J. Anthony Gaughan, *Austin Stack – Portrait of a Separatist*, Kingdom Books, Dublin, 1977, p36.
19. BMH, Miss Bridget O'Mullane Witness Statement, WS450.
20. *Irish Volunteer*, 19 June 1915.
21. Margaret Skinnider, *Doing My Bit for Ireland*, Century, New York, 1917, p9-10.
22. BMH, Sorcha McDermott Witness Statement, WS945.
23. UCDA, Eithne Coyle O'Donnell Papers, P61/4.
24. *Irish Volunteer,* 23 October 1915.
25. Ibid, 6 November 1915.
26. The addresses given by the *Irish Volunteer* throughout 1914-16 were; 206 Great Brunswick St, 19 Parnell Square, 12 D'Olier Street, 8 D'Olier Street, 25 Parnell Square, 41 Kildare Street and 2 Dawson Street.
27. *Irish Volunteer*, June-October 1915.
28. Ibid, 29 January 1916.
29. Ibid, 30 October 1915.

30. Ibid, 26 February 1916.
31. NLI, Cumann na mBan Constitution 1919, LOLB161. This document claims 43 branches in the immediate aftermath of the rising.
32. UCDA, Sighle Humphreys' Papers, P106/1427. See also, *Irish Volunteer*, 6 November 1915.
33. Jacqueline Van Voris, *Constance de Markievicz – In the Cause of Ireland*, The University of Massachusetts Press, Massachusetts, 1967, p157. Although Van Voris claims that Markievicz was president of the organisation in 1915, no contemporary account makes any mention of her presidency in 1915 and several of her more recent biographers (Norman, McGowan, Moriarty and Sweeney) all agree that she did not take that office until 1916.
34. *Irish Volunteer*, 11 September 1915.
35. Ibid, 29 August 1914.
36. NLI, Leabhar na mBan, 3B2531.
37. *National Volunteer*, 17 October 1914. See also, NLI, Cumann na mBan Constitution 5/10/1914, Ir94108 P48.
38. *Irish Volunteer*, 17 October 1914.
39. *National Volunteer*, 28 November 1914.
40. *Irish Independent*, 7 October 1914.
41. NLI, Leabhar na mBan, 3B2531.
42. Writing in (or after) 1939, Kathleen Clarke indicated that the majority of the Central branch supported Redmond and membership fell from about 200 members to about 24. This completely contradicts Wyse Power's 1919 account. Whilst Clarke's account was hardly intended as propaganda (and Wyse Power's was) it was written at least 25 years after the events in question (Helen Litton [ed], Kathleen Clarke, *My Fight for Ireland's Freedom*, O'Brien Press, Dublin, 1991, p49).
43. *Irish Volunteer*, 1 May 1915. The exact date would appear to have been Sunday 13 December (See Hilary Pyle [ed] *Cesca's Diary*, Woodfield Press, Dublin 2005, p181.)
44. UCDA, Sighle Humphreys' Papers, P106/1404.
45. BMH, Madge Daly Witness Statement, WS855.
46. *The Irish Times*, 17 October 1914.
47. *National Volunteer*, 24 October 1914. The diary of one prominent Cumman na mBan member refers to nineteen branches having defected by 2 November 1914 (Pyle, *Cesca's Diary*, p170).
48. The *National Volunteer* printed news of these women's corps throughout 1914 and 1915.
49. Keyes McDonnell, *There is a Bridge at Bandon*, pp27-29.
50. *Irish Citizen*, 4 July 1914.

51. It would appear that Wyse Power's mention of a 'Volunteer Aid Society' must have been a reference to the Volunteer Aid Association mentioned in *The Irish Times* of 13 October 1914.
52. For a list of Volunteer Aid Association senior personnel see the *National Volunteer*, 31 October 1914.
53. *Irish Citizen*, 4 July 1914.
54. *Irish Volunteer*, 15 August and 5 September 1914. By 5 September Cumann na mBan had replaced the words 'belonging to' with the phrase 'in connection with'.
55. *National Volunteer*, 31 October 1914 and 3 April 1915.
56. *Irish Volunteer*, 31 October 1914.
57. NLI, Cumann na mBan Constitution 1919, LOLB161.
58. *Irish Volunteer*, October 1914-April 1916.
59. BMH, Mrs Maire Fitzpatrick, Eily O'Hanrahan O'Reilly and Mrs Margaret Lucey Witness Statements, WS1345, WS270 and WS1561.
60. BMH, Mrs Maire Fitzpatrick Witness Statement, WS1344.
61. BMH, Dr Nancy Wyse Power Witness Statement, WS587.
62. F.X. Martin, *The Irish Volunteers*, Duffy, Dublin, 1963, pp192-193.
63. *Irish Volunteer*, 27 June 1914.
64. Ibid, 31 October 1914.
65. Ibid, 25 July 1914.
66. Wage rates as advertised in various issues of *The Irish Times* during the period in question.
67. BMH, Mrs Mary Josephine Mulcahy Witness Statement, WS399.
68. Máire Nic Shúibhlaigh, *The Splendid Years*, James Duffy, Dublin, 1955, p160.
69. Conlon, *Cumann na mban*, p14.
70. Ibid.
71. Deirdre McCarthy, 'Cumann na mBan – The Limerick Link' in Bernadette Whelan (ed), *Clio's Daughters – Essays on Irish Women's History 1845-1939*, University of Limerick Press, Limerick, 1997, p57.
72. *Irish Volunteer*, 29 August, 26 September and 7 November 1914.
73. UCDA, Sighle Humphreys' Papers, P106/1419.
74. *Irish Volunteer*, 5 September 1914.
75. Barry Delaney, 'Cumann na mBan – The Women's Auxilliary of the Irish Army', in William Fitzgerald (ed), *The Voice of Ireland*, Virtue and Co Ltd, Dublin and London, Undated, p162.
76. NLI, Leabhar na mBan, 3B2531.
77. *Irish Volunteer*, 16 October 1915.
78. NLI, Leabhar na mBan, 3B2531.

79. *Irish Volunteer*, 17 July 1915.
80. BMH, Peg Duggan Witness Statement, WS1576.
81. Eithne Ní Chumhaill, 'The History of Cumann na mBan' in *An Phoblacht*, 8 April 1933.
82. BMH, Mrs Kitty O'Doherty Witness Statement, WS355.
83. Lily O'Brennan, 'The Dawning of the Day' in *The Cappuchin Annual*, 1936.
84. The first contemporary reference to this activity occurs in the *Irish Volunteer* of 11 December 1915.
85. *Irish Volunteer*, 1 January 1916.
86. Ibid, 8 January 1916. See also, Éilis Ní Chorra, 'A Rebel Remembers' in *The Capuchin Annual* 1966. Ní Chorra states that the Belfast branch used miniature rifles as service rifles were too precious to be used in practice. However, HQ's suggestion that service rifles be converted to the smaller calibre suggests that there may also have been a stereotypical concern regarding the inability of women to handle the recoil of larger firearms.
87. *Irish Volunteer*, 4 December 1915.
88. NLI, Cumann na mBan Pamphlets, I94109 P4.
89. UCDA, Sighle Humphreys Papers, P106/1205. This title was published by the 'O'Donovan Rossa Funeral Committee', in which several senior Cumann na mBan personnel were engaged. See also, NLI, Rossa – born 1831. Died 1915, Ir320p60.
90. *Irish Volunteer*, October 1915-April 1916.
91. *Irish Volunteer*, 6 November 1915.
92. Ibid.
93. *The Spark*, 31 October 1915.

CUMANN NA MBAN AND THE RISING

1. See, J.J. Lee, 'In Search Of Patrick Pearse, Michael Laffan, Insular Attitudes: The Revisionists and their Critics and Seamus Deane, Wherever Green is Read', in *Revising the Rising*, Field Day, Derry, 1991. See also, Ruth Dudley Edwards, *Patrick Pearse: the Triumph of Failure*, Gollancz, London, 1977, F.S.L. Lyons, *Culture and Anarchy in Ireland 1890-1939*, Oxford University Press, Oxford, 1979, pp90-92 and Roy Foster, *Modern Ireland 1600-1972*, Penguin Press, London, 1988.
2. Taillon, *The Women of 1916*, p38.
3. BMH, Miss Margaret Kennedy and Mrs Annie O'Brien Witness Statements, WS185 and WS805. After the rising the UCD students, who had not been permitted to form their own branch due to the perception that they wished to be exclusive, were allowed to form a separate branch

and that was attached to the 3rd Volunteer battalion (BMH, Mrs Eileen McCarvill Witness Statement, WS1752.).

4. BMH, Miss Rose MacNamara Witness Statement, WS482.

5. O'Brennan, 'The Dawning of the Day', in *Capuchin Annual* 1966.

6. UCDA, Sighle Humpreys' Papers, P106/1404 and BMH, Mrs Annie O'Brien Witness Statement, WS805.

7. O'Brennan, 'The Dawning of the Day' in *Capuchin Annual* 1966.

8. Joseph O'Connor, 'In Boland's Mills' in *Capuchin Annual* 1966.

9. Ward, *Unmanageable Revolutionaries*, p110.

10. Taillon, *The Women of 1916*, p59.

11. UCDA, Eithne Coyle O'Donnell Papers, P61/4.

12. BMH, Mrs Michael Foley Witness Statement, WS539.

13. UCDA, Sighle Humphreys' Papers, P106/1404.

14. BMH, Mairead O'Kelly, Mrs Tom Barry, Eilis Bean Ui Chonaill, Mrs Anna Fahy and Phyllis Morkan Witness Statements, WS925, WS1754, WS568, WS202 and WS210.

15. BMH, Phyllis Morkan Witness Statement, WS210.

16. BMH, Mrs Mary Josephine Mulcahy Witness Statement, WS399.

17. BMH, Mrs Phyllis Morkan and Eilis Bean Ui Chonnaill Witness Statements, WS210 and WS568.

18. BMH, Mairead O'Kelly, Mrs Tom Barry, Eilis Bean Ui Chonnaill and Phyllis Morkan Witness Statements, WS925, WS1754, WS568 and WS210.

19. NLI, Programme for a Concert at 41 Parnell Square 16/04/1916, Ir94109 P40. Programme lists four Dublin branches as Central, Inghindhe, Collumcille and Caitlin Ní Houlihan. Caitlin Ní Houlihan was the official name for the Fairview branch (BMH, Miss Molly Reynolds Witness Statement, WS195).

20. A smaller part of the 2nd battalion was to join up with Thomas Ashe's 5th battalion in north Dublin.

21. BMH, Miss Molly Reynolds Witness Statement, WS195 and Kilmainham Archives, Gertie Colley Murphy Papers.

22. Anon, 'A Dublin woman's story of the rebellion', in *The Gaelic American*, 18 November 1916 as quoted in Luddy, *Women in Ireland 1800-1918*, p314.

23. Taillon, *The Women of 1916*, p57. See also, McCoole, *No Ordinary Women*, p37.

24. Skinnider, *Doing My Bit for Ireland*, p124.

25. NLI, Cumann na mBan Vol II no.10 - Easter Week Commemoration Number-1926, ILB94109p4.

26. Accounts of Keogh's death differ according to the source, although she was a professional nurse and wore the uniform of same. See *An Phoblacht*,

25 June 1932. See also, Taillon, *The Women of 1916*, pp60-61.
27. Nic Shiúbhlaigh, *The Splendid Years*, p168.
28. BMH, Mrs Eileen Murphy Witness Statement, WS480.
29. UCDA, Eithne Coyle O'Donnell Papers, P64/4.
30. McCoole, *No Ordinary Women*, p39.
31. UCDA, Sighle Humphreys' Papers, P106/1165.
32. UCDA, Eithne Coyle O'Donnell Papers, P64/4.
33. BMH, Phyllis Morkan Witness Statement, WS210.
34. Taillon, *The Women of 1916*, p51.
35. BMH, Louise Gavan Duffy Witness Statement, WS216.
36. Price was not sure where the order to disband had come from, but stated (WS1754) that she 'gathered' it had come from Ned Daly.
37. BMH, Mrs Tom Barry Witness Statement, WS1754.
38. Sinéad McCoole, *Guns and Chiffon – Women Revolutionaries and Kilmainham Gaol 1916-1923*, The Stationery Office, Dublin, 1997, p28. See also, *Wexford People*, 10 May 1916. One of the wounded treated by Cumann na mBan in Enniscorthy was a local RIC member (BMH, Micheal Kirwan Witness Statement, WS1175).
39. BMH, Mrs Maire Fitzpatrick Witness Statement, WS1345.
40. BMH, Patrick Ronan Witness Statement, WS299.
41. Taillon, *The Women of 1916*, p68.
42. BMH, Mrs Nora O'Brien Witness Statement, WS286.
43. Conlon, *Cumann na mBan*, p26.
44. Seamus O Dubhghaill, 'Activities in Enniscorthy' in *Capuchin Annual* 1966.
45. McCoole, *No Ordinary Women*, p177.
46. Nic Shúibhlaigh, *The Splendid Years*, p174.
47. Taillon, *The Women of 1916*, pp68-71. See also, McCoole, *No Ordinary Women*, pp34-58.
48. McCoole, *No Ordinary Women*, p42.
49. Taillon, *The Women of 1916*, p98.
50. Annie Ryan, *Witnesses – Inside the Easter Rising*, Liberties Press, Dublin, 2005, pp129-130.
51. NLI, GPO Area in Easter Week, MS5173.
52. Nic Shúibhlaigh, *The Splendid Years*, p185.
53. McCoole, *No Ordinary Women*, p44.
54. Taillon, *The Women of 1916*, p98.
55. BMH, Miss Rose MacNamara Witness Statement, WS482.
56. UCDA, Sighle Humphreys' Papers, P106/1165.
57. *Irish Citizen*, May 1916.

58. Ibid, October 1916.
59. *The Irish Times*, 2 May 1916.
60. UCDA, Sighle Humphreys' Papers, P106/384. Fighting had occurred near the Humphreys' home on Northumberland road.
61. Taillon, *The Women of 1916*, p98. On the other hand, a unionist barrister (W.E. Wylie) who interviewed the women imprisoned after the rising, later formed the impression that only four of them knew what they were fighting for, and the rest had joined merely because the movement was popular with their peers. However, it is quite likely that prisoners who wished to be released would say such things. See, Leon Ó Broin, *W.E. Wylie and the Irish Revolution 1916-1921*, Gill and Macmillan, Dublin, 1989, p36.
62. BMH, Mrs Tom Barry Witness Statement, WS1754.

FROM THE GUN TO THE BALLOT BOX 1916 -18
1. McCoole, *No Ordinary Women*, pp51-58.
2. Ibid, p50. See also, Jacqueline Van Voris, *Constance de Markievicz – In the Cause of Ireland*, University of Massachusetts Press, Massachusetts, 1967, p210.
3. Anne Haverty, *Constance Markievicz – An Independent Life*, Pandora, London, 1988, p162.
4. Leon Ó Broin, *W.E. Wylie and the Irish Revolution*, p27. Ó Broin's account is drawn from the unpublished memoir of W.E. Wylie, a barrister at Markievicz's trial. The memoir was written at least 23 years after the event, although rumours of the alleged breakdown did circulate Dublin in May 1916. There is no reference to Markievicz having begged for her life in the formal trial record in which she was reported to have said, 'It doesn't matter what happens to me. I did what I thought was right and I stand by it'. It seems unlikely that the court would fabricate such defiant words if they had seen Markievicz beg for her life. It seems equally unlikely that a woman who had begged for her life, would, in the same sitting, utter such defiant words. Thus, the Wylie account seems somewhat suspect. However, as Townshend has commented, Wylie's motive for any alleged fabrication on his part remains obscure. See, Charles Townshend, *Easter 1916: The Irish Rebellion*, Penguin, London, 2006, pp285 and 286. See also, Barton, *From Behind a Closed Door*, p80.
5. Ward, *Unmanageable Revolutionaries*, p123.
6. Public Record Office (PRO)/Colonial Office (CO)/904/100 and 101 RIC County Inspectors (CI) Reports, Galway East May 1916, Cork West June 1916, Longford June 1916, Waterford June and October 1916, Sligo October 1916 and Inspector Generals (IG) Report August 1916.

7. UCDA, Sighle Humphreys' Papers, P106/1405.
8. NLI, Leabhar na mBan, 3B2531.
9. Clarke, *Revolutionary Woman*, p130.
10. BMH, Peg Duggan Witness Statement, WS1576.
11. Clarke, *Revolutionary Woman*, p137.
12. UCDA, Eligin O'Rahilly Papers, Máire Comerfird Memoir, P200/65.
13. PRO/CO904/100, CI Reports, Louth, Monaghan and Kilkenny, May - July 1916.
14. BMH, Dr Nancy Wyse Power and Mrs Eileen Murphy Witness Statements, WS587 and WS480.
15. PRO/CO904/100, IG Report, June 1916.
16. Clarke, *Revolutionary Woman*, p127.
17. Ibid, p132. See also, BMH, Mrs Kitty O'Doherty Witness Statement, WS355.
18. BMH, Dr Nancy Wyse Power Witness Statement, WS587.
19. PRO/CO904/100, IG Report, August 1916.
20. The British authorities (including the Inspector General) continued to mistakenly refer to republicans as Sinn Féiners.
21. UCDA, Sighle Humphreys' Papers, P106/1425.
22. Ibid.
23. Clarke, *Revolutionary Woman*, p131.
24. Conlon, *Cumann na mBan*, p34.
25. Ibid, p52.
26. Ibid, p70.
27. PRO/CO904/100, CI Report, Galway East, May 1916.
28. PRO/CO904/100, CI Report, Galway East, August 1916.
29. Conlon, *Cumann na mBan*, p45
30. BMH, Mrs Sean Beaumont and Eilis Bean Ui Chonaill Witness Statements, WS385 and WS568.
31. UCDA, Elgin O'Rahilly Papers, Máire Comerford Memoir, P200/65.
32. BMH, Mrs Sean Beaumont Witness Statement, WS385.
33. BMH, Eilis Bean Ui Chonaill Witness Statement, WS568.
34. Keyes McDonnell, *There is a Bridge at Bandon*, pp78 - 88.
35. BMH, Mrs Sidney Czira Witness Statement, WS909.
36. See, Margaret Ward, *Hanna Sheehy Skeffington – A Life*, Attic Press, Cork, 1997, pp201 and 202.
37. UCDA, Sighle Humphreys' Papers, P106/1165.
38. NLI, Life of Mary L Butler, MS7321.
39. Brian Feeney, *Sinn Féin – A Hundred Turbulent Years*, O'Brien Press, Dublin, 2002, p42.

40. Clarke, *Revolutionary Woman*, p138; See also, Feeney, *Sinn Féin*, p94.
41. Feeney, *Sinn Féin*, p57.
42. After the Sinn Féin convention of 1917 Cumann na d'Teachtaire was formed by a group of Cumann na mBan, Irish Women Workers Union and Citizen Army women, in order to 'secure women's role in the national movement and to promote their claims for equality, including suffrage'. See McCoole, *No Ordinary Women*, p65. See also, Cullen Owens, *A Social History of Women in Ireland*, pp117-119.
43. PRO/CO904/105, CI Report, Fermanagh, March 1918.
44. PRO/CO904/106, CI Report, Tipperary South, June 1918.
45. PRO/CO904/105, CI Report, Cavan, March 1918.
46. UCD's Archives contain two incomplete, and almost certainly unrepresentative, surveys of Cumann na mBan members, among the excellently catalogued papers of Sighle Humphreys and Eithne Coyle.
47. UCDA, Sean MacEoin Papers, P151/1366-1488.
48. *Nationality*, 8 February 1919.
49. BMH, Madge Daly Witness Statement, WS855.
50. Peter Hart, *The IRA and its Enemies – Violence and Community in Cork 1916 -1923*, Oxford University Press, Oxford, 1998, p235 and John J. Duggan, *Grenagh and Courtbrack During the Struggle for Independence*, published privately, Cork, undated.
51. UCDA, Sighle Humphreys' Papers, Cumann na mBan Convention Report 1918, P106/1128.
52. PRO/CO904/106, CI Report, Longford, June and July 1918.
53. PRO/CO904/105, CI Report, Fermanagh, March 1918.
54. PRO/CO904/105, CI Report, Donegal, March 1918.
55. PRO/CO904/106, IG Report, May 1918.
56. David Fitzpatrick, *Politics and Irish Life 1913-1921 – Provincial Experience of War and Revolution*, Cork University Press, Cork, 1998, p122.
57. BMH, Dr Brigit Lyons Thornton Contemporary Documents, CD134. See also, NLI, Liberty League Pamphlet, Ir94109 P65.
58. Fitzpatrick, *Politics and Irish Life*, p173. See also, BMH, Dr Nancy Wyse Power Witness Statement, WS587 and Hart, *The IRA and its Enemies*, p219.
59. Patrick Maume, *The Long Gestation – Irish Nationalist Life 1891-1918*, Gill and Macmillan, Dublin, 2000, pp156-7.
60. NLI, Leabhar na mBan, 3B2531.
61. Ibid.
62. PRO/CO904/105, CI Report, Donegal, April 1918.
63. PRO/CO904/105, CI Report, Roscommon, April 1918.
64. PRO/CO904/105 and106, CI Reports, Donegal, April 1918 and Laois,

August 1918.
65. BMH, Miss Mollie Cunningham Witness Statement, WS1681.
66. PRO/CO904/157, Military Intelligence Report, Connaught/Midlands Region, September 1917.
67. NLI, Leabhar na mBan, 3B2531.
68. McCoole, *No Ordinary Women*, p66.
69. *Freeman's Journal*, 7 June 1918.
70. PRO/CO904/106, CI Report, Longford, June 1918.
71. Conlon, *Cumann na mBan*, p64.
72. *Freeman's Journal*, 10 June 1918.
73. *Irish Independent*, 10 June 1918.
74. *Kerryman*, 15 June 1918.
75. *Kilkenny People*, 15 June 1918.
76. *Irish Independent*, 10 June 1918.
77. PRO/CO904/106, CI Report, Monaghan, June 1918.
78. *Galway Express*, 8 June 1918.
79. PRO/CO904/106, CI Report, Tipperary SR, June 1918.
80. *Longford Leader*, 5 May 1917 and PRO/CO904/105, CI Report, Longford, April 1918.
81. *Anglo Celt*, 20 April 1918.
82. UCDA, Sighle Humphreys' Papers, P106/1405.
83. *Freeman's Journal*, 2 December 1918.
84. *Cork Examiner*, 10 December 1918.
85. Ibid, 9 December 1918.
86. Ibid, 10 December 1918.
87. Ibid, 14 December 1918.
88. NLI, Leabhar na mBan, 3B2531.
89. *Waterford News*, 6 December 1918.
90. NLI, Coyle Memoir, MS 28818 (1).
91. For examples see, UCDA, Sighle Humphreys' Papers, P106/1425, Eithne Coyle Papers, P61/4, and Conlon, *Cumann na mBan*, pp 73-74.
92. Maume, *The Long Gestation*, p213.
93. BMH, Mrs Bridget Doherty and Mrs Margaret Brady Witness Statements, WS1193 and WS1257.
94. BMH, Eilis Bean Ui Chonaill, Witness Statement, WS568.
95. *The Irish Times*, 16 January 1920.
96. *Nationality*, 13 April 1918.
97. UCDA, Sighle Humphreys' Papers, P106/1425.
98. The Irish Party actually returned seven MPs with T.P. O'Connor elected for an English constituency.

99. NLI, Leabhar na mBan, 3B2531. Text in brackets is my own.
100. Feeney, *Sinn Féin*, p110 and John A. Murphy, *Ireland in the Twentieth Century,* Gill and Macmillan, Dublin, 1989, p4.
101. R.C. Owens, *Smashing Times, A History of the Irish women's suffrage movement 1889-1922,* Attic Press, Dublin, 1984 , p48.
102. Conlon, *Cumann na mBan*, pp74-75.
103. See Murphy, *Ireland in the Twentieth Century,* pp5-7 (first published in 1975). See also, Joseph Lee, *The Modernisation of Irish Society*, Gill and Macmillan, Dublin, 1992, p161 and Cal McCarthy, 'The 1918 General Election: The Swing to Sinn Féin', MPhil Thesis, UCC, 2005.
104. NLI, Leabhar na mBan, 3B2531.
105. UCDA, Sighle Humphreys' Papers, P106/1414
106. Clarke, *Revolutionary Woman*, p133.
107. UCDA, Sighle Humphreys' Papers, P106/1427.
108. BMH, Dr Nancy Wyse Power Witness Statement, WS587.
109. NLI, Leabhar na mBan, 3B2531.
110. NLI, Cumann na mBan Constitution 1916, P2119. Although this document is undated it can be traced to the 1916 convention for a number of reasons. Firstly, it refers to the 1915 convention meaning that it was written after that date. Secondly, Markievicz is named as president, meaning it was written after the rising. Thirdly it is significantly different from the 1917 document, which is dated, and was the first to give allegiance to a republic. Fourthly it gives the organisation's post rising HQ address at 6 Harcourt Street.
111. UCDA, Sighle Humphreys' Papers, P106/1427.
112. Clarke, *Revolutionary Woman*, p134.
113. McCoole, *No Ordinary Women*, p198.
114. Ibid, p146 and 201.
115. NLI, Cumann na mBan Constitution 1916, P2119.
116. Ibid
117. NLI, Cumann na mBan Constitution 1917, IR94109P68.
118. Ibid.
119. Ibid.
120. Ibid.
121. UCDA, Sighle Humphreys' Papers, 1918 Convention Report, P106/1128.
122. Ibid.
123. NLI, Cumann na mBan Constitution 1919, LOLB161.
124. NLI, Cumann na mBan Constitution 1916, P2119.
125. NLI, Cumann na mBan Constitution 1917, IR94109/P68.

126. Ibid.
127. *Nationality*, 17 August 1918.
128. UCDA, Sighle Humphreys' Papers, 1921 Convention Report, P106/1131.
129. NLI, *Cumann na mBan*, June 1925, IR3205/P64.
130. NLI, Cumann na mBan Constitution 1917, IR94109/P68.
131. *Nationality*, 20 April 1918.
132. *Nationality*, 23 March 1918.
133. *Nationality*, 11 May 1918.
134. UCDA, Sighle Humphreys' Papers, P106/1405.
135. UCDA, Sighle Humphreys' Papers, Cumann na mBan 1918 Convention Report, P106/1128.
136. County Inspectors for Donegal and Fermanagh both reported Cashel's presence in those counties in March 1918 (PRO/CO904/105, CI Reports, Donegal and Fermanagh, March 1918).
137. UCDA, Sighle Humphreys' Papers, Cumann na mBan 1918 Convention Report, P106/1128.
138. Conlon, *Cumann na mBan*, p68.
139. Ibid, p61-64. See also, BMH, Miss Mollie Cunningham Witness Statement, WS1681 and Keyes McDonnell, *There is a Bridge at Bandon*, p42.
140. Indeed, when the number of County Inspectors not tabulating Cumann na mBan statistics is taken into account, the 112 reported branches is actually quite close to the number of branches (150) represented at the 1918 convention.
141. Membership estimates for both are frequently in excess of 100,000.
142. PRO/CO904/105, CI Report, Donegal, April 1918.
143. PRO/CO904/106, CI Report, Laois, August 1918.

THE WAR OF INDEPENDENCE 1918-1921

1. Liam Deasy, *Towards Ireland Free – The West Cork Brigade in the War of Independence 1917-21*, Royal Carbery Books, Cork, 1973, pp19 - 20.
2. Ibid, p21.
3. The likelihood of any other southern Irish group arming itself at this time must have been considered slim.
4. On 26 October 1918 the *Irish Independent* reported that two British army privates 'on their way to duty were attacked by 5 men who took away a rifle'. And on 25 October the *Freeman's Journal* contained more reports of arms raiding.
5. For a county by county breakdown of revolutionary activity see Hart, Peter, *The IRA at War*, Oxford University Press, Oxford, 2003, pp30 - 61.

6. NLI, Cumann na mBan Constitution 1914, LOLB161.
7. NLI, Cumann na mBan Constitution 1919, LOLB161.
8. NLI, Cumann na mBan Constitution 1920, LOLB162
9. UCDA, Sighle Humphreys' Papers, Cumann na mBan Convention Report 1918, P106/1128.
10. *Nationality*, 20 April 1918.
11. UCDA, Sighle Humphreys' Papers, Cumann na mBan Convention Report 1918, P106/1128.
12. See p30.
13. UCDA, Elgin O'Rahilly Papers, Máire Comerford Memoir, P200/65.
14. The Cork IRA had been slow to trust Tom Barry (who was an ex-British army sergeant) and he was interviewed by senior IRA officers before being invited to join the West Cork Brigade (Deasy, *Towards Ireland Free*, p141).
15. Joost Augusteijn, *From Public Defence to Guerrilla Warfare – The Experience of Ordinary Volunteers in the Irish War of Independence 1916-1921*, Irish Academic Press, Dublin, 1998, p77. For further examples of Cumann na mBan's co-operation with the IRA throughout the conscription crisis see pp91-92.
16. Louis Whyte, *The Wild Heather Glen – The Kilmichael Story of Grief and Glory*, The Kilmichael/Crossbarry Commemoration Committee, Cork, 1995, pp51 -125.
17. Tom Barry, *Guerrilla Days in Ireland*, Anvil Books, Dublin, 1981, p208.
18. BMH, Mrs Margaret Broderick Nicholson Witness Statement, WS1682.
19. BMH, Madge Daly Witness Statement, WS855.
20. Family ties have also been established in County Longford. See, Marie Coleman, *County Longford and the Irish Revolution 1910-1923*, Irish Academic Press, Dublin, 2002 pp183 and 184.
21. Hart, *The IRA and its Enemies*, pp234 - 235.
22. BMH, Mrs Eileen MacCarvill Witness Statement, WS1752. MacCarvill (Eileen McGrane) stated that she first proposed this scheme at the 1919 Convention. However she may actually have done so in 1920, as the 1921 Convention report, reports on its implementation.
23. UCDA, Sighle Humphreys' Papers, 1921 Convention Report, P106/1131.
24. Charlie Browne, *The story of the 7th : A concise history of the 7th battalion, Cork No. 1 Brigade, Irish Republican Army, from 1915 to 1921*, Undated, pp74 -87 and BMH, Miss Mollie Cunningham Witness Statement, WS1681.
25. UCDA, Richard Mulcahy Papers, P7a/27 and Eithne Coyle O'Donnell Papers, P61/4.

26. BMH, Paul Mulvey, Hugh Brady, Patrick Doherty, Mrs Bridget Doherty and Mrs M Brady Witness Statements, WS1265, WS1266, WS1195, WS1193 and WS1257. Witness Statements 1193 and 1257 claim that there may have been more than sixteen branches in South Leitrim. However, it is unlikely that both witnesses had forgotten any more than one or two branches.
27. BMH, IRA Personnel for Divisions, Brigades and Battalions as on 11th July 1921, CD322 and UCDA, Sighle Humphreys' Papers, 1921 Convention Report, P106/1131.
28. *Nationality*, 15 February 1919.
29. PRO/CO904/111, IG Report, February 1920.
30. Augusteijn, *From Public Defence to Guerrilla Warfare*, p122.
31. NLI, Leabhar na mBan, 3B2531.
32. Ibid.
33. UCDA, Elgin O'Rahilly Papers, Máire Comerford Memoir, P200/65.
34. NLI, Coyle Memoir, MS28818.
35. UCDA, Sighle Humphreys' Papers, P106/1425.
36. Fitzpatrick, *Politics and Irish Life*, p183. See also, Hart, *The IRA and its Enemies*, p258.
37. BMH, Seamus Babington Witness Statement, WS1595.
38. For IRA tributes to Cumann na mBan see, Barry, *Guerrilla Days in Ireland*, pp208 -209, Deasy, *Towards Ireland Free*, p356 and UCDA, Sighle Humphreys' Papers, 1921 Convention Report, P106/1131. For an interesting sociological analysis of such tributes see, Louise Ryan, 'In the Line of Fire: representations of women and war (1919-1923) through the writings of republican men', in Louise Ryan and Margaret Ward (eds), *Irish Women and Nationalism – Soldiers, New Women and Wicked Hags*, Irish Academic Press, Dublin, 2004, p48.
39. PRO/CO904/112, CI Report, Cork East, June 1920.
40. PRO/CO904/113, CI Report, Cork West, November 1920.
41. PRO/CO904/113, CI Report, Longford, November 1920.
42. PRO/CO904/113, CI Report, Sligo, November 1920.
43. PRO/CO904/113, CI Report, Fermanagh, December 1920.
44. Barry, *Guerrilla Days in Ireland*, p218.
45. UCDA, Sighle Humphreys' Papers, 1921 Convention Report, P106/1131.
46. BMH, Mrs Sean Beaumont (nee Maureen McGavock) Witness Statement, WS385.
47. PRO/CO904/114, CI Report, Tyrone, February 1921.
48. Extract from a lecture by Lieutenant General A.E. Percival. Taken

from, William Sheehan, *British Voices from the Irish War of Independence 1918-1921 – The Words of British Servicemen who were there*, The Collins Press, Cork, 2005, pp104 - 106. Text in brackets is my own.

49. PRO/CO904/114, CI Report, Galway West, January 1921.

50. PRO/CO904/157, Dublin Castle Statement, December 1920.

51. BMH, Mrs M. Brady Witness Statement, WS1257.

52. PRO/CO904/114, CI Reports, Galway East, January 1921, Tyrone, February 1921 and Offaly, March 1921.

53. BMH, Miss Nora Cunningham Witness Statement, WS1690. See also, Conlon, *Cumann na mBan*, p210.

54. BMH, Mrs M Brady Witness Statement, WS1257.

55. PRO/CO904/115, CI Report, Meath, June 1921.

56. BMH, Mrs Bridget Doherty and Mrs M Brady Witness Statements, WS1193 and WS1257.

57. PRO/CO904/115, CI Report, Laois, May 1921.

58. Republicans later claimed that an unnamed British officer had stated in an interview with an unnamed American magazine that the British military would 'make minced meat of those fellows in a very short time only for the women'. (*Poblacht na hEireann – The Republic of Ireland*, 21 February 1922).

59. PRO/CO904/114, CI Report, Kilkenny, March 1921.

60. UCDA, Elgin O'Rahilly Papers, Máire Comerford Memoir, P200/65.

61. McCoole, *No Ordinary Women*, p72.

62. BMH, Miss Mollie Cunningham Witness Statement, WS1681.

63. BMH, Peg Duggan Witness Statement, WS1576.

64. NLI, Cumann na mBan Constitution 1920, LOLB161.

65. BMH, Miss Annie Barrett Witness Statement, WS1133.

66. Gaughan, *Austin Stack*, p64.

67. Tim Pat Coogan, *Michael Collins*, Arrow Books, London, 1991, pp375-376.

68. NAI, Department of the Taoiseach, Appointments in the Public Interest, Miscellaneous Group 1931, S5778. This file refers to the claim for establishment in the Civil Service of Miss K. Fleming and details her activities during the revolution.

69. BMH, Miss Moira Kennedy O'Byrne Witness Statement, WS1029.

70. BMH, Eilis Bean Ui Chonnaill Witness Statement, WS568. Ui Chonaill states that the woman (McDonagh) was not a member of Cumann na mBan as they had nobody free to fill the vacancy. However, for a job within the walls of Dublin Castle it is unlikely that Collins would have selected a known member of Cumann na mBan.

71. Lt. Gen A.E. Percival in, Sheehan, *British Voices*, p104.

72. Ibid.
73. PRO/CO904/168, Dublin Castle Documents, May 1921.
74. BMH, Miss Mollie Cunningham Witness Statement, WS1681.
75. BMH, Bernard Sweeney Witness Statement, WS1194.
76. BMH, Miss Nora Cunningham Witness Statement, WS1690.
77. Meda Ryan, *Tom Barry – IRA Freedom Fighter*, Mercier Press, Cork, 2003, p100.
78. BMH, Mrs Bridget Doherty, Mrs Margaret Brady, Maire Bean Mhic Giolla Phadraig and Miss Nora Cunningham Witness Statements, WS1193, WS1257, WS1345 and WS1690. Cunningham reported troop movements to IRA scouts on the perimeter of IRA actions, almost like a scout for the scouts themselves.
79. UCDA, Sighle Humphreys' Papers, P106/1166.
80. BMH, Dr Nancy Wyse Power Contemporary Documents, CD200. For report of a Cumann na mBan member being caught in possession of a leaflet urging 'social boycott' of the police, see *Tipperary People*, 1 April 1921.
81. BMH, Mrs Bridget Doherty Witness Statement, WS1193.
82. Kilmainham Archives, Record of Máire McDonald (nee Dooley).
83. BMH, Miss Mary McGeehin Witness Statement, WS902.
84. For examples see, *The Irish Times*, 21, 26, 28 July 1920, *Tipperary People*, 7 May and 30 July 1920 and *Leitrim Observer*, 29 May 1920. In some areas the cutting of women's hair proved so popular with the IRA that they continued the activity even after the truce had been declared (PRO/CO904/116, CI Reports, Carlow July 1921 and Tyrone August 1921).
85. BMH, Daniel Byrne Witness Statement, WS1440.
86. BMH, Mrs Margaret Broderick-Nicholson Witness Statement, WS1682.
87. BMH, Madge Daly and Mrs Margaret Broderick-Nicholson Witness Statements, WS855 and WS1682. See also, Conlon, *Cumann na mBan*, p224.
88. *Limerick Leader*, 11 April 1921.
89. Conlon, *Cumann na mBan*, pp186, 188, 211, 222 and 225.
90. Ibid, p179. See also, Ward, *Unmanageable Revolutionaries*, p143.
91. PRO/CO904/114, IG Report, March 1921. Although the Inspector General alleges that the young woman in Fermoy was shot because she was in the company of two soldiers it should be borne in mind that the soldiers might have been the intended targets of the attack.
92. *Sligo Champion*, 1 January 1921 and *Leitrim Observer*, 1 January 1921.
93. PRO/CO904/115, IG Report, May 1921. In the Galway case police alleged that District Inspector Blake's wife was 'riddled with bullets while

she lay on the ground' after an IRA ambush. In the same month a District Inspector and his wife were ambushed in Mayo. The DI was wounded but his wife survived unscathed (CI Report, Mayo, May 1921).

94. McCoole, *No Ordinary Women*, p75. See also, Conlon, *Cumann na mBan*, p198. In addition to the two alleged spies, a third woman was shot dead in Monaghan. Although the traditional IRA notice proclaiming that she had been convicted of spying was found on the corpse, police suspected that she had been killed as a result of a feud over poteen making and that the real perpetrators were merely 'sheltering behind' the IRA (PRO/CO904/115, IG Report, April 1921).

95. BMH, Miss Mollie Cunningham Witness Statement, WS1681 and UCDA, Eithne Coyle O'Donnell Papers, P61/4.

96. BMH, Miss Bridget O'Mullane Witness Statement, WS450.

97. For an explanation of how 'Flying Columns' operated and were supported see, Augusteijn, *From Public Defence to Guerrilla Warfare*, pp124-164.

98. BMH, Miss Bridget O'Mullane Witness Statement, WS450.

99. BMH, Mrs Margaret Brady Witness Statement, WS1257.

100. NLI, Open Letter on behalf of Cumann na mBan Prisoners Committee, LOLB161.

101. *Freeman's Journal*, 5 June 1918.

102. UCDA, Sighle Humphreys' Papers, 1918 Convention Report, P106/1128.

103. The 'German Plot' was an allegation by the British authorities that senior Sinn Féin members were in league with the Germans. Over the years no evidence has come to light to support the allegation and historians generally agree that the plot was invented in order to scupper Sinn Féin's electoral chances.

104. *Nationality*, 11 January 1919.

105. UCDA, Sighle Humphreys' Papers, P106/1405.

106. BMH, Madge Daly Witness Statement, WS855.

107. BMH, Eilis Bean Ui Chonaill Witness Statement, WS568.

108. BMH, Madge Daly Witness Statement, WS855.

109. Ryan, *Tom Barry*, p73. See also, Barry, Tom, *Guerrilla Days in Ireland*, p56.

110. Ryan, *Tom Barry*, p106.

111. *The Irish Times*, 25 August 1919.

112. UCDA, Sighle Humphreys' Papers, P106/1405.

113. PRO/CO904/107, CI Reports, Kerry, October and December 1918. See also, Conlon, *Cumann na mBan*, p75.

114. PRO/CO904/108, CI Report, Cork East, April 1919.

115. PRO/CO904/114, CI Reports, Clare February 1921, Kilkenny and Belfast, March 1921.
116. UCDA, Sighle Humphreys' Papers, 1921 Convention Report, P106/1131 and Conlon, *Cumann na mBan,* p182.
117. BMH, Madge Daly Witness Statement, WS855.
118. PRO/CO904/108, CI Report, Cork East, April 1919.
119. BMH, Peg Duggan Witness Statement, WS1576.
120. PRO/CO904/110, CI Report, Fermanagh, October 1919.
121. BMH, Dr Nancy Wyse Power Witness Statement, WS587.
122. BMH, Mrs Margaret Brady Witness Statement, WS1257. See also, *Tipperary People*, 2 April 1920, *Waterford News*, 11 and 24 March 1921 and *Limerick Leader*, 11 March 1921. Urban branches of Cumann na mBan were also frequently involved in Volunteer funerals (see Conlon, *Cumann na mBan*, pp111, 120, 122, 123, 126, 127, 172, 201, 218 and 231).
123. BMH, Eilis Bean Ui Chonaill Witness Statement, WS568.
124. BMH, Mrs Catherine Rooney Witness Statement, WS648.
125. BMH, Eilis Bean Ui Chonaill Witness Statement, WS568. See also, UCDA, Elgin O'Rahilly Papers, Máire Comerford Memoir, P200/65.
126. UCDA, Elgin O'Rahilly Papers, Maire Comerford Unpublished Memoir, P200/65 and *Tipperary People*, 5 November 1920.
127. *Sligo Champion*, 19 March 1921, Conlon, *Cumann na mBan*, p185 and McCarthy, *Cumann na mBan – The Limerick Link*, p68. It should be stated that vast numbers of Volunteers and the general population were also involved in most of these protests.
128. UCDA, Elgin O'Rahilly Papers, Maire Comerford Unpublished Memoir, P200/65.
129. PRO/CO904/111, CI Report, Monaghan, January 1920.
130. *The Irish Times*, 21 July 1919.
131. *Cork County Eagle and Munster Advertiser*, 14 July 1919.
132. Hart, *The IRA and its Enemies*, p235. 'Separation women' had husbands or sons in the British armed forces during the First World War.
133. *Cork County Eagle and Munster Advertiser*, 14 June 1919.
134. *The Irish Times*, 14 December 1920.
135. Dermot Keogh, *The Vatican, The Bishops and Irish Politics 1919-39,* Cambridge University Press, 1988, p60.
136. Ibid p51.
137. *Tipperary People*, 1 April 1921.
138. *Kerryman*, 23 January 1921. See also, McCoole, *No Ordinary Women,* p81 and Conlon, *Cumann na mBan*, p34.
139. *Tipperary People*, April 1st 1921.

140. NLI, Coyle Memoir, MS28818(1).
141. *Tipperary People*, 25 February 1921, *Roscommon Herald*, 8 January 1921, *Sligo Champion*, 1 January, 19 February and 26 March 1921. See also, Conlon, *Cumann na mBan*, pp221 (refers to Linda Kearns who was not a member of Cumann na mBan) and 229.
142. NAI, Dáil Eireann Papers, DE 5/5/72. Mary MacSwiney did encounter considerable difficulty in reclaiming substantial moneys she had paid from her own pocket. By August 1922, she was still owed at least £1000, but the exact amount was still debated and thus MacSwiney had received no payment.
143. Joanne Mooney Eichacker, *Irish Republican Women in America – Lecture Tours 1916 - 1925*, Irish Academic Press, Dublin, 2003, pp93-111. Muriel MacSwiney returned home in January 1921, but Mary remained, at the request of de Valera.
144. *Limerick Leader*, 3 January 1921.
145. UCDA, Sighle Humphreys' Papers, 1921 Convention Report, P106/1131.
146. NAI, Dáil Eireann Papers, DE 2/10.
147. BMH, Madge Daly Witness Statement, WS855.
148. PRO/CO904/114, CI Report, Wexford, March 1921.
149. UCDA, Elgin O'Rahilly Papers, Maire Comerford Memoir, P200/65.
150. University College Cork, Boole Library, Report of the Irish White Cross, Bielenberg361.7Iris. See also, Aine Ceannt, *The Story of the Irish White Cross 1920-1947*, At the Sign of the Three Candles, Dublin, Undated, *Waterford News*, 8 and 29 April 1921, *Limerick Leader*, 1 April 1921 and *Kerryman*, 2 March 1921.
151. Uinseann MacEoin, *Survivors*, Argenta, Dublin, 1980, p152.
152. Conlon, *Cumann na mBan*, p205.
153. NLI, IRPDF – A Further Appeal, ILB300 P12, NLI, IRPDF – Third Appeal, LOP115 [Item 138], NLI, Cumann na mBan – Howth, MS33368, UCDA, Eithne Coyle O'Donnell Papers, P61/4, NAI, Dept of Taoiseach, S14182 and IMA, Captured Documents, Lot 12.
154. UCC, Boole Library, Report of the Irish White Cross, Bielenberg361.7Iris.
155. *Sligo Champion*, 26 March 1921. Quinn admitted to 'being a lieutenant in a girls club pledged to work for an Irish Republic' (Conlon, *Cumann na mBan*, p207). In a separate incident two Liverpool members were accused, but acquitted, of setting fires at Liverpool docks (*Sligo Champion*, 19 February 1921). See also, UCDA, Eithne Coyle O'Donnell Papers, P61/4.
156. BMH, Mrs Mary A. Cremin Witness Statement, WS924.

157. BMH, Sorcha McDermott Witness Statement, WS945.
158. UCDA, Sighle Humphreys' Papers, P106/1405.
159. BMH, Dr Nancy Wyse Power Witness Statement, WS587.
160. Michael J. Rafter, *The Quiet County*, Alderin Publishing, Portlaoise, 2005, pp50 and 65.
161. *Kerryman*, 8 July 1918.
162. Hart, *The IRA at War*, pp30-61.
163. Ibid. It is also worth noting that an obvious inconsistency occurs in the 1921 Convention Report with regard to District Councils. Leslie Price refers to the formation of seventeen DCs in Kerry. Yet she later states that only ten DCs existed in that county. The most likely explanation is that of a typographical error. In listing the number of DCs existing in each Munster county (22 in Cork, ten in Kerry, five in Limerick, six in Tipperary, six in Waterford and two in Clare) the report falsely declares that the total number of DCs in Munster was 57. Clearly the total was actually 51. As the report was most likely typed from Price's handwriting, the error is probably in the interpretation of same. If Kerry had seventeen or more DCs the error would have been much more than the basic confusion of a one and a seven. Thus it is assumed that no more than ten DCs existed in Kerry and it is most likely that seven of them were formed in 1921.
164. UCDA, Sighle Humphreys' Papers, 1921 Convention Report, P106/1131.
165. The other Waterford attendees were from, Waterford city (two), Tramore, Ballyduff, Villierstown, Colligan, Old Parish, Lismore, Touraneena, Sleady and Brickey.
166. The other Limerick attendees were from Limerick (three), Kildimo (two), Newcastlewest, Rathkeale, Carrigerry, and Foynes. The Drumcollegher delegate may have been affiliated with a DC in Newcastlewest or Rathkeale.
167. *Nationality*, 25 January 1919.
168. UCDA, Sighle Humphreys' Papers, 1921 Convention Report, P106/1131.
169. BMH, Eilis Aughney Witness Statement, WS1054.
170. NLI, Cumann na mBan Constitution 1920, LOLB162.
171. UCDA, Sean MacEoin Papers, P151/1366-1488.
172. Military Service Pensions Act 1934, First Schedule, Section 7. For rounded estimates see, UCDA, Eithne Coyle O'Donnell Papers, P61/4, Sighle Humphreys' Papers, P106/1425, BMH, Mrs Bridget Doherty, Mrs Margaret Brady, Miss Mollie Cunningham and Peg Duggan Witness Statements, WS1193, WS1257, WS1681 and WS1576.

173. UCDA, Eithne Coyle O'Donnell Papers, P61/4.
174. BMH, Mrs Maire Fitzpatrick Witness Statement, WS1345.
175. See, Aideen Sheehan, Cumann na mBan-Policies and Activities in David Fitzpatrick (ed), *Revolution? Ireland 1917-1923*, Trinity History Workshop, Dublin 1990, p89. See also, Appendix.
176. In an interview with Margaret Ward, Eithne Coyle later declared that Cumann na mBan had had about 3,000 members. It is difficult to know exactly how Coyle had arrived at this figure. However, she may have been referring to the most militantly active members.
177. UCDA, Eithne Coyle O'Donnell Papers, P61/4.
178. Not all the Ulster, Leinster and Connaught delegates are prefixed by a title and thus we can only say that 'at least' the number titled Miss were unmarried.
179. Duggan, *Grenagh and Courtbrack During the Struggle for Independence*, p64 and Browne, *The Story of the Seventh*, pp86-87
180. BMH, Mrs Bridget Doherty Witness Statement, WS1193.
181. BMH, Mrs Kitty O'Doherty Witness Statement, WS355. Eileen Murphy (WS480) also stated that she ceased Cumann na mBan activity after her marriage, whilst her husband remained an active Volunteer.
182. Matthews, 'Cumann na mBan', pxi.
183. Sheehan, *Cumann na mBan – Policies and Activities*, pp189-190.
184. Ó Ríordáin, John J., *Kiskeam versus the empire*, Kerryman, Tralee, 1985; Duggan, *Grenagh and Courtbrack During the Struggle for Independence* and Browne, *The Story of the Seventh*, pp64-71.
185. The fathers occupations of the seven members categorised as other, were as follows: one cattle drover, two in the merchant navy, four dairymen.
186. Hart, *The IRA at War*, p116.
187. UCDA, Sighle Humphreys' Papers, 1921 Convention Report, P106/1131.
188. BMH, Eilis Aughney Witness Statement, WS1054.
189. UCDA, Sighle Humphreys' Papers, 1921 Convention Report, P106/1131.
190. Markievicz's presidential address paid tribute to the organisation by telling the delegates of the praise given them by many IRA leaders.
191. See p49.
192. UCDA, Sighle Humphreys' Papers, 1921 Convention Report, P106/1131.
193. BMH, Dr Nancy Wyse Power and Sorcha Nic Diarmada Witness Statements, WS587 and WS945.
194. Michael Hopkinson, *The Irish War of Independence*, Gill and Macmillan,

Dublin, 2002, p128.

DIVISION AND CIVIL WAR 1921-1923

1. Charlotte Fallon, *Soul of Fire – A Biography of Mary MacSwiney*, Mercier Press, Cork, 1986, p78.
2. Ward, *Unmanageable Revolutionaries*, p166.
3. Ibid, p171. See also, *Kilkenny People*, 7 July 1922.
4. UCDA, Sighle Humphreys' Papers, P106/743 and *Irish Independent*, 6 February 1922.
5. NAI, Dáil Eireann Papers, DE 2/486. The document in question is undated. However, its order of filing would suggest that it dated from mid January. In addition, a note attached to a duplicate copy confirms that it was passed to Michael Collins on 1/2/1923. Thus it definitely pre-dates the Cumann na mBan convention. See also, Gaughan, *Austin Stack*, p190.
6. Conlon, *Cumann na mBan*, p255.
7. Ibid and *Poblacht na hEireann – The Republic of Ireland*, 17 January 1922.
8. BMH, Miss Bridget O'Mullane Witness Statement, WS486.
9. UCDA, Sighle Humphreys' Papers, P106/745.
10. *Freeman's Journal*, 6 February 1922.
11. BMH, Miss Bridget O'Mullane Witness Statement, WS486.
12. UCDA, Sighle Humphreys' Papers, P106/743. Text in brackets is my own.
13. Although originally scheduled for 28 January the Convention was subsequently deferred for one week (Conlon, *Cumann na mBan*, p256).
14. *Freeman's Journal*, 6 February 1922.
15. *Irish Independent*, 6 February 1922.
16. Ibid.
17. Ibid. This reserved tribute to Wyse Power was paid after the votes had been cast.
18. *Freeman's Journal*, 6 February 1922.
19. *Irish Independent*, 6 February 1922. See also, *Poblacht na hEireann – The Republic of Ireland*, 14 February 1922.
20. *Irish Independent*, 6 February 1922.
21. UCDA, Sighle Humphreys' Papers, P106/743.
22. *Freeman's Journal*, 6 February 1922.
23. *The Irish Times*, 6 February 1922.
24. BMH, Aine Ryan Witness Statement, WS887.
25. IMA, Captured Documents, Lot No 51.
26. In a letter to the *Irish Independent* on 8 February 1922, Hanna Sheehy Skeffington claimed that she 'understood' Cumann na mBan had 1,100

branches. However, the purpose of Sheehy Skeffington's letter was to highlight the political activity of women and their right to equality of suffrage. Bearing in mind the figures provided at the 1921 convention, Sheehy Skeffington was almost certainly exaggerating the organisation's size. If she was not, the number of branches not present at the special convention increases dramatically.

27. UCDA, Sighle Humphreys' Papers, 1921 Convention Report, P106/1131 and IMA, Captured Documents, List of Anti-Treaty branches, Lot 51. Cork and Kerry branches that were not in attendance but were alleged to have been anti-Treaty are included in this analysis.

28. See pp36-37.

29. *Freeman's Journal*, 23 February 1922. It seems very likely that the writer (Anna Joyce) is writing about pre-convention drop outs as the 'minority of opinion' of which she wrote, is surely that which was reflected by the conventions voting pattern and not by anything which had occurred in the days after the convention.

30. Conlon, *Cumann na mBan*, p257-8.

31. *Cork Examiner*, 16 February 1922.

32. UCDA, Sighle Humphreys' Papers, P106/743.

33. *Freeman's Journal*, 18 February 1922. Letter to Editor from 'Siobhan Bean an Phaoraigh'.

34. *Poblacht na hEireann – The Republic of Ireland*, 17 January-4 May 1922.

35. *Irish Independent*, 9 January-11 February 1922.

36. Cullen Owens, A *Social History of Women in Ireland 1870-1970*, p125.

37. *Freeman's Journal*, 3 March 1922.

38. UCDA, Sighle Humphreys' Papers, P106/742 and 745.

39. *Freeman's Journal*, 9 March 1922.

40. *Irish Independent* and *Freeman's Journal*, 14 March 1922.

41. *Irish Independent*, 6 February 1922.

42. Ibid, 14 March 1922.

43. Ibid.

44. *Irish Independent, The Irish Times* and *Freeman's Journal*, 12 February 1923.

45. UCDA, Richard Mulcahy Papers, P7b/199. These were the draft rules and constitution of the organisation, dated 5 Januray 1923. They appear to have been sent to Mulcahy for his approval. His only comment was that the word 'war' should be removed from the draft and replaced with the words; 'armed revolt against the government'.

46. IMA, Captured Documents, Lot 12.

47. IMA, Captured Documents, Lot 34.

48. IMA, Captured Documents, Lot 79. As early as July 6th 1922 the repub-

lican propaganda sheet; *Poblacht na hEireann* had carried a similar warning.
49. UCDA, Ernie O'Malley Papers, P17a/34.
50. IMA, Captured Documents, Lot 233.
51. UCDA, Ernie O'Malley Papers, P17a/34.
52. *The Times*, 5 February 1923.
53. Ibid, 11 December 1922.
54. Ibid, 17 February 1922.
55. IMA, Operations Reports Cork Command, CW/OPs/13/C and Conlon, *Cumann na mBan*, p287.
56. *Freeman's Journal*, 6 June 1923.
57. *Free State*, 5 July 1922.
58. IMA, Communications Reports Kerry Command, CW/OPs/12/E.
59. *The Irish Times*, *Irish Independent* and *Freeman's Journal*, 12 February 1923. See also, Conlon, *Cumann na mBan*, pp276-282.
60. IMA, Captured Documents, Lot 34. The *Manchester Guardian* described Kilkenny as a Free State stronghold on April 23rd 1923 (Reported in *Kilkenny People*, 28 April 1923).
61. *The Irish Times*, *Irish Independent* and *Freeman's Journal*, 12 February 1923.
62. Marie O'Neill, *From Parnell to De Valera – A Biography of Jennie Wyse Power 1858-1941*, Blackwater Press, Dublin, 1991, p 140.
63. UCDA, Richard Mulcahy Papers, P7b/199. See also, *The Irish Times*, *Irish Independent* and *Freeman's Journal*, 12 February 1923. It seems that the executive had considered the word 'directed' but had eventually opted for 'advised', in relation to their members joining Cumann na nGaedheal.
64. Conlon, *Cumann na mBan*, pp276-282.
65. *Cork Examiner*, 14 February 1922.
66. Ibid, 16 February 1922 and UCDA, Mary MacSwiney Papers, P48a/24.
67. *Cork Examiner*, 16 February 1922.
68. BMH, Eilis Aughney Witness Statement, WS1054. Aughney 'thinks' that executive members were dispatched to the country after the convention. O'Mullane (WS486) clearly states that this occurred 'before the convention'.
69. These 'Baby Clubs' had been used as fronts for Cumann na mBan operations since the Anglo-Irish war.
70. IMA, Captured Documents, Lot 34.
71. IMA, Captured Documents, Lots 34 and 51.
72. IMA, Captured Documents, Lot 51.
73. UCDA, Ernie O'Malley Papers, P17a/144. Although the list is undated, the papers up to that point run in sequence. Thus, it is quite likely the document dates from late December 1922.

74. IMA, Operations Reports, Dublin Command (Carlow District), Dublin Command (Dundlak District), Kerry Command and Cork Command, CW/OPs/9/E, CW/OPs/9/G, CW/OPs/12/L, CW/OPs/12/E, CW/OPs/13/C and CW/OPs/13/D. In Carlow, Dundalk and Cork arrests did not begin until 1923. However the first arrests of republican women in Kerry occurred in October 1922.
75. UCDA, Sighle Humphreys' Papers, P106/1169.
76. UCDA, Eithne Coyle Papers, P61/4.
77. BMH, Madge Daly Witness Statement, WS855.
78. BMH, Eilis Aughney Witness Statement, WS1054.
79. NLI, Coyle Memoir, MS28818(1).
80. UCDA, Ernie O'Malley Papers, P17a/144.
81. IMA, Captured Documents, Lot 34 and UCDA, Ernie O'Malley Papers, P17a/144.
82. PRO/CO904/115, CI Report, Longford, June 1921.
83. NLI, Coyle Memoir, MS28818(1).
84. *Belfast Telegram*, 12 April 1922 in NLI, Coyle Memoir, MS28818(1).
85. *Derry Sentinel*, 18 April 1922 in NLI, Coyle Memoir, MS28818(1).
86. *Poblacht na hEireann – The Republic of Ireland*, 29 March 1922.
87. Ryan, *In the Line of Fire: representations of women and war (1919 - 1923) through the writings of republican men*, p48.
88. IMA, Communications Report Kerry Command, CW/OPs/12/E.
89. BMH, Mrs Eileen McCarvill Witness Statement, WS1752.
90. BMH, Miss Bridget O'Mullane Witness Statement, WS486, UCDA, Sighle Humpreys' Papers, P106/752 and *Poblacht na hEireann – War News* No 13, 11 July 1922.
91. BMH, Madge Daly and Mrs Brigid Ryan Witness Statements, WS855 and WS1573.
92. IMA, Captured Documents, Lots 34 and 79.
93. BMH, Miss Nora Cunningham Witness Statement, WS1690.
94. Ibid.
95. *Irish Independent*, 11 May 1923.
96. IMA, Operations Reports Cork Command, CW/OPs/13/C.
97. IMA, Operations Reports Cork Command, Unnumbered file.
98. IMA, Operations Reports Cork Command, CW/OPs/13/D.
99. UCDA, Ernie O'Malley Papers, P17a/144.
100. BMH, Madge Daly Witness Statement, WS855. See also, McCoole, *No Ordinary Women*, p98.
101. *Eire – The Irish Republic*, 23 June 1923.
102. IMA, Captured Documents, Lot 34.

103. Ibid.
104. IMA, Captured Documents, Lot 109.
105. BMH, Miss Bridget O'Mullane Witness Statement, WS486.
106. UCDA, Ernie O'Malley Papers, P17a/144.
107. Matthews, Cumann na mBan, p58. See also, Karen Steele, 'Constance Markievicz and the politics of memory', in Ryan and Ward (eds), *Irish Women and Nationalism*, p65, UCDA, Eithne Coyle O'Donnell Papers, P61/4, and IMA, Captured Documents, Lot 127.
108. UCDA, Ernie O'Malley Papers, P17a/193.
109. UCDA, Ernie O'Malley Papers, P17a/144.
110. IMA, Operations Reports Kerry Command, CW/OPs/12/L.
111. IMA, Operations Reports Kerry Command, CW/OPs/12/M.
112. IMA, Communications Reports Kerry Command, CW/OPs/12/E.
113. IMA, Operations Reports Cork and Kerry Commands, CW/OPs/14/A and CW/OPs/12/L.
114. UCDA, Ernie O'Malley Papers, P17a/144. Some of these single sheets were taken south by women going home for Christmas.
115. Ernie O'Malley, *The Singing Flame*, Anvil Books, Dublin, 1992, p101.
116. BMH, Mrs Brigid Ryan Witness Statement, WS1573. See also, *The Irish Times*, 1 January 1923.
117. IMA, Captured Documents, Lot 34 and BMH, Mrs Margaret O'Callaghan Witness Statement, WS747. The purchase of weaponry from Free State troops was not always advantageous and eventually the IRA had to warn their membership of Free State soldiers selling Mills bombs with instantaneous fuses to republicans (IMA, Captured Documents, Lot157(1)).
118. BMH, Mrs Brigid Ryan Witness Statement, WS1573 and IMA, Captured Documents, Lot 34.
119. UCDA, Ernie O'Malley Papers, P17a/144.
120. IMA, Captured Documents, Lot 34 and UCDA, Ernie O'Malley Papers, P17a/144.
121. A list which was kept by Cumann na mBan for propaganda purposes named 44 women who were arrested under the DORA regulations. The list contains four sets of sisters or duplicated names (BMH, Mrs Sean Beaumont Contemporary Documents, CD167).
122. BMH, Mary Rigney Witness Statement, WS752. Rigney states that her record was obtained directly from Mountjoy jail.
123. BMH, Mrs Bernard O'Donnell Witness Statement, WS750. Even the police report does not imply that the women were guilty of anything other than 'running through the fields' close to where the incident had occurred

(PRO/CO904/115, CI Report, Cork East, June 1921).
124. *Tipperary People*, 4 March 1921 and *Kerryman*, 5 March 1921.
125. *Sligo Champion*, 1 January 1921 and *Limerick Leader*, 27 May 1921.
126. BMH, Mrs Mairin Ryan Witness Statement, WS416.
127. The initials F. MacH. do appear on the 3 March article entitled 'Women and the Treaty'. Although similar in style and content, this article was not a part of the 'A Woman's View' series.
128. *Free State*, 13 July 1922.
129. Of course, there were many families that were torn apart by the Civil War, but they remain the exceptions rather than the rule.
130. NLI, Coyle Memoir, MS28828(1).
131. BMH, Mrs Bernard O'Donnell Witness Statement, WS750.
132. NLI, Coyle Memoir, MS28818(1).
133. Ibid.
134. BMH, Miss Bridget O'Mullane Witness Statement, WS486.
135. IMA, Operations Report, Dublin Command, CW/OPs/9/B.
136. MacEoin, *Survivors*, p49.
137. *Free State*, 20 July 1922 and IMA, Captured Documents, Lot 227.
138. BMH, Mrs Bernard O'Donnell, WS750 and UCDA, Sighle Humhpreys' Papers, P106/750.
139. McCoole, *No Ordinary Women*, pp111-112.
140. Matthews, *Cumann na mBan*, p66. See also, Oonagh Walsh, 'Testimony from Imprisoned Women' in David Fitzpatrick (ed), *Revolution? Ireland 1917-1923*, pp77-79.
141. Kilmainham Archives, Cumann na mBan Minute Book of Prisoners Council, NDU 1923.
142. MacEoin, *Survivors*, p49. See also, McCoole, *No Ordinary Women*, p126.
143. IMA, Operations Reports, Dublin Command, CW/OPs/9/B. See also, *Irish Independent*, 10 May 1923 and McCoole, *No Ordinary Women*, p126.
144. NLI, Coyle Memoir, MS28818(1).
145. IMA, Captured Documents, Lot 157(1). See also, McCoole, *No Ordinary Women*, p126 and Margaret Buckley, *The Jangle of the Keys*, James Duffy and Co. Ltd, Dublin, 1938, pp87-94.
146. *Eire – The Irish Nation*, 30 June 1923. Some republican activists had been arrested by the authorities in Britain and deported to Ireland. These were known as deportees.
147. Buckley, *The Jangle of the Keys*, pp18-19.
148. BMH, Miss Bridget O'Mullane Witness Statement, WS486.
149. NLI, May Bowen Kilmainham Jail Autograph Book, MS27981.
150. McCoole, *No Ordinary Women*, p123.

151. *The Irish Times*, 8 May 1923.
152. *The Irish Times*, 5 May 1923.
153. Charlotte Fallon, 'Civil War Hunger Strikes: Women and Men', in *Eire*, Vol 22, 1987.
154. McCoole, *No Ordinary Women*, p135.
155. Ibid, p115.
156. *Poblacht na hEireann – War News* No 14, 7 July 1922.
157. Buckley, *The Jangle of the Keys*, p30.
158. McCoole, *No Ordinary Women*, pp218-239.
159. For references to women serving time in Buncranna and Cork see *Eire – The Irish Nation*, 9 and 23 June 1923.
160. IMA, Operations Reports Kerry Command, CW/OPs/12/J.

BIBLIOGRAPHY

PUBLISHED

Augusteijn, Joost, *From Public Defiance to Guerrilla Warfare: The Experience of Ordinary Volunteers in the Irish War of Independence 1916-1921*, Irish Academic Press, Dublin, 1998.

Benton, Sarah, 'Women Disarmed: The Militarization of Politics in Ireland 1913-23', in *Feminist Review* 50, 1995.

Barry, Tom, *Guerrilla Days in Ireland*, Anvil, Dublin, 1981.

Breen, Dan, *My Fight for Irish Freedom*, Talbot Press, Dublin, 1926.

Broderick, Marian, *Wild Irish Women*, O'Brien Press, Dublin, 2001.

Buckley Margaret, *The Jangle of the Keys*, James Duffy and Co. Ltd, Dublin, 1938.

Ceannt, Áine, *The Story of the Irish White Cross 1920-1947*, At the Sign of the Three Candles, Dublin, Undated.

Clarke, Kathleen, *Revolutionary Woman: My Fight for Ireland's Freedom*, Helen Litton (ed), O'Brien Press, Dublin 1991.

Coleman, Marie, *County Longford and the Irish revolution 1910-1923*, Irish Academic Press, Dublin, 2002.

Colum, Padraig, *Arthur Griffith*, Browne and Nolan, Dublin, 1959.

Conlon, Lil, *Cumann na mBan and the Women of Ireland 1913-1925*, Kilkenny People Ltd, Kilkenny, 1969.

Coogan, Oliver, *Politics and War in Meath 1913-1923*, privately published, Kildare, 1983.

Coogan, Tim Pat, *The IRA*, Fontana, London 1966.

— *Michael Collins*, Arrow, London, 1991.

— *DeValera*, Arrow, London, 1995.

Cowell, John, *A Noontide Blazing: Brigid Lyons Thornton: Rebel, Soldier, Doctor*, Currach Press, Dublin, 2005.

Coxhead, Elizabeth, *Daughters of Erin: Five Women of the Irish Renaissance*, Colin Smythe, Gerrards Cross, 1979.

Coyle, Eithne, 'The History of Cumann na mBan', *An Poblacht*, 8 April, 1933.

Craig, F.W.S., *British Electoral Facts 1832-1937*, Parliamentary Research Services, Dartmouth, 1988.

Cullen Owens, Rosemary, *Smashing Times: A History of the Irish Women's Suffrage Movement 1889-1922*, Attic Press, Dublin 1984.

— *A Social History of Women in Ireland*, Gill and Macmillan, Dublin, 2005.

Cullen, Mary and Luddy, Maria, *Female Activists, Irish Women and Change 1900-1960*, The Woodfield Press, Dublin, 2001.

De Paor, Mairéad and Siobhán, 'Blaze Away With Your Gun' in *Kerryman*, 21 December 1968, 28 December 1968, 3 January 1969.

Deasy, Liam, *Towards Ireland Free*, Royal Carbery Books, Cork, 1973.

Desmond, Shaw, *The Drama of Sinn Féin*, W Collins Sons and Co Ltd, London, 1923.

Dudley Edwards, Ruth, *The Triumph of Failure*, Victor Gollanez Ltd, London, 1977.

Fallon, Charlotte H., Soul of Fire – *A Biography of Mary MacSwiney*, Mercier Press, Dublin, 1986.

— 'Civil War Hunger Strikes – Women and Men' in *Eire*, Vol. 22, 1987.

Farrell, Brian (ed), *The Creation of the Dáil*, Blackwater Press, Dublin, 1994.

— *The Scholarly Revolutionary*, Irish University Press 1973.

Feeney, Brian, *Sinn Féin A Hundred Turbulent Years*, O'Brien Press, Dublin, 2002.

Figgis, Darrell, *Recollections of the Irish War*, Ernest Benn Ltd, London, 1927.

Fitzpatrick, David, *Politics and Irish Life: Provincial Experience of War and Revolution*, Cork University Press, Cork, 1998.

Foster, Roy, *Modern Ireland 1600-1972*, Allen Lane, London 1988.

Fox, R.M., *Rebel Irishwomen*, Progress House, Dublin, 1935.
Garvin, Tom, *1922: The Birth of Irish Democracy*, Gill and Macmillan, Dublin, 1996.
Gaughan, J. Anthony, *Austin Stack: Portrait of a Separatist*, Kingdom Books, Dublin, 1977.
Gore-Booth, Constance (ed), *Prison Letters of Countess Markevicz*, Longmans Green and Co, London, New York and Toronto, 1934.
Greaves, Desmond C., *Liam Mellows and the Irish Revolution*, Lawrence and Wishart, London, 1971.
Grenan, Julia, 'Events of Easter Week' in *The Catholic Bulletin*, June, 1917
— 'After the Surrender' in *Wolfe Tone Annual* – Special 1916 Number.
Hart, Peter, *The IRA at War 1916-1923*, Oxford University Press, Oxford, 2003.
— *The IRA and its Enemies: Violence and Community in Cork 1916-1923*, Oxford University Press, Oxford, 1998.
Haverty, Ann, *Constance Markievicz: An Independent Life*, Pandora, London, 1988.
Henry, R.M., *The Evolution of Sinn Féin*, Talbot Press, Dublin, 1920.
Hill, Myrtle, *Women In Ireland: A Century of Change*, Blackstaff Press, Belfast, 2003.
Hopkinson, Michael, *The Irish War of Independence*, Gill and Macmillan, Dublin, 2002.
Joy, Sinéad, *The IRA in Kerry 1916-1921*, The Collins Press, Cork, 2005.
Kearns, Linda, *In Times of Peril*, Talbot Press, Dublin, 1922.
Keogh, Dermot, *The Vatican, The Bishops and Irish Politics 1919-39*, Cambridge University Press, 1988.
Kinsella, Anna, *Women of Wexford 1798-1998*, Courtown Publications, Wexford, 1998.
Lee J., *The Modernisation of Irish Society*, Gill and Macmillan, Dublin, 1992.
Longford, Earl of, and O'Neill T.P., *Eamon de Valera*, Hutchinson, London, 1970.
Luddy, Maria, *Women in Ireland 1800-1918: A Documentary History*, Cork University Press, Cork, 1999.
Luddy, Maria and Murphy, Cliona (eds), *Women Surviving: Studies in Irish*

Women's History in the 19th and 20th Centuries, Poolbeg Press, Dublin, 1990.

Lyons, F.S.L., *Ireland since the Famine*, Charles Scribner's Sons, New York, 1971.

MacArdle, Dorothy, *The Irish Republic*, Irish Press Ltd, Dublin, 1951.

MacEoin, Uinseann, *Survivors*, Argenta, Dublin, 1980.

Manseragh, Nicholas, *The Irish Question 1840-1921*, Allen and Unwin, London, 1965.

Markievicz, Countess Constance, *Cumann na mBan* 11, no 10, 1926.

Marreco, Anne, *The Rebel Countess: The Life and Times of Constance Markievicz*, Weidenfield and Nicholson, London, 1967.

Maume, Patrick, *The Long Gestation: Irish Nationalist Life 1891-1918*, Gill and Macmillan, Dublin, 2000.

McCoole, Sinéad, *No Ordinary Women: Irish Female Activists in the Revolutionary Years 1900-1923*, O'Brien Press, Dublin, 2004

— *Guns and Chiffon: Women Revolutionaries and Kilmainham Gaol 1916-1923*, The Stationery Office, Dublin, 1997.

McDonnell, Kathleen Keyes, *There is a Bridge at Bandon: A Personal Account of the Irish War of Independence*, Mercier Press, Cork, 1972.

Mooney Eichacker, Joanne, *Irish Republican Women in America: Lecture Tours 1916-1925*, Irish Academic Press, Dublin, 2003.

Mulholland, Marie, *The Politics and Relationships of Kathleen Lynn*, Woodfield Press, Dublin, 2002.

Neilan, Mattie, 'The Rising in Galway' in *The Cappuchin Annual*, 1966.

Ní Chorra, Eilis, 'A Rebel Remembers' in *The Capuchin Annual*, 1936.

Ní Dhonnchadha, Mairin and Dorgan, Theo (eds), *Revising the Rising*, Field Day, Derry, 1991.

Nic Shiúbhlaigh, Máire, *The Splendid Years*, James Duffy, Dublin, 1955.

Norman, Diana, *Terrible Beauty: A life of Constance Markievicz*, Hodder and Stoughton, London, 1988.

Ó Céirin, Kit and Cyril, *Women of Ireland*, TirEolas, Galway, 1996.

O Cleirigh, Nellie, 'A Political Prisoner in Kilmainham Jail: The Diary of Cecilia Saunders Gallagher', *Dublin Historical Record* Vol. LVI No1, Spring 2003.

Ó Duigneáin, Proinnsíos, *Linda Kearns*, Drumlin Publications,

Manorhamilton, 2002.
Ó Dúlaing, Donnacha (ed), *Voices of Ireland*, The O'Brien Press, Dublin, 1984.
O' Brennan, Lily, 'The Dawning of the Day' in *The Capuchin Annual*, 1936.
O'Ceallaigh, Pádraig,, 'Jacob's Factory Area' on *The Cappuchin Annual*, 1966.
O'Ceirín, Kit and Cyril, *Women of Ireland: A Biographic Dictionary*, TirEolas, Galway.
O'Connor, Joseph, 'Boland's Mills Area' in *The Cappuchin Annual*, 1966.
O'Delaney, Barry, 'Cumann na mBan: The Women's Auxiliary of the Irish Army', in William G. Fitgerald (ed.), *Voice of Ireland*, Virtue and Co Ltd, London, Undated.
O'Dubhghaill, Seamus, 'Activities in Enniscorthy' in *The Capuchin Annual* 1966.
O'Farrell, Elizabeth, 'Recollections' in *An Poblacht*, 2 April, 3 May, 10 May 1930.
O'Hegarty, P.S., *The Victory of Sinn Féin: How it won and How it used it*, The Talbot Press, Dublin, 1924.
O'Malley, Ernie, *On Another Man's Wound*, Anvil, Dublin, 1979.
— *The Singing Flame*, Anvil, Dublin, 1978.
O'Neill, Marie, *From Parnell to de Valera: A Biography of Jennie Wyse Power*, Blackwater Press, Dublin, 1991.
O'Sullivan, Donal J., *Irish Constabularies*, Brandon Books, Dingle 1999.
Pyle, Hilary, *Cesca's Diary*, Woodfield Press, Dublin 2005.
Regan, John M., *The Irish Counter Revolution*, Gill and Macmillan, Dublin, 2001.
Reynolds, M., 'Cumann na mBan in the GPO' in *An t-Óglach*, March, 1926.
Ruiseal, Liam, 'The Position in Cork' in *The Cappuchin Annual* 1966.
Ryan, Annie, *Witnesses: Inside the Easter Rising*, Liberties Press, Dublin, 2005.
Ryan, Louise, 'In the Line of Fire: representations of women and war (1919-1923) through the writings of republican men', in Louise Ryan and Margaret Ward (eds), *Irish Women and Nationalism: Soldiers, New Women and Wicked Hags*, Irish Academic Press, Dublin, 2004.
Ryan, Meda, *Michael Collins and the Women in his Life*, Mercier Press, Cork, 1996.

Tom Barry, IRA Freedom Fighter, Mercier Press, Cork, 2003.
Sheehan, Aideen, 'Cumann na mBan-Policies and Activities' in David Fitzpatrick (ed), *Revolution? Ireland 1917-1923*, Trinity History Workshop, Dublin 1990.
Sheehan William (ed), *British Voices from the Irish War of Independence 1918-1921: The Words of British Servicemen who were there*, The Collins Press, Cork, 2005.
'Sinn Féin Rebellion Handbook: Easter 1916', *Weekly Irish Times*, Dublin, 1917.
Skinnider, Margaret, *Doing My Bit for Ireland*, Century, New York, 1917.
Taillon, Ruth, *When History Was Made: The Women of 1916*, Beyond the Pale, Belfast, 1999.
Urquhart, Diane, *Women in Ulster Politics 1890-1940*, Irish Academic Press, Dublin, 2000.
Van Voris, Jacqueline, *Constance de Markievicz: In the Cause of Ireland*, University of Massachusetts Press, 1967.
Walsh, Oonagh, 'Testimony from Imprisoned Women' in David Fitzpatrick (ed), *Revolution? Ireland 1917-1923*, Trinity History Workshop, Dublin, 1990.
Ward, Margaret, *Unmanageable Revolutionaries: Women in Irish Nationalism*, Pluto Press, London, 1995.
— *In Their Own Voice*, Attic Press, Dublin, 1995.
— *Hanna Sheehy Skeffington: A Life*, Attic Press, Cork, 1997.
— 'From Marginality and Militancy: Cumann na mBan 1914-36', in Morgan, Austin and Purdie, Bob (eds), *Ireland: Divided Nation*, Divided Class, London, 1980.
Wyse Power, Jennie, 'The Political Influence of Women in Modern Ireland' in William G. Fitgerald (ed.), *Voice of Ireland*, Virtue and Co Ltd, London, Undated.
Younger, Calton, *Arthur Griffith*, Gill and Macmillan, Dublin, 1981.

NEWSPAPERS AND PERIODICALS
An Saoghal Gaedhealach
An tÓglác
Anglo Celt

Belfast Newsletter
Belfast Telegram
Clare Champion
Clare Journal and Ennis Advertiser
Cork County Eagle and Munster Advertiser
Cork Examiner
Derry Journal
Derry Sentinel
Eire – The Irish Republic
Free State
Freeman's Journal
Galway Express
Irish Citizen
Irish Independent
Irish Opinion
Irish Times (The)
Irish Volunteer
Kerryman
Kilkenny People
Leitrim Observer
Limerick Leader
London Times
Longford Leader
National Volunteer
Nationality
New Ireland
Poblacht na hEireann – The Republic of Ireland
Poblacht na hEireann – War News
Roscommon Herald
Sligo Champion
Southern Democrat
The Spark
Tipperary People
Tipperary Star

Waterford News
Weekly Observer
Wexford People
Wicklow Newsletter and Arklow Advertiser

UNPUBLISHED
Bureau of Military History
Aughney, Eilis, Witness Statement, WS1054.
Barry, Mrs Tom, Witness Statement, WS1754.
Beaumont, Mrs Sean, Witness Statement, WS385 and Contemporary Documents, CD167.
Bloxham, Elizabeth, Witness Statement, WS632 and Contemporary Documents, CD216.
Boyce, Mary, Contemporary Documents, CD314.
Brady, Margaret, Witness Statement, WS1267.
Ní Bhriain, Maire, Witness Statement, WS363.
Broderick-Nicholson, Margaret, Witness Statement, WS1682.
Cahill, Bessie, Witness Statement, WS1143.
Cashel, Alice M, Witness Statement, WS366 and Contemporary Documents, CD174.
Ui Chonnaill, Eilis, Witness Statement, WS568 and Contemporary Documents, CD202.
Clarke, Josephine, Witness Statement, WS699.
Colum, Mary M., Contemporary Documents, CD30.
Comerford, Maire, Contemporary Documents, CD59.
Corr, Elizabeth and Nell, Witness Statement, WS179.
Cremin, Mary A., Witness Statement, WS924.
Cunningham, Mollie, Witness Statement, WS1681.
Cunningham, Nora, Witness Statement, WS1690.
Curran, Lily, Witness Statement, WS805.
Czira, Sidney, Witness Statement, WS909 and Contemporary Documents, CD186 and CD252.
Daly, Madge, Witness Statements, WS209 and WS855.
De Burca, Aoife, Witness Statement, WS359.

Doherty, Bridget, Witness Statement, WS1193.
Ui Donnchadha, Bean, Contemporary Documents, CD160.
Dore, Nora, Witness Statement, WS154.
Duggan, Peg, Witness Statement, WS1576.
Fahy, Anna, Witness Statement, WS202.
Fay, Bridget, Witness Statement, WS484 and Contemporary Documents, CD182.
Fitzpatrick, Maire, Witness Statements, WS1344 and WS1345.
Foley, Mrs Michael, Witness Statement, WS539.
Gavan-Duffy, Louise, Witness Statement, WS216.
Heron, Aine, Witness Statement, WS293 and Contemporary Documents, CD130.
Heron, Ina, Witness Statement, WS919.
Keating, Pauline, Witness Statement, WS432 and Contemporary Documents, CD22.
Kennedy, Margaret, Witness Statement, WS185.
Lalor, Molly Hyland, Witness Statement, WS295 and Contemporary Documents, CD311.
Lucey, Margaret, Witness Statement, WS1561.
Martin, Bridget, Witness Statement, WS398 and Contemporary Documents, CD164 and CD168.
Moloney, Katherine Barry, Witness Statement, WS731.
Molony, Helena, Witness Statement, WS391 and Contemporary Documents, CD119.
Morkan, Phyllis, Witness Statement, WS210.
Mulcahy, Mary Josephine, Witness Statement, WS399.
Murphy, Eileen, Witness Statement, WS480.
MacGarry, Maeve, Witness Statement, WS826.
MacNeill, Agnes, Witness Statement, WS213 and Contemporary Documents, CD7.
MacCarvill, Eileen, Witness Statement, WS1752.
McDermott, Sorcha, Witness Statement, WS945.
McGeehin, Mary, Witness Statement, WS902.
McGrath, M.A., Witness Statement, WS1704.

McNamara, Rose, Witness Statement, WS482.
McNeill, Josephine, Witness Statement, WS303.
McWhinney, Linda, Witness Statement, WS404.
Nolan, Nan, Witness Statements, WS1441 and WS1747.
O'Brien, Annie, Witness Statement, WS805.
O'Brien, Nora, Witness Statement, WS286.
O'Byrne, Maire Kennedy, Witness Statement, WS1029.
O'Callaghan, Margaret, Witness Statement, WS747.
O'Doherty, Kitty, Witness Statement, WS355 and Contemporary Documents, CD141, CD142 and CD201.
O'Donnell, Mrs Bernard, Witness Statement, WS750.
O'Donoghue, Sheila, Contemporary Documents, CD160.
O'Kelly, K., Witness Statement, WS180.
O'Kelly, Mairead, Witness Statement, WS925.
O'Mahony, Anna Hurley, Witness Statement, WS540.
O'Mullane, Bridget, Witness Statements, WS450 and WS485.
O'Rahilly, Aine, Witness Statement, WS333.
O'Reilly, Eily O'Hanrahan, Witness Statements, WS270 and WS415.
Reynolds, Molly, Witness Statement, WS195 and Contemporary Documents, CD290.
Rigney, Mary, Witness Statement, WS752.
Rooney, Catherine, Witness Statement, WS648.
Ryan, Aine, Witness Statement, WS887.
Ryan, Bridget, Witness Statement, WS1488.
Ryan, Brigid, Witness Statement, WS1573.
Ryan, Mairin, Witness Statement, WS416 and Contemporary Documents, CD171.
Stack, Una C., Witness Statements WS214 and WS416 and Contemporary Documents, CD190 and CD199.
Thornton (nee Lyons), Bridget, Witness Statement, WS259 and Contemporary Documents, CD134.
Walsh, Mary, Witness Statement, WS556.
Woods, Mary Flannery, Witness Statement, WS624.
Wyse Power, Nancy, Witness Statements WS541, WS587 and WS732

and Contemporary Documents, CD193, CD194 and CD200.

IRISH MILITARY ARCHIVES

Captured Documents Lots, 34, 51, 79, 109, 157(1), 227 and 233.

Free State Army Operations Reports, Various Commands, June 1922-June 1923.

UNIVERSITY COLLEGE DUBLIN, ARCHIVES DEPARTMENT

Eithne Coyle Papers, P61.

Elgin O'Rahilly Papers, P200.

Ernest O'Malley Papers, P17a and P17b.

Mary MacSwiney Papers, P48a.

Sighle Humphreys Papers and Eithne Coyle O'Donnell Papers P106.

General Richard Mulcahy Papers, P7.

Lily O'Brennan Papers P13.

General Sean MacEoin Papers P151.

NATIONAL ARCHIVES OF IRELAND

Department of the Taoiseach, File Nos., S5778 and S14182.

Dáil Eireann Papers.

See also www.nationalarchives.ie/wh/whp.html.

NATIONAL LIBRARY OF IRELAND

Appeal to join Cumann na mBan, LOLB/161(29).

Bulmer Hobson Papers, MS12177.

Cumann na mBan – Howth, MS33368.

Cumann na mBan Pamphlets, I94109 P4.

Cumann na mBan Rules and Constitution 1920, LOLB162.

Cumann na mBan Rules and Constitution 1914, LOLB 161(2).

Cumann na mBan Rules and Constitution 1916, P2119.

Cumann na mBan Rules and Constitution 1917, IR94109/P68(10).

Cumann na mBan Rules and Constitution 1919, LOLB161(3).

Cumann na mBan Vol II no.10 – Easter Week Commemoration Number-1926, ILB94109P4.

Eithne Coyle Memoir, MS 28818 (1).
GPO Area in Easter Week, MS5173.
IRPDF – A Further Appeal, ILB300 P12.
IRPDF – Third Appeal, LOP115 [Item 138].
Leabhar na mBan, 3B2531.
Life of Mary L. Butler, MS7321.
May Bowen Kilmainham Jail Autograph Book, MS27981.
Open Letter on behalf of Cumann na mBan Prisoners
Committee, Lolb161(6).
Programme for a Concert at 41 Parnell Square 16/04/1916, Ir94109 P40.
Sheehy Skeffington Papers, MS22259.
NB: The dates of the various 'Rules and Constitution' documents are provided by the author based on the date of the 'policy' section of each document.

PUBLIC RECORD OFFICE, LONDON

COLONIAL OFFICE PAPERS

INDEX

5021 6